# Toward
# A Catholic
# Constitution

# Toward A Catholic Constitution

## Leonard Swidler

*A Crossroad Book*
The Crossroad Publishing Company
New York

1996

The Crossroad Publishing Company
370 Lexington Avenue, New York, NY 10017

Printed in the United States of America

**Library of Congress Cataloging-in-Publication Data**

Swidler, Leonard J.
    Toward a Catholic constitution / Leonard Swidler.
      p.  cm.
    Includes bibliographical references and index.
    ISBN 0-8245-1626-5 (pbk.)
    1. Catholic Church – Government. 2. Church renewal – Catholic Church. 3. Catholic Church – Doctrines. 4. Catholic Church – Membership. 5. Catholic Church – History – 1965-    I. Title.
BX1802.S95   1996
262′.02 – dc20                    96-21857
                                        CIP

# Contents

# Foreword

It is strange that the Catholic Church does not yet have a Constitution. In the turbulence of the early Middle Ages after the definitive collapse of the Roman Empire, the Church was the only institution which was able to preserve some remnants of a legal order. It developed a theory of human rights when the robber barons were running wild in the forests and hills of Europe. While its own legal procedures were often abused, it nonetheless did support due processes of a sort when the feudal lords were a law unto themselves. Recent research in Spain demonstrates that the Inquisition, as horrific as it was, was far less abusive to human rights and executed far fewer people than did the witchcraft trials in northern Europe.

Yet when the emergent democracies began to codify their legal systems and their bills of rights in written Constitutions (with the exception of England), the Church somehow never got around to the same task, perhaps because its legal creativity had deteriorated under the pressure of its conflict with the Reformation and then the Enlightenment. The best it could do was to produce a "Code" of Canon Law in 1919.

In the revision of this code after the Second Vatican Council it did indeed produce a "bill of rights" for the laity, but, in effect, it didn't tell anyone about it. Attempts were made to produce this list of rights in a separate document, but these efforts were blocked, perhaps because those who revised the code wanted the lay people to have rights but it didn't want them to know that they had rights.

Moreover, while the rights (to the reception of the sacraments for example) are clearly spelled out, there are no procedures for the vindication of these rights against oppressive pastors and bishops. Thus priests and religious educators all over America have added extracanonical regulations for the reception of the sacraments and often deny the sacraments to those who don't live up to the regulations. It would appear that neither bishops nor pastors nor the laity know that the laity have rights and that these rights are violated constantly.

A distinguished theologian has been cited by religious educators as saying that baptism cannot simply be administered "on demand" — an unfortunate allusion to the abortion controversy. In fact, according to the code, the laity have the right to demand baptism for their children and rarely if ever should that right be denied.

This abuse of simple human rights is but one example — though one which impinges on the lives of many of the laity — of the reasons why the Church needs a Constitution which spells out clearly how the Church should work. Obviously there will be a strong opposition to the notion of a Constitution for the Church. It would severely limit the absolute power that many church persons think they have.

Lord Acton, himself a Catholic, had the Church in mind when he said that absolute power corrupts absolutely.

It will be argued that other human institutions might need Constitutions, but that the Church because of its "divine origin" is immune from this need — an argument which has often sounded to be like saying that the Lord Jesus, because of his special relationship with God, did not need to sleep.

So one does not expect hierarchs to sign on *en masse* to Professor Swidler's proposals. Eventually, however, his vision will become a reality. The Church does eventually catch up: it did decide, for example, that slavery was wrong — though only after it had been abolished in most countries.

Maybe when it has a Constitution the Church will not always have to play catch-up ball.

ANDREW GREELEY
*Wednesday of the Third Week in Lent*
*Feast of St. Colette*

# Introduction

A Constitution for the Catholic Church? An oxymoron? Hardly: set up a Constitution for the Catholic Church. Those were the instructions of Pope Paul VI during the Second Vatican Council (1962–65). Not only is there no inherent contradiction in the idea of a Constitution for the Catholic Church, there have in fact been many elements of a Constitution in the history of the Catholic Church. Further, there are even substantial portions of a *written* Constitution which are now part of the 1983 Code of Canon Law. However, that written partial Constitution is not complete, nor is it as democratic or responsibility-sharing as many of the past governance structures of the Catholic Church. Flowing from the vision projected and the energies released at the Second Vatican Council (1962–65) is a movement toward the completion of the task of writing, adopting, and living a Constitution in the Catholic Church that is both in the spirit of Jesus' gospel of liberation and love and adaptive of the most mature governance principles available at the edge of the third millennium.

After a period of deep depression in the 1980s, concern for Catholic church renewal and needed structural reform in the spirit of Vatican II is beginning once again to swell on the grassroots level both in North America and Europe. This is not a revolutionary wave like the one which poured forth from the sixteenth-century Protestant Reformation, nor is it an enthusiastic wave like the one which sprang from the dam-burst-like release after Vatican Council II. It is a much more sober, chastened swell which on the one hand has no illusions that the situation in the Church will be quickly and radically transformed, but on the other hand so treasures values in Catholicism that energies are being recommitted to making those values truly available to a society living now at the edge of the third millennium, and beyond. Moreover, those energies are today being expended in increasingly "savvy" and coordinated ways.

In these pages I will sketch briefly a picture of the five revolutionary "Copernican turns" which took place at Vatican II and its immediate aftermath, the subsequent slump into restorationism and resignation, then the current reenergized church-renewal movement, focusing on how it developed, what it looks like now, and what it is trying to accomplish. Concerning the latter I will also be at some pains to provide the justifications offered by

1

its participants. My final section will deal with the effort to "*re*-democratize" the Church — for the ancient Church was for many a "limited democracy" — climaxing in the call for a "Catholic Constitutional Convention" to usher in the third millennium after the birth of Jesus.

# 1

# The Copernican Turn of Vatican II

The 1960s were a momentous turning-point decade for the world: (1) American Catholics broke out of their ghetto in the election of President Kennedy; (2) the American civil rights movement began a transformation of the Western psyche; (3) the antiwar, environmentalist, antiestablishment and related movements in the West brought the transformation to a fever pitch; (4) through Vatican Council II the Catholic Church leapt into modernity, and edged even beyond.

The Copernican turn that occurred in the Catholic Church at Vatican II took place in five major ways:

## The Turn Toward This World

Until very recently the term "salvation" was understood exclusively to mean going to heaven after death; its root meaning from *salus*, of a "full, healthy life," was largely lost in Christianity after the third century.[1] Marx was not far from the mark when he claimed that Christianity (and religion in general) was mainly concerned about "pie in the sky bye and bye." But that focus shifted radically with Vatican II, especially as reflected in the document "The Church in the Modern World," which in effect, though without the name, launched liberation theology.

## The Turn Toward Dialogue

Far too often religion has held men and women back from their neighbor in their deepest dimension, their religious dimension, because their religion was different. There are still many Catholics and Protestants who hate each other, many Christians who hate Jews, many Christians and Jews who hate Muslims — religiously. When this happens, religion, including Christianity, becomes an enslaving force; religion — Christianity — becomes the anti-Christ, for the truth of Christ should make women and men free and open to all men and women, to all reality, to all paths to God.

At Vatican II Catholics were taught — especially in the Constitution on the Church, the Declaration on Religious Liberty, the Decree on Ecumenism, and the Declaration on the Relationship with Non-Christian

3

Religions — that to be authentically Christian, Christians must cease being enslaved by their tribal forms of Christianity; they must stop their fratricidal hate; they need to recall their Jewish roots and the fact that the Jewish people today are still God's chosen people, for God's promises are never revoked; they need to turn from their imperialistic convert-making among Muslims, Hindus, and other religious peoples and turn toward bearing witness to Jesus Christ by their lives and words, toward helping the Muslims be better Muslims and the Hindus better Hindus. This will make Christians love their own liberating traditions not less, but more, for these traditions will then be even more fully Christian.

Nowhere was this proclaimed more forcefully than in the Vatican document *Humanae personae dignitatem:*

> Doctrinal discussion requires recognizing the truth everywhere, even if truth demolishes one so that one is forced to reconsider one's own position, in theory and in practice, at least in part...in discussion the truth will prevail by no other means than by the truth itself. Therefore the liberty of the participants must be ensured by law and reverenced in practice.[2]

## The Turn Toward the Historical/Dynamic

For centuries the thinking of official Catholicism was dominated by a static understanding of reality; it resisted not only the democratic and human rights movements of the nineteenth and twentieth centuries, but also the growing historical, dynamic way of understanding the world, including religious thought.

That changed dramatically with Vatican II where the historical, dynamic view of reality and doctrine was officially fully embraced (unfortunately the present leadership largely resists this, and the other, Copernican turns of the Council).[3]

## The Turn Toward Freedom

The image Catholicism projected at the end of the 1950s was of a giant monolith, a community of hundreds of millions who held obedience in both action and thought as the highest virtue. If the pope said, "Have babies," Catholics had babies; if he said, "Don't associate with Protestants and Jews," Catholics avoided them like the plague; if he said, "Believe in papal infallibility, in Marian dogmas," they believed. For a hundred years — but really not much more than that! — Catholics were treated like children in the Church, acted like children, and thought of themselves as children.

With the Second Vatican Council, however, this very unfree image, and reality, was utterly transformed. Suddenly it seemed humanity, including Catholics, became aware of their "coming of age," hence, their freedom and responsibility. This was clearly expressed in many places, but perhaps nowhere clearer than in the Declaration on Religious Liberty.

## The Turn Toward Inner-Church Reform

Since the sixteenth century, inside the Catholic Church even the word "reform" was forbidden, to say nothing of the reality (there were periods of notable exception,[4] but they were largely obliterated — even from our church history textbooks!). At the beginning of the twentieth century Pope Pius X, leapfrogging back to his predecessor Pope Pius IX, launched the heresy-hunting Inquisition of antimodernism, crushing all creative thought in Catholicism for decades. In the middle of the twentieth century, leading theologians were again censured and silenced (e.g., Jean Daniélou, Henri de Lubac, Pierre Teilhard de Chardin, John Courtney Murray, Karl Rahner).

But Pope Saint John XXIII (so canonized by the traditional method of popular acclamation by the Association for the Rights of Catholics in the Church — ARCC) burst those binding chains and called the Second Vatican Council. He spoke about "throwing open the windows of the Vatican" to let in fresh thought, about *aggiornamento,* bringing the Church "up to date."

Indeed, the Vatican II documents even used that neuralgic word "reformation": "Christ summons the Church, as she goes her pilgrim way, to that continual reformation of which she always has need"; "*All* [Catholics] are led to . . . , wherever necessary, undertake with vigor the task of renewal and reform." And the Council insisted that *all* Catholics' "primary duty is to make an honest and careful appraisal of whatever needs to be renewed and achieved in the Catholic household itself" (Decree on Ecumenism).

# 2

# Vatican II and the Turn
# Toward This World

## Historical Background

As noted, with Vatican II there was a decided Copernican "turn toward this world," a renewing of the effort to overcome the destructive dualism that has plagued Christianity (and many other religions) from the very first century. During the Middle Ages the Church was very much involved in this world, with bishops and abbots being secular as well as spiritual princes. However, in many ways even the concern for the neighbor's physical well-being of the medieval feudal world, which the Church helped construct, began to turn inward as that feudal world gave way to modernity.

Even during the feudal period, however, efforts to help disadvantaged human beings were pretty much done on a remedial, individualistic basis. "Charitable" institutions were founded — actually in quite extraordinary richness. The situation began to change drastically, however, with the coming of the Industrial Revolution in England in the late eighteenth century and elsewhere in Europe and America starting in the nineteenth century: the old guild and feudal systems no longer functioned for the increasing millions caught in the transfer of populations to the cities. Whereas most people had died quite young and a much smaller population lived in relative social and geographical stability before the nineteenth century, suddenly a massive and exploding population problem burst upon the world, and neither civil society nor religion was prepared for it. Individual acts of charity and charitable institutions were increasingly swamped in the growing flood of social misery that rose as the nineteenth and twentieth centuries wore on.

At the same time the structures of society and their workings were being studied. Plans on how to shape and reshape those structures were laid and tested, adjusted and retested. Such awareness, planning, and action also took place within Western religions. One need only remember the large number of Jews involved in the history of socialism (starting with Marx) and the labor movement, including Jewish social justice organizations from the Jüdischer Bund to Israeli Kibbutzim. Christian socialism started in England with people like Charles Kingsley (1819–75) and Frederick Denison Maurice

(1805–72) and in Germany with people like Bishop Wilhelm von Ketteler (1811–77); in France religious social justice work was led by activists like Count Albert de Mun (1841–1914), Count René de la Tour du Pin (1834–1925), and Marc Sagnier (1873–1950); in America there were Terence Powderley (1849–1924) and the Knights of Labor, Walter Rauschenbusch (1861–1918) and his highly influential "Social Gospel" message. Even the popes moved in this direction: Leo XIII issued the first papal social encyclical, *Rerum novarum*, in 1893, followed by Pius XI's *Quadragesimo anno* in 1933, John XXIII's *Pacem in terris* (1963), and Paul VI's *Populorum progressio* (1968).

The most recent developments include European political theology, Latin American liberation theology, North American black theology and feminist theology and Korean *minjung* or people's theology. Around the globe Christian churches spend hundreds of millions of dollars annually on social justice issues, a significant portion of which is aimed at changing the structures of society to benefit more people. The notion is spreading among Christians that the mission of the Church is to preach the Good News of the gospel to all humanity, not just quantitatively in terms of individual persons, but also qualitatively in the sense that every portion of the human being and the human patterns one lives in are an essential part of one's humanity.

## Liberation Theologies

Paul Knitter has persuasively pointed out that there are four contemporary critical areas in desperate need of *global* liberation — (1) physical suffering, (2) socioeconomic oppression, (3) nuclear holocaust, and (4) ecological catastrophe — which must be addressed by all religions (and ideologies) if they are to have any credibility in any sphere in the future. In fact, as he pointed out, the major religions of the world are, to a greater or lesser extent, beginning to address those issues and to some degree are also entering into cooperation on them. Without a doubt, the growing awareness of these *global* threats provides a basis, indeed, an impulse, even a compulsion, for the religions and ideologies to enter into dialogue and cooperation.

Thus, it is increasingly clear that there are *patterns* of injustice that need to be changed, that the structures of unjust dominance must be unmasked and dismantled wherever they are to be found, and that demands a constant searching within and without. But, at the same time, there is also an increasing awareness that it is not possible for the "haves" in a material sense to eliminate the material poverty of the "have-nots" simply by "external" changes, such as by modifying the social structures, or heavier taxes, or lowering their own material standard of living. Some, or perhaps even all of these and more, are seen to be doubtless necessary, but not sufficient.

Liberation theology has spoken movingly of a "preferential option for the poor." Nevertheless, it is not mainly in the direction of "giving up things" on the part of the "haves" that the "poor," and other "nonpersons," will be liberated, but rather in the direction of doing more, both qualitatively and quantitatively. We have learned in the last two centuries that material wealth is not limited, static; it is essentially linked with "spiritual wealth," with mental creativity, which is dynamic, unending. It is essentially, though not only, this latter, spiritual wealth, that needs to be expanded, shared; the former, material wealth, will then follow. This lesson is being learned today, the hard way, by former Marxist countries, such as Hungary: "Our existing socialism had to realise that *structural changes* either in the economy or in the very society itself *do not involve automatic changes in the mentality* of the people."[1]

I would like to suggest that the "Other" toward whom our "altruistic" ethical action should reach might be named not the poor, but simply the oppressed, the *unfree,* in any dimension — and who is completely free? Logic, of course, also directs that those in greatest need should receive the greatest attention, but it likewise directs that each person should contribute according to her or his gifts, and in a preeminent though not exclusive way to those before them *now* in need, whether that need be material, spiritual, social, esthetic, or any other: producing good material things for the well-to-do as well as the poor, teaching the poor as well as the well-to-do, making democracy work better for the well-to-do as well as the poor, creating beauty for the poor as well as the well-to-do.

In the U.S., for example, the material poverty of the 30 million "poor" must be eradicated, but at the same time the various spiritual poverties of the 220 million "well-to-do" must likewise be diminished. This "preferential option for the unfree" in no way rules out the "preferential option for the poor." Rather, it includes it — in eminent fashion — but expands it.

It seems to me that the question of timing is also all-important. Both Christianity (as well as other religions) and Marxism have in practice far too often sacrificed the present generation to both the past and the future. Because of its age, Christianity has been much more guilty than Marxism of sacrificing the present to the past, but both have been equally guilty of sacrificing the present to the future: Christians have often been taught to accept their lot as God's will, not to try to change the social structure of things but to look forward to a future reward. Populations in Marxist countries have often been told that they ought not to try to change the economic order of things but to give up "consumer goods" so future generations could benefit from their development of "heavy industry" — which led to their economic and political collapse, for neither consumer goods nor heavy industry were adequately developed.

Here again, former Marxist Hungary has been learning this lesson the hard way — but it is learning it!

What is more, individual persons are not only citizens to be governed, but also autonomous living beings with specific needs and rights. Their basic needs and rights cannot be neglected for a long period without considerable damage even to society, and in consequence to the state.... The socialist system in Hungary aimed to achieve social justice.... But in the recent past the fact had to be faced and acknowledged that *a new type of poverty* emerged: ... *in the financial sense ... in a moral and human sense.*[2]

Each person, each society must find the delicate balance whereby the past is properly appreciated and reverenced, the future responsibly cared for, and the present lived as fully and intensely as possible, *now*.

Without diminishing in the least the burning need for the "haves" of this world, largely, though by no means only, Christians and Jews — or in short, the "First World" — to move out from its *amour propre* to a commitment to socioeconomic liberation, I believe it is also important for all to remember that until very modern times life for the vast majority (that is, in the magnitude of 90 percent!) of the people of the world was, as Thomas Hobbes said, "short, nasty, and brutish." It is only with the advances of the West in science, medicine, economics, and social/political structures that there could even be a Third World as differentiated from the First World. In many ways much of the "Second World," that is, the Communist world, was really Third World in its economic and socio/political underdevelopment, which it too is now admitting and beginning to try to overcome. Until modern times the whole world was what we today call Third World.

Hence, it doesn't make sense to accuse the present First World of having *created* the Third World. What does make sense is to call the First World to move from its appropriate, indeed necessary, prior love of self to its appropriate, indeed necessary, continuance of the act of love to the Other. For not only can I not love my neighbor if I do not love myself, I also cannot truly love myself if I do not also love my neighbor. In fact, I become an "I" only in encounter with the Other. In the social, economic, and political spheres that means that the First World must strive to "do unto others as it would have them do unto it," that is, cease policies and practices that worsen or continue the underdevelopment of the Third World, as well as facilitate an ever more human social, economic, political reality for it, and thereby also for itself.

Perhaps another way to express the needed integration of the several essential elements of the Catholic "turn toward this world" can be found in the changeling child of Catholicism, the Enlightenment, and in the American and French Revolutions. Surprising as it may be to many Catholics, the slogan of the French Revolution really encapsulates the essence of Catholicism and the fundamental Good News of Jesus: *Liberté, égalité, fraternité.* The essence of the love of neighbor is freely (*liberté*) to treat *all* men and women as brothers and sisters (*fraternité* — today we would eliminate the sexist language and probably say *solidarité*), especially the powerless of society (*égalité*).

# 3

# Vatican II and the Turn Toward Dialogue

## Catholic Commitment to Dialogue

Unfortunately, for centuries, especially since the sixteenth century, the Catholic Church was largely trapped in a kind of solipsism, talking only to itself and shaking its finger at the rest of the world. When, e.g., a committee of Protestant churchmen shortly after World War I visited Pope Benedict XV to invite the Catholic Church to join in launching the ecumenical movement to work for church reunion, he told them that he was happy they were finally concerned about church unity, but that he already had the solution to the problem of Christian division: "Come home to mama!" The Vatican's forbidding of Catholic participation in dialogue was subsequently constantly repeated, e.g., *Mortalium animos* (1928), *Monitum* (1948), *Instructio* (1949), and barring of Catholics at the Evanston, Illinois, World Council of Churches World Assembly (1954).

Again, Saint John XXIII and Vatican II changed all that navel-staring radically. Ecumenism was now not only not forbidden, but "pertains to the whole Church, faithful and clergy alike. It extends to everyone" (Decree on Ecumenism). Pope Paul VI issued his first encyclical (*Ecclesiam suam*, 1964), specifically on dialogue:

> Dialogue is *demanded* nowadays.... It is *demanded* by the dynamic course of action which is changing the face of modern society. It is *demanded* by the pluralism of society and by the maturity man has reached in this day and age. Be he religious or not, his secular education has enabled him to think and speak and conduct a dialogue with dignity.

We are now poised at the entrance to the Age of Dialogue. We travel all over the globe, and large elements of the entire globe come to us. There can hardly be a U.S. campus which does not echo with foreign accents and languages. Our streets, businesses, and homes are visibly filled with overseas products. We constantly hear about the crises of our massive trade deficit and the overwhelming debts second and third world countries owe us. Through our Asian-made television sets we invite into our living rooms myriads of people of strange nations, cultures, and religions.

10

Perhaps even more important than these vital external changes that have helped prepare the contemporary world for dialogue is the fundamental paradigm-shift that has occurred to our understanding of truth, our epistemology. Whereas our Western notion of truth was largely absolute, static, and monologic or exclusive up to the past century, it has since become deabsolutized, dynamic, and dialogic — in a word, it has become "relational." This new view of truth came about in at least six different, but closely related, ways. In brief they are:

1. *Historicism:* Truth is deabsolutized by the perception that reality is always described in terms of the circumstances of the time in which it is expressed.

2. *Intentionality:* Seeking the truth with the intention of acting accordingly deabsolutizes the statement.

3. *Sociology of knowledge:* Truth is deabsolutized in terms of geography, culture, and social standing.

4. *Limits of language:* Truth as the meaning of something and especially as talk about the transcendent is deabsolutized by the nature of human language.

5. *Hermeneutics:* All truth, all knowledge, is seen as interpreted truth, knowledge, and hence is deabsolutized by the observer who is always also interpreter.

6. *Dialogue:* The knower engages reality in a dialogue in a language the knower provides, thereby deabsolutizing all statements about reality.

Before the nineteenth century in Europe *truth, that is, a statement about reality,* was conceived in quite an absolute, static, exclusivistic either-or manner. If something was true at one time, it was always true; not only empirical facts but also the meaning of things or the oughtness that was said to flow from them were thought of in this way. At bottom, the notion of truth was based exclusively on the Aristotelian principle of contradiction: a thing could not be true and not true in the same way at the same time. Truth was defined by way of exclusion; A was A because it could be shown not to be not-A. Truth was thus understood to be absolute, static, exclusivistically either-or. This is a *classicist* or *absolutist* view of truth.

1. *Historicism:* In the nineteenth century many scholars came to perceive all statements about the truth of the meaning of something as partially the products of their historical circumstances. Those concrete circumstances helped determine the fact that the statement under study was even called forth, that it was couched in particular intellectual categories (for example, in abstract Platonic or concrete legal language), in particular literary forms (for example, mythic or metaphysical language), and in particular psychological settings (such as a polemic response to a specific attack). These scholars argued that only if the truth statements were placed in their historical situation, in their historical *Sitz im Leben,* could they be properly understood. The understanding of the text could be found only in *context.* To express

that same original meaning in a later *Sitz im Leben* one would require a pro-portionately different statement. Thus, all statements about the meaning of things were now seen to be deabsolutized in terms of time.

This is a *historical* view of truth. Clearly at its heart is a notion of *relationality:* Any statement about the truth of the meaning of something has to be understood in relationship to its historical context.

2. *Intentionality:* Later thinkers like Max Scheler added a corollary to this historicizing of knowledge; it concerned not the past but the future. Such scholars also saw truth as having an element of intentionality at its base, as being oriented ultimately toward action, praxis. They argued that we perceive certain things as questions to be answered and set goals to pursue specific knowledge because we wish to do something about those matters; we intend to live according to the truth and meaning that we hope to discern in the answers to the questions we pose, in the knowledge we decide to seek. The truth of the meaning of things was thus seen as deabsolutized by the action-oriented intentionality of the thinker-speaker.

This is an *intentional* or *praxis* view of truth, and it too is basically *relational:* A statement has to be understood in relationship to the action-oriented intention of the speaker.

3. *The sociology of knowledge:* Just as statements of truth about the meaning of things were seen by some thinkers to be historically deabsolutized in time, so too, starting in this century with scholars like Karl Mannheim, such statements began to be seen as deabsolutized by such things as the culture, class, and gender of the thinker-speaker, regardless of time. All reality was said to be perceived from the perspective of the perceiver's own world view. Any statement of the truth of the meaning of something was seen to be perspectival, "standpoint-bound," *standortgebunden,* as Karl Mannheim put it, and thus deabsolutized.

This is a *perspectival* view of truth and is likewise *relational:* All statements are fundamentally related to the standpoint of the speaker.

4. *The limitations of language:* Following Ludwig Wittgenstein and others, many thinkers have come to see that any statement about the truth of things can be at most only a partial description of the reality it is trying to describe. Although reality can be seen from an almost limitless number of perspectives, human language can express things from only one, or perhaps a very few, perspectives at once. If this is now seen to be true of what we call "scientific truths," it is much more true of statements about the truth of the meaning of things. The very fact of dealing with the truth of the "meaning" of something indicates that the knower is essentially involved and hence reflects the perspectival character of all such statements. A statement may be true, of course — it may accurately describe the extramental reality it refers to — but it will always be cast in particular categories, language, concerns, etc., of a particular "standpoint," and in that sense will be limited, deabsolutized.

This also is a *perspectival* view of truth, and therefore also *relational.*

This limited and limiting, as well as liberating, quality of language is especially clear in talk of the transcendent. The transcendent is by definition that which "goes beyond" our experience. Any statements about the transcendent must thus be deabsolutized and limited far beyond the perspectival character seen in ordinary statements.

5. *Hermeneutics:* Hans-Georg Gadamer and Paul Ricoeur recently led the way in developing the science of hermeneutics, which, by arguing that all knowledge of a text is at the same time an *interpretation* of the text, further deabsolutizes claims about the "true" meaning of the text. But this basic insight goes beyond knowledge of texts and applies to all knowledge.

This is an *interpretive* view of truth. It is clear that *relationality* pervades this hermeneutical, interpretive view of truth. (It is interesting to note that one dimension of this interpretive understanding of truth can already be found in St. Thomas Aquinas, who states that "things known are in the knower according to the mode of the knower — *cognita sunt in cognoscente secundum modum cognoscentis.*"[1]

6. *Dialogue:* This insight is developed further below.

In sum, our understanding of truth and reality has been undergoing a radical shift. This new paradigm which is being born understands all statements about reality, especially about the meaning of things, to be historical, intentional, perspectival, partial, interpretive, and dialogic. What is common to all these qualities is the notion of *relationality,* that is, that all expressions or understandings of reality are in some fundamental way related to the speaker or knower.

Consequently, instead of automatically rejecting the understanding of reality of someone from a different religion, we now increasingly see that we need to be in dialogue with that person so we might learn something about reality, the meaning of life, that we cannot perceive from our particular perspective.

This turn toward dialogue naturally was directed toward the first obvious dialogue partners for Catholics: fellow Christians, Protestants and Orthodox. But this turn outward from an inward gazing had its own inner dynamic: why stop at talking with Protestants and Orthodox; why not continue on to dialogue with Jews, and then Muslims, Hindus, Buddhists, etc., and even nonbelievers? And so it is now happening in an explosion of interreligious/interideological dialogue of exponentially increasing magnitude. One need only look at the flood of books now appearing in the field.

Moreover, this dimension of the Copernican turn is at least as radical in its creative transformation of Catholic, Christian self-understanding as the other three, and hence profoundly affects all aspects of Christian life. For example, since in this new Age of Dialogue we Christians understand that our Jewish or Muslim neighbors can be "saved" without becoming Christian, our relationship to them ceases being one of "convert-making," and becomes dialogue and cooperation.

## A Radically New Age

Those scholars who earlier in the twentieth century with a great show of scholarship and historical/sociological analysis predicted the impending demise of Western civilization were "dead wrong." After World War I, in 1922, Oswald Spengler wrote his widely acclaimed book *The Decline of the West*.[2] After the beginning of World War II Pitirim A. Sorokin published in 1941 his likewise popular book, *The Crisis of Our Age*.[3] Given the massive, worldwide scale of the unprecedented destruction and horror of the world's first global war, 1914–18, and the even vastly greater terror of the second global conflict, 1939–45, the pessimistic predictions of these scholars and the great following they found are not ununderstandable.

In fact, however, those vast world conflagrations were manifestations of the dark side of the unique breakthrough in the history of humankind in the modern development of Christendom-become-Western Civilization, now becoming Global Civilization. Never before had there been world wars; likewise, never before had there been world political organizations (League of Nations, United Nations). Never before had humanity possessed the real possibility of destroying all human life — whether through nuclear or ecological catastrophe. These unique negative realities/potentialities were possible, however, only because of the correspondingly unique accomplishments of Christendom-Western-Global Civilization — the like of which the world has never before seen. On the negative side, from now on it will always be true that humankind can self-destruct. Still, there are solid empirical grounds for reasonable hope that the inherent, infinity-directed life force of humankind will nevertheless prevail over the parallel death force.

The prophets of doom were correct, however, in their understanding that humanity is entering into a radically new age. Earlier in this century the naysayers usually spoke of the doom of only Western civilization (e.g., Spengler, Sorokin), but after the advent of nuclear power and the Cold War, the new generation of pessimists — as said, not without warrant: *corruptio optimae pessima* — warned of *global* disaster. This emerging awareness of global disaster is a clear, albeit negative, sign that something profoundly, radically new is entering onto the stage of human history.

There have, of course, also recently been a number of more positive signs that we humans are entering a radically new age. In the 1960s there was much talk of "The Age of Aquarius," and there still is today the continuing fad of "New Age" consciousness. Some may be put off from the idea of an emerging radically new age because they perceive such talk to be simply that of fringe groups. I would argue, however, that the presence of "the crazies" around the edge of any idea or movement, far from being a sign of the invalidity of that idea or movement, is on the contrary a confirmation precisely of its validity, at least in its core concern. I would further argue that if people are involved with a movement which does not eventually develop its "crazies," its extremists, the movement is not touching the core of human-kind's concerns — they should get out of the movement, they are wasting their time!

Moreover, there have likewise recently been a number of very serious scholarly analyses pointing to the emergence of a radically new age in human history. One is the concept of the "paradigm-shift," particularly as expounded by Hans Küng.[4] The second is the notion of the "Second Axial Period," as articulated by Ewert Cousins.[5] Including these two, but setting them in a still larger context, I see the movement of humankind out of a multimillennia long "Age of Monologue" into the newly inbreaking "Age of Dialogue," indeed, an inbreaking "Age of Global Dialogue."[6]

Of course there is a great deal of continuity in human life throughout the shift from one major "Paradigm" to another, from one "Period" to another, from one "Age" to another. Nevertheless, even more striking than this continuity is the ensuing break, albeit largely on a different level than the continuity. This relationship of continuity and break in human history is analogous to the transition of water from solid to fluid to gas with the increase in temperature. With water there is throughout on the chemical level the continuity of $H_2O$. However, for those who have to deal with the water, it makes a fantastic difference whether the $H_2O$ is ice, water, or steam! In the case of the major changes in humankind, the physical base remains largely the same, but on the level of consciousness the change is massive. And here too it makes a fantastic difference whether we are dealing with humans whose consciousness is formed within one paradigm or within another, whose consciousness is Pre-Axial, Axial-I, or Axial-II, whose consciousness is Monologic or Dialogic.

## The Age of Global Dialogue

Ewert Cousins has basically affirmed everything Hans Küng has described as the newly emerging contemporary paradigm-shift (largely in terms of moving from the static to the dynamic), but he sees the present shift as much more profound than simply another in a series of major paradigm-shifts of human history. He sees the current transformation as a shift of the magnitude of the First Axial Period which will similarly reshape human consciousness. I too want to basically affirm what Küng sees as the emerging contemporary major paradigm-shift, as well as with Cousins that this shift is so profound as to match in magnitude the transformation of human consciousness of the Axial Period, so that it should be referred to as a Second Axial Period.

More than that, however, I am persuaded that what humankind is entering into now is not just the latest in a long series of major paradigm-shifts, as Hans Küng has so carefully and clearly analyzed. I am also persuaded that it is even more than the massive move into the consciousness transforming Second Axial Period, as Ewert Cousins has so thoroughly demonstrated. Beyond these two radical shifts, though of course including both of them, humankind is emerging out of the "from-the-beginning-till-now" millennia-long "Age of Monologue" into the newly dawning "Age of Dialogue."

The turn toward dialogue is, in my judgment, *the most fundamental, the most radical and utterly transformative* of the key elements of the newly emerging paradigm, which Hans Küng has so penetratingly outlined and which Ewert Cousins also perceptively discerns as one of the central constituents of the Second Axial Age. However, that shift from monologue to dialogue constitutes such a radical reversal in human consciousness, is so utterly new in the history of humankind *from the beginning,* that it must be designated as literally "revolutionary," that is, it turns everything absolutely around.

Up until almost the present just about *all* were convinced that they alone had the absolute truth. Because all were certain that they had the truth — otherwise they wouldn't have held that position — therefore others who thought differently necessarily held falsehood. But with the growing understanding that all perceptions of, and statements about, reality were — even if true — necessarily limited (the opposite of "ab-solute," that is, literally "un-limited"), the permission, and even the necessity, for dialogue with those who thought differently from us became increasingly apparent.

Thus dialogue — which is a conversation with those who think differently, the *primary* purpose of which is *for me* to learn from the other — is *a whole new way of thinking* in human history.

At the heart of this new dialogic way of thinking is the basic insight that I learn not by being merely passively open or receptive to, but by being in dialogue with, extramental reality. I not only "hear" or receive reality, but I also — and, I think, first of all — "speak" to reality. I ask it questions, I stimulate it to speak back to me, to answer my questions. In the process I give reality the specific categories and language in which to respond to me. The "answers" that I receive back from reality will always be in the language, the thought categories, of the questions I put to it. It can "speak" to me, can really communicate with my mind, only in a language and categories that I understand.

When the speaking, the responding, grow less and less understandable to me, if the answers I receive are sometimes confused and unsatisfying, then I probably need to learn to speak a more appropriate language when I put questions to reality. If, for example, I ask the question, "How far is yellow?" of course I will receive a non-sense answer. Or if I ask questions about living things in mechanical categories, I will receive confusing and unsatisfying answers. Thus, I will receive confusing and unsatisfying answers to questions about human sexuality if I use categories that are solely physical, biological. Witness the absurdity of the answer that birth control is forbidden by the natural law; the question falsely assumes that the nature of humanity is merely physical, biological. This dialogic view of truth, like the five other shifts in modern epistemology described above, is *relational,* as its very name, *dia-logos* (literally, "word-across"), indicates.

With the new and irreversible understanding of the meaning of truth resulting from modern epistemological advances, culminating in the insight of a dialogic view of truth, the modern critical thinker has undergone a radical Copernican turn. Recall that just as the vigorously resisted shift in astronomy from geocentrism to heliocentrism revolutionized that science, the paradigm or model shift in the understanding of truth statements has revolutionized all the humanities, including theology and ideology. The macroparadigm with which critical thinkers operate today (or the "horizon" within which they operate, to use Bernard Lonergan's term) is characterized by historical, social, linguistic, hermeneutical praxis and dialogic — *relational* — consciousness. This paradigm shift is far advanced among thinkers and doers; but as in the case of Copernicus, and even more dramatically of Galileo, there of course are still many resisters in positions of great institutional power.

Our perception, and hence description, of reality is like our view of an object in the center of a circle of viewers. My view and description of the object, or reality, may well be true, but it will not include what someone on the other side of the circle perceives and describes, which also may well be true. So, neither of our perceptions and descriptions of reality can be total, complete, "absolute" in that sense, or "objective" in the sense of not in any way being dependent on a "subject" or viewer. At the same time, however, it is also obvious that there is an "objective," doubtless "true" aspect to each perception and description, even though each is relational to the perceiver, or "subject."

## Conclusion

To sum up and reiterate: in the latter part of the twentieth century humankind is undergoing a macro-paradigm-shift (Hans Küng). More than that, at this time humankind is moving into a transformative shift in consciousness of the magnitude of the Axial Period (800–200 B.C.E.) so that we must speak of the emerging of the Second Axial Period (Ewert Cousins). Even more profound, however, now at the edge of the third millennium humankind is slipping out of the shadowy Age of Monologue, where it has been since its beginning, into the dawn of the Age of Dialogue (Leonard Swidler). Into this new Age of Dialogue Küng's macro-paradigm-shift and Cousins's Second Axial Period are sublated (*aufgehoben,* in Hegel's terminology), that is, taken up and transformed. Moreover, as Ewert Cousins has already detailed, humankind's consciousness is becoming increasingly global. Hence, our dialogue partners necessarily must also be increasingly global. In this new Age of Dialogue, dialogue on a global basis is now not only a possibility; it is a necessity. As I noted in a title of a recent book — humankind is faced ultimately with two choices: Dialogue or Death![7]

# 4

# Vatican II and the Turn Toward History: A New Freedom

One of the most powerful forces within Western civilization in the last century and a half has been the burgeoning sense of history, the growing awareness of change, dynamism, evolution, in all of reality and, most particularly, in humanity — individually and communally. The impact of this new sense of history only recently began to be felt within the Catholic Church, but the delayed impact rapidly effected wondrous changes, including the setting free of manifold forces of church renewal. Hence, to understand adequately the dynamics of freedom at work in the Catholic Church today, one must analyze the bases of the turn toward, of this new sense of, history and its relationship to the Church.

## The Nature of Historical Knowledge

History is a kind of knowledge, a knowledge of the past of at least part of a human community. As the knowledge of history spreads in a community, it becomes a sort of communal self-awareness; and it is this self-awareness, already on an individual level, that marks humans off from all other earthly creatures. This self-awareness of each individual person includes, not only a consciousness of her/his own unique being, but also an ever-expanding knowledge of things that are not him/herself. In fact, the knowledge of the self and the knowledge of other are bound together by an indissoluble and proportionately developing dialogue.

The more I learn to know the world about me, both in the sense of piling up fact on fact, and in the sense of penetrating somewhat the very structure of a thing, of grasping its reality, both in its essentiality and its particularity, the more I learn to know myself. This occurs partly by analogy with what I have learned of the other; having grasped something of the reality of the other, I may suddenly become aware of the existence of something similar in me. It also occurs partly by direct differentiation from the other: in a negative, but not therefore unimportant, way my knowledge of myself grows by learning more about what I am not. And finally, it occurs when in the very

19

act of knowing the other I at the same time perceive myself knowing, how I am knowing, and, therefore, to some extent, how I am not knowing.

But all of this "growing" knowledge on the part of the human being does not happen simply in a moment-to-moment fashion. People have memories whereby they are able to accumulate the knowledge garnered from each moment. The memory, however, is a faculty which produces not only a quantified build-up of information, but also a qualified change in the ability to perceive the reality of the other. One of the startling discoveries of the relatively young discipline of psychology has been to see just how much the "recollection" of past events restructures our human apparatus for perceiving the reality that is the other and our self. This is true even though, and perhaps especially if, the recollection has faded from our conscious memory into our unconscious. A second great discovery was the realization that the simple act of recovering the past knowledge from the unconscious realm places the individual in a position to evaluate and integrate it into a more coherent structure of perceiving, assimilating, and reacting to current reality. This is one among many areas the words of Jesus, "The truth will make you free," apply with unsuspected aptness.

Everyone, of course, lives in a community, or rather many communities, and these communities also provide some kind of collective memories. One does not have to be a nineteenth-century romantic or an avid devotee of Carl Jung to affirm such a notion; one need simply be a sensitive observer. The Church is one of the communities the Christian lives in — in many ways one of the most humanly important communities — and it also has a communal memory. It manifests itself in an almost limitless variety of ways: doctrines, functional relationships of offices, liturgies, alleged recollections of the past, postures toward all other aspects of life. The Church's memory embraces all of life because the Church is, or should be, a totally comprehensive community; there can be no portion of reality toward which it does not take a stance. This comprehensiveness, of course, in no way necessarily implies an exclusivity, but if the Church is functioning rightly it will provide a vital integrating overview of all reality for its members.

At almost the same time psychology was uncovering the profound importance to the individual of memory, conscious and unconscious, in the perceiving of current reality, and the liberating force of the act of transferring knowledge from the unconscious to the conscious memory, history was making somewhat similar findings for communities. History in the eighteenth century was often thought to be merely a recounting of the past so as to find examples of the universal qualities of humanity: what was not of universal character was not looked upon as really human, and hence was often distorted and even more often ignored or not even seen. But in the nineteenth century a passion developed for the particular, for the unique, and in the very growth of this knowledge men and women became aware of growth and finally perceived how this growth metamorphosed their perception of reality;

that is, the nineteenth-century positivist view of history — the purist searching for "how it really was," *wie es eigentlich gewesen ist* — gave way to an ever growing awareness of just how much the history a person writes is formed by what that person brings to this study of the documents.

## Impact on the Church of the New Sense of History

It is rather dramatically apparent how this sense of history, this awareness of growth in all things, has influenced the Church in its liturgy. The very act of learning how we arrived at the various rigid forms of the liturgy was sufficient to release us from an unwarranted bondage to these forms. The past experiences could then be evaluated for what they really were and placed in proper perspective and integrated into all the rest of the Church's experience — proper to the Church's current needs, that is. The Church, like all vital communities, must be constantly "updated," *"aggiornamento*-ized" to fulfill its proper function. Good history has here deabsolutized historical reality, e.g., the Latin silent canon did not preexist in some pseudo-Platonic world of ideas and wait until the ninth century to incarnate itself forever thereafter. It developed out of a specific set of concrete, temporal circumstances and must be evaluated accordingly.

In the area of doctrine the Vatican II "coming of age" of the Church began to produce even more spectacular results. First of all, the Catholic community began to acquire a new awareness of how important it is to know the whole history of a dogmatic formula in order to interpret it accurately. Where before an analytic, scholastic approach was often used exclusively, the problems of theology now are placed first in historical perspective, with the result that many of the old impasses dissolve. Instead of merely taking a dogmatic formula and analyzing it, as it were, on the table in front of them, contemporary Catholic theologians — who are also half historians — study the original documents bearing on the problem.

### Contextualization Example

A timely example might be the final phrase that was added at the last moment to the statement of Vatican Council I (1869–70) which sweepingly argued that papal statements were irreformable of themselves and not by consent of the Church, *ex sese non ex consensu ecclesiae*. Such a statement might easily be construed to indicate that the pope can, merely by fulfilling the prerequisites outlined in the rest of Vatican I's decree, issue an irreformable decree quite apart from the consensus, that is, the general mind, or faith, of the Church. However, when one becomes aware of the long history of Gallicanism[1] and its influence even into the nineteenth century, and adds to that the awareness of the tendency to associate Gallicanism with the French Revolution — and all the agony for the institutional Church it entailed — it is not difficult to understand how many bishops would have been so intent upon crushing out every possible ember of Gallicanism, which included the tenet that decrees of the pope could enjoy infallibility and, hence, irreformability, only if the body of bishops indicated their consent (*ex consensu episcoporum*).

It is apparent from the speeches and writings of the minority bishops at Vatican I that one of their major concerns was to see that the final formulary did not give the impression that the pope could somehow be isolated from the rest of the Church in his role as infallible teacher. Except for a handful of extremists like Cardinal Manning of England (a vigorous opponent of his fellow convert from Anglicanism, the theologically liberal John Henry Newman, later made cardinal), the members of the majority seemed to answer the resisting minority: "Yes, yes, we agree that the pope is not to be isolated from the Church in his infallible teaching, but that is clear enough; what we must make certain of is that the old virus of Gallicanism, now veiled in the democratic notion that the consent of the bishops must be somehow obtained before the pope can make an infallible statement, be absolutely stamped out."

Hence, one can make a case for arguing that the phrase *non ex consensu ecclesiae* was intended to eliminate the requirement that the consent of the bishops be obtained (*ex consensu episcoporum*), as in a poll; it did not intend at all to say that the pope could speak infallibly outside the consensus of the Church. Such a "historical," "contextual" understanding of this statement in fact opened up many more avenues of development than the former nonhistorical interpretation. (However, as will be discussed below, the very notion of infallibility was even more radically questioned by further historical analysis of the teaching going back to the Middle Ages.)

It should also be pointed out that just as one attains a greater knowledge of oneself by an ever fuller differentiation of oneself from the other — and this, paradoxically, enables one to identify oneself with the other in love much more profoundly because a possible veiled egoism is thereby eliminated — so also does a community, in this instance, the Church. Theologians, often having sympathetically immersed themselves in history, are today much more deeply aware that dogmatic formularies have functioned largely as delimiting factors. Dogmatic definitions state that outside of certain areas the truth of specific mysteries of the faith is not to be found (literally, *de-finis*); which of the many possible understandings of the formulary is the true one the formulary itself, of course, cannot say; only the actual life of the Church can provide the key to this. One student of Catholic theology has stated this notion very well:

> To use a metaphor, what a dogma does is to draw a line across an indefinitely wide expanse of possible affirmations. On the one side are the affirmations which it excludes, which, if it is well-formulated, it clearly and unambiguously says are false. On the other side, is an indefinitely large number of mutually incompatible religious meanings and theological interpretations which it admits as possibly true, but only one of which is actually true. It would be nonsense to

demand of a dogma that it designate which one of its possible interpretations is the true one. It is no more possible to do this than to square a circle....

The positive theological meaning and concrete religious significance of a dogmatic formulation must be viewed as coming from outside, from the Bible, the worship and the life of the Christian community, and the general cultural and intellectual context. The primary function of a dogma must therefore be to exclude error; its role, not only as a matter of historical fact but in the very nature of the case, must be primarily negative and defensive.[2]

## Development of Doctrine

But perhaps most deep-going of all the changes the modern sense of history is beginning to work in the Church and its doctrine is the growing acceptance that doctrine grows or develops in a much more profound way than was previously thought. Development of doctrine is not just a making explicit, by way of logical deduction, of what was previously implicit. It certainly is not a simple, always progressive, "organic" growth as from the acorn into the oak tree — to use Newman's image — for there have been some obvious reversals, such as in the teaching on religious freedom in the last 150 years. Nor is it sufficient to say that the substance of the doctrine remains the same in each age, but the formulation of it can be changed and perhaps improved, as good Pope John stated in such quiet revolutionary fashion. What is demanded as the community of the Church attains a greater knowledge of itself and the other (in dialogic fashion) is not just a reformulation of the mysteries of the faith, but also a reconceptualization.

As the community becomes more fully human (the element of hope grows ever stronger here, for as we scale the mountain of our potentialities, the heights become ever more dizzying and could lead to an ever more disastrous fall), it is naturally going to require a proportionately greater degree of freedom in conceptualizing and expressing the mysteries of the faith. This by no means implies a complete sort of relativism; there are a number of definite constants: the revelation as found in the Scriptures and the Apostolic Church (*Scriptura*); Tradition (*Traditio*), which will provide us with a sort of series of proportionalities (for example, what transubstantiation was to the mystery of the Real Presence in the Middle Ages, "transsignification" and other attempts at reconceptualization are trying to be today); the living Church — the People of God with the hierarchy within it, not above it — under the guidance of the Holy Spirit (*magisterium latum*, the magisterium broadly understood).

## Historical Creativity

These, of course, are not the building blocks of a mechanistic kind of system which can produce the eternal verities in concepts and formularies eternally valid for all people, times, and places. They are more like the living tissues which in vital organic interaction can transcend themselves.

Here we fumble with the latest gift of the new sense of history; the past leads to the present but it also implies the future, which contains the radically unknown; for history shows us that because of human freedom the present is not limited to an unfolding of the potential of the past. Human freedom, despite all its restrictions, places in our hands the power of creativity. This has always been potentially available, but now that the new sense of history has made the Christian more profoundly aware of it, its operation on the communal level of the Church will be the more profound.

# 5

# Vatican II and the Turn
# Toward Freedom

## Freedom and Unfreedom

If one were asked to put the most central, burning issue of the decade of Vatican II, the 1960s, into one word, that word would be "freedom." In fact, for the last two hundred years it has been the central word in one or other of its variant forms from *liberté* of the French Revolution, or "Give me liberty or give me death" of the American Revolution, to *Uhuru* in postcolonial Africa of the 1960s. Moreover, there is no sign that the passionate search for freedom is about to abate, for within the last decades the intensity of the search has both increased and broadened.

The 1950s were the days of "McCarthyism," of the "Organization Men," of conformity and complacency, when the aim of college and career for men was to sink themselves ever more deeply into the folds of a giant American Linus blanket; for women the aim was to retreat into the pseudo-sanctuary of the unfulfilling fulfillment of the "feminine mystique."

But that era ended with the demise of the 1950s, and a new era was inaugurated in a preeminent way by two men named John — John F. Kennedy and John XXIII. One treated the secular as sacred, the things of humankind as pertaining to God; the other treated the sacred as secular, the things of God as pertaining to humankind. They thereby freed the objects of their own primary concern to be what they were supposed to be. John F. Kennedy treated his human tasks as a sacred trust and thereby helped lift politics, human life, out of self-centeredness to a service of others: "Ask not what your country can do for you, but what you can do for your country." John XXIII embraced the world (as he symbolically did in his response to a life convict who asked him if God could ever forgive a murderer — Pope John threw his arms around him). He embraced the world, with all its joys and miseries, as God's gift to and task for humanity. Each with his own approach, these two men saw that only by freeing the secular from a cramped sort of selfish secularism and the sacred from a twisted sort of Manicheistic sacralism could the secular and the sacred really be fully secular and sacred,

25

that is, when they were seen to be the same reality viewed from two different aspects.

Not accidentally, both men, one for the secular world and one for the Church, were also deeply committed to openness to and concern for others, to freedom and responsibility, for they saw that contemporary men and women can no longer continue to exist in a closed ghetto unconcerned about their neighbor, that they will not live without freedom, and therefore they cannot live long without responsibility. These two men symbolized and partly inspired the new concerns of the 1960s: freedom and responsibility, which also are two aspects of a single reality — human life.

In the 1960s the cry of freedom for American Blacks was raised; there were sit-ins, marches, demonstrations, and even violence, under the banner of freedom for Blacks. Also in that decade the cry of freedom for the poor from their grinding degradation was raised, but the "war on poverty" was no more than engaged when its outcome was threatened by the escalating war in Vietnam. That war in turn called forth another cry of freedom by many Americans from what they said was the myth of America's infallible right-eousness. In the years since the beginning of Vatican II the cry of freedom in the Catholic Church was also raised — freedom for Catholics from restrictive ecclesiastical traditions to fulfill their true gospel-centered tradition of service to God's world. American Catholics lived in the "land of the free" and were nurtured in a religious tradition which stated that "the truth will make you free." They maintained that they are free, or that they had a right to be free.

For some philosophers freedom is humanity's greatest gift. For others, freedom is that to which humanity is condemned. It is well to reflect briefly on what this freedom is that everyone is talking about, that everyone is yearning and striving for.

To be free is to be unbound, to be unrestricted. But when one speaks of human freedom, one must ask what the human person is freed from, what the human being is freed for, and what the consequences of freedom and unfreedom are. It is logical to consider the last-named first, since that is where the human person, as an infant, starts, in a state of unfreedom. The theological word for unfreedom is "sin." What is meant by that is not so much sins in the plural, but sin in the singular, not so much sinful acts as the sinful state out of which those acts naturally and regularly flow. The focus, then, is not so much on acts which are "wrong," a common definition of sins, but on the state in which a person is, whereby that person's actions tend to be "wrong." This wrongness, this state of sin, basically is a lack of freedom from self-centeredness. Put positively, sin is being bound to, being restricted by, one's self.

It may be asked why being self-centered is wrong, is sinful. One answer is this: experience teaches that it is the peculiar nature of the human person to be potentially open to all other beings. Indeed, this capacity is in some ways infinite, that is, unlimited. In many ways a woman or man can be united to other beings even to the point of being identified with them. This is what happens in love, when, for example, a woman identifies with her beloved, her *alter ego*. It is the nature of humans to be able to move beyond themselves, to embrace an ever-expanding universe of persons, of beings, of all reality, even the ultimate source of all reality. Hence, to remain within the closed case of one's self is to act contrary to one's very structure; in more traditional terms, it is to violate the "natural law." It is like a seed refusing to break out of itself and put forth the plant. Such a seed is "bad seed." In scriptural terms, in the Jewish and Christian "law," all men and women are to love their neighbor as themselves. The fact is that if people do not love, are not open to, their neighbor, they do not even really love themselves, for they are shut up within themselves in the pain of utter loneliness.

Once this human unfreedom or state of sin is recognized as being locked inside the case of one's self, then the way is clear to seeing what it is the human person has to be freed from. To be really humanly free, humans must be liberated from anything and everything that restricts their openness to, their knowledge of, their love of, themselves and the other. The things that restrict a person's openness and freedom are far too numerous to begin to list all of them, but it is well to look briefly at a few of those that have special significance today.

By way of prolegomenon, it should be noted that almost everything that expands a person's universe by knowledge and love can also in turn serve as a restriction, as a somewhat larger or more heavily gilded cage. Only the attainment of an open and dynamic view of life can transform each new experience from being something like the bars of a prison into the cables of a bridge to an expanding reality.

A dominant force in the lives of many is the religious tradition in which they were reared. If a religion (in brief: "an explanation of the ultimate meaning of life, and how to live accordingly") is what it should be, it will help free women and men from the tyranny of the mountain of meaningless moments and experiences that life can appear to be. It can, in a preeminent fashion, help to open men and women to their neighbor, to all reality, and to its Source. It can give them an explanation of the meaning of life, help them to bring some sort of order into, to make sense out of, the day-to-day and year-to-year events.

A religion can, however, and often has been, a very restrictive, unfree influence in women and men's lives. But when religion becomes restrictive, it is in reality inhuman and, therefore, irreligious.

Far too often the religions or churches people have been brought up in have weighed them down with a myriad of religious, ecclesiastical traditions that may, or may not, have had some meaning at one time, but which have long since lost any significance. Of course, the challenging of constrictive traditions does not mean that all traditions are to be eliminated: for, even if that were possible, humanity would then be thrown into a state of anarchy, of lawlessness — and there is nothing more destructive of freedom than lawlessness. Religious traditions should not be peremptorily abrogated, but, where possible, be preserved and updated, be made effective and meaningful.

## Freedom and Responsibility

It is now proper to consider what men and women are freed *for* by turning to the other aspect of human reality adjoining freedom, namely, responsibility. If people choose one action rather than another, then they must answer for their choice. They must *respond* to the question: "Who made this choice? Who is *respons-ible*?" Those who are free, who are open and turned toward the other, are also those who will answer for their actions. Those who will run and leave others to answer for their actions, those who are irresponsible, are not open and turned toward the other, but are turned in on themselves, are self-centered, are unfree.

Therefore, if people yearn to be free, if they yearn to be open to self, other persons, all reality, and its Source, God, as they learn to know more fully self, others, and God, they must also answer to their knowledge of them. They must be responsible to them. As much as possible and in an ever broadening and deepening fashion, they must unite and identify with them; they must respond to their needs. In fact, they must make the other's needs their needs. This is the message Jesus preached by his life: "Lord, when did we see you hungry or thirsty or without a job or discriminated against or killed unjustly?" "What you have done to one of these the least of my brothers or sisters, you have done to me" (Mt 25:40). "My friends... God is love... and anyone who says 'I love God,' and hates his sister or brother, is a liar, since whoever does not love the brother or sister who can be seen, cannot love God who has never been seen" (1 John 4:8, 20).

The development of this concern for others, that is, of the capacity of the individual to make free decisions in a responsible fashion, in other words, the development of maturity, is one of the ultimate goals of every educative process, whether it be in the family, school, or other institution. Such responsible decisions require a certain knowledge concerning the area of decision and a willingness to accept the consequences of the decision. They also of necessity include the ability to make the decisions and carry them out; that is, responsible decisions presume freedom. If a person is not free to make a choice, that person cannot be held responsible for the consequences. If there is no freedom, there is no responsibility, since the irresponsible person is trapped within his or her own self. Hence, the process of education must also include a proportioned involvement of freedom. This parallel development can be seen in a very simple way in the curricula of the various educational systems; the first years of study in general, and of a particular discipline, are rather stringently prescribed, whereas with the development of a certain amount of maturity students are allowed more freedom of choice in following their own interests in specialization. The same pattern, of course, can be seen in the well-run family. Very small children have almost no freedom of choice, nor are they held responsible for their actions, but a real effort is made as the children grow to give them proportionately greater freedom, for they are able to accept greater responsibility.

The Church, of course, is in a position similar to that of the parent and the teacher. In fact, the Church is often referred to as "Holy Mother Church," and one of the most vital functions of the Church is to fulfill its mission to proclaim the gospel, to be a teacher of the nations, to exercise magisterium. If this is true, then at least one of the major goals of the Church must also be that of the parent and the teacher — the development of maturity in those for whom it has concern. In many ways the Church in the past has worked vigorously toward this goal. For example, it fostered learning and the spread of learning in the Middle Ages when no other institution could. However, in recent centuries, as the masses of men and women have advanced in learning and commensurate maturity, the Church has often tended not to allow them their proportional freedom. It has tended to continue to treat most women and men like children who cannot be trusted to make responsible decisions, and therefore cannot be given the necessary freedom. However, such a situation cannot continue indefinitely. Mature adults will either find a way to act freely and responsibly within the institution or in their eventual frustration and embitterment will attempt to withdraw from the institution or even destroy it.

Fortunately, with Vatican II Catholics began to find ways for increasing numbers of the faithful to act as free, responsible adults in the Church.

# 6

# The Vatican II Attitude
# Toward History and Freedom

## Responsibilities of the Historian and the Catholic

Because we humans are most profoundly the product of our past, we must study that past very carefully so that we may know ourselves more precisely. This is doubly mandatory for Christians since Christianity is a historical religion. Yet if the history of humankind could be summed up in one or two words, they would be, as Lord Acton indicated, "freedom" and "unfreedom." Hence it is very important today, as the new sense of history and freedom dawns on us both as humans and as Christian humans, to analyze carefully what our understanding of and attitude toward history and freedom have been.

In studying our own past, we must approach the task as diligently, critically, and sympathetically as possible, taking care to be as objective as we can. However, at times we must also take on another task when reviewing our past, a task that is incumbent upon us not specifically as students of the past, as historians, but rather as human persons, namely, making a judgment about the object studied. Again, this obligation will be doubled when a Christian and the study of the Christian past is involved.

After an event or an institution has been studied in true historicist fashion — that is, after it has been discerned with meticulous objectivity, using all the sources possible, and leaving no evidence aside because it does not seem to fit an a priori schema, and after the subject has been evaluated in terms of the principles of its time and not ours — there will, I believe, be occasions when a judgment should be made by the Christian on the "Christian-ness" of an institution; and obviously no one is in a better position to render such a judgment than the intelligent Christian who has carefully studied the institution in question. Some would side with Herbert Butterfield and say that the student of the past should never make moral judgments — except in the historicist fashion;[1] some would agree with Isaiah Berlin and maintain that women and men studying their past cannot avoid making moral judgments.[2] What I am suggesting here is that "for the sake of argument" Butterfield be granted his point — although I personally am inclined to side with Berlin —

30

but that the student of the past, not as historian, but as Christian, decide whether or not the spirit of Jesus was in the institution under study. I am suggesting this for institutions, not persons, for, as Butterfield points out, the hearts of men are hard to read for anyone who is not God.

Perhaps an example will help make the point clearer. In studying the Inquisition, the Christian — and here permit me to narrow the category to Catholic in order to eliminate the possibility of polemics — will, like every other student of the past, have the obligation of describing the institution and the conditions of its time. This person will have to point out that in this period of Western civilization Church and State, the sacred and secular, were so interwoven that a revolt against one would most probably have involved a revolt against the other. Any one who preached heresy was also a disturber of the civil peace. Moreover, the Church as such did not perform the execution, but handed the culprit over to the State authorities. Torture was a common practice among civil officials in attempting to extract confessions, and so this inquisitorial practice must be seen as a reflection of the cruelty of the times. At the same time it must be recalled that there was a great deal of hypocrisy and abuse in the practice of the Inquisition, although of course an institution cannot be condemned because of the abuse of it.

But after all this has been said, the Catholic must then step back and as a Catholic hold up the Inquisition to the most objective standard of Christianity to be found: the life of Jesus as found in the New Testament. Of course some subjectiveness will creep in here. But this is an inevitability in the human structure of things. However, in this instance I believe the facts in the documents loom so large that they cannot be pulled out of focus by the honest person. When this comparison is made, the conclusion must be that the Inquisition is essentially unchristian in almost every aspect. The very idea that adherence to a belief in Jesus and a loving worship of God can be forced is inimical to the whole spirit of the gospel. The "joyful news" cannot be crammed down someone's throat under the threat of the torch. Fortunately, Catholic historians finally took this position even before Vatican II. One Catholic scholar referred to the erecting of the Papal Inquisition in the thirteenth century as one of the darkest pages in the history of the Church, a phenomenon that no one today will justify.[3]

## Special Catholic Temptations

In the light of past experiences, it would seem that Catholics have been especially prone to certain temptations when they considered specifically Catholic institutions.

The first temptation is one peculiar to all who are committed to an institution of long standing, and is particularly acute when the institution is one with claims of infallibility: witness the mid-twentieth-century writing of history by some Russian Marxists. The temptation for the Catholic has been to defend everything that the Church, or that Church authorities, have done in the past. By starting out with this attitude, even unconsciously, Catholics destroy themselves as honest men and women. They become instead more or less technically sophisticated polemicists. They are not seeking the truth really; they are seeking to discomfit their enemy and win an argument. In this they do God and the Church a grave disservice. God is pleased by nothing less than the complete truth; how could God be other since God is Truth? And when the Church is defended by something less than the whole truth, it is stained and contaminated by the falsity involved; it to some extent becomes captive to the "lie," and one lie always leads to other, bigger ones and to a constriction of freedom. And when the truth does finally come out, there is a horrible disillusionment and very painful catharsis for all the faithful.

Perhaps an example will again help to clarify this point. Catholics for centuries felt called upon to defend the late medieval and early modern Church in almost all its aspects. The most they would admit was that there were *some* unhappy conditions, but not nearly so many as non-Catholics had insisted; besides, these "peccadillos" are to be expected in all human institutions, and the Protestant churches were just as bad or worse. Somehow the Calvinist execution of Servetus "justified" the St. Bartholemew's Day Massacre by French Catholics.

Older Catholics are all familiar with this approach; we have seen it in our grade school, high school, and even college textbooks, in the pamphlets at the rear of the churches, and heard it in sermons from the pulpit and talks in parish halls and at Church banquets. But what were the conditions of religious life in Christendom at the beginning of the sixteenth century? They were indeed bad, so bad that one Catholic scholar, Josef Lortz, stated that the Reformation was "historically necessary."[4] Catholic historians like Lortz, Jedin, and other European scholars at last began to admit the evils that were rife in the Catholic Church at that time, not in some sort of gleeful masochism, but with penitent *nostra culpa*s before God and the world — both of whom Catholics have offended. And this action did not injure the Church. On the contrary, it improved the Church in the eyes of those within and outside it.

Another temptation for Catholics, quite similar to the one just discussed, is an inordinate falling back on Providence in describing Christian history. One Catholic thinker remarked that there can be really no philosophy of history, but only a theology of history.[5] The inclination of many Catholics in the past had been in effect to play God. They often saw all sorts of divine patterns in events, patterns that frequently had a greater reality in their imaginations than in God's Providence — which we refer to as inscrutable. It seems to me that it is inscrutable not only in the present and future, but also most often in the past. Saying that all history is in God's hands says so much that, as far as seeing patterns in concrete details is concerned, it comes close to saying nothing. We may be able to make out some very large and very general patterns and faint glimmerings here and there. But we should be very careful not to try to apply these patterns in too specific a fashion or even be too wedded to the general patterns, for they may appear to need adjustment at some future date. Otherwise there will arise the problems of Leibnitz's best of all possible worlds.

This aspect of the problem concerning the relationship of history and Providence may not be quite so pressing today as another side of the problem, which is most closely related to the tendency to defend everything. Catholics who cannot bring themselves to controvert the unpleasant facts they find in the history of Christianity or the history of the Church may succumb to the temptation to say that it was obviously all in the Providence of God, that God must have willed it that way so that something better could grow out of it. Here we come very close to the ancients' concept of fate: whatever happened did so because it had to; it was inevitable. The pseudo-Christian version is that it had to happen because it was in God's Providence.

Obviously there is a sense in which this is true: all things happen because God permits them. But this fact in no way eliminates intermediate causes. It was all right for the scientifically naive person to stop with saying that the grain grows because God makes it grow; but the agronomist surely must search for more immediate, physical causes. So too must students of history: they also need to search for the more immediate, historical causes, whether they be social, political, economic, geographic, or a combination of several of these. Moreover, it must be especially noted that here a free creature is involved; and although God's omnipotence is not to be frustrated, God's dealings with humanity do not, cannot — by God's own fiat found in the natural structure of reality — destroy this freedom.

There have been endless discussions about determinism and free will, God's omnipotence and the human being's freedom on the natural level, and about grace and free will on the supernatural. But we must remember that two mysteries are involved here: the ultimately "unexplainable" free will of the human being, and the essential omnipotence of God. Not being able to completely analyze the two, humans find it impossible ever to see clearly how the two intermesh.

Another kindred temptation for the Catholic is, after having found unpleasant facts in the history of the Church, to attempt to explain them away with specious, *post factum* arguments and maintain that the actions taken were necessary, were the best possible at that time and under those circumstances, and that if those measures had not been taken matters would have been even worse. Sometimes, many times, this will be true. But to assume that it is always true is to canonize the past merely because it is past, a slightly paraphrased version of Alexander Pope's dictum, "whatever is, is right." It has already been pointed out that the best contemporary Catholic historians have complained that the founding day of the Inquisition was a dark day for the Church. It was a dark day, not only as seen from the twentieth century, but an evil day, a day injurious to the Church, in the thirteenth century. If the Church had not inaugurated the Inquisition but had met the problem — it was profound, widespread, and demanded drastic action — with positive approaches in preaching and teaching that were compatible with the spirit of the gospel, the Church and society would have been better then, and now, for it. True, the Albigensian and other heresies were suppressed after many bloody decades. But the cure was worse than the disease; the reforms that were called for explicitly or implicitly by the Waldensians, Lollards, and others were merely postponed until the day of reckoning came in 1517, and consequently the Church was splintered into hundreds of pieces.

After Vatican II the *Index of Forbidden Books* was abolished, and many Catholics took the attitude that the Index had then become outmoded and therefore a change was in order. The temptation for Catholics is to say that, of course, in the sixteenth and ensuing centuries it was necessary and good that the Church established and maintained the Index (it was first drawn up by the extremist Cardinal Caraffa, then Pope Paul IV, in 1559). The fact that the Index has been in the Church for four hundred years is *prima facie* evidence that it was a good thing. But the intelligent Catholic cannot stop with such superficial evidence. The evil of nepotism was a long time with the Church, but that does not justify it at its beginning or anywhere during its history. A thorough study of the facts will indicate, I believe, that the Index caused more harm than good even in the sixteenth century.

Any number of events happened in the Church during the Reformation and Counter-Reformation periods that intelligent Catholics find shocking today: the almost absolute freezing of the liturgy in the Latin language, the forbidding even of the translation of the prayers of the Mass into a modern language (renewed by Pope Pius IX in 1857 and in force until the time of Pope Leo XIII),[6] the extremely severe restrictions on possessing and reading the Bible by Catholic laity,[7] and many more. Catholics in the past leapt to the "defense" of the Church here again, as they also did in the very embarrassing Galileo case — only in the 1990s laid to rest by the Vatican's admission of guilt. But again I believe a case for challenging the value of these proscriptions may be made by an objective Catholic who has studied the facts thoroughly without an a priori inclination to assume that they must have been good for the Church, at least at that time. For example, many "concessions" on the vernacular in the liturgy were made to countless Germans to good effect as far as the Catholic Church was concerned. The historical research of Lortz, Veit, Lenhart, and others strongly indicates that a more open, permissive policy on the vernacular by Catholic authorities in the sixteenth century would have been far wiser;[8] from just the Counter-Reformation point of view it would have "stolen some of the thunder" of the Protestants.

## Special Catholic Tasks

Several special tasks confront Catholics when they consider the past history of the Catholic Church. One task may be well designated as an apologetical one, not in the sense of "leaping to the Church's defense," a tactic which has already been discussed, but in the sense of translating the significance of the past history of the Church to the world, a sort of demythologization of the Church. Obviously there will be times when deliberate misrepresentations will have to be set aright. But what is meant here is a kind of "kerygmatic" presentation of Christianity and the Church to the world; this is in some way a participation in the bringing of the Word of God to the world, but the Word as extended in the Church over the centuries. This in no way means a distortion of facts or a covering of blemishes in the body of the Church; all must be made bare so that it may be cleansed. Catholics should be able to understand the central Christian meaning of historical Christian institutions — whether they be distorted in outward form or no — and explain them to their contemporaries in a language that will speak to them and their problems.

*Mutatis mutandis* this is the perennial task of all students of the past. The presentation of the facts, all the facts, and their significance is all that is necessary — but it is all necessary. This is what Leo XIII had in mind when he opened the Vatican archives to scholars and admonished them to report only and all the truth. Leo's admonition was needed not only by non-Catholics but even, sadly, by Catholics who were members of the hierarchy. For example, the editor of Lord Acton's correspondence, Cardinal Gasquet, muted or even suppressed many of Acton's stronger expressions, presumably in Acton's and the Church's interests.[9] More recently Johannes Neuhäusler, auxiliary bishop of Munich, was accused of altering and suppressing portions of documents on Catholic Church-State relations under the Nazis, which he edited in the book *Kreuz und Hakenkreuz* (Munich, 1946).[10] These and the like, of course, are unforgivable sins for the non-Catholic scholar; they do not become less so for the Catholic.

Another task the student of history must perform for all society, and this is also a task the Catholic must perform for Christian culture, is to prevent temporal, historical conditions from becoming absolutized. This is a particularly critical task in such a long-enduring — and hence tradition-revering and authoritarian-oriented — institution as the Catholic Church. Many of the customs of the Catholic religion and the institutions and cultures it has inspired are presumed to be absolute essentials, whereas they are merely the results of historical accident.

An example of an "absolutized" custom is the notion that lay people per se cannot engage in preaching, that this is a responsibility and a privilege that belongs essentially and exclusively to the cleric. One may try to argue from philosophical or theological grounds that this is not so, but that is not even necessary. Using the principle "if it happened, it's possible," *ab esse ad posse,* the student of history needs only to point out the many times in past history that Catholic Church authorities, indeed Pope Innocent III himself, empowered lay people to preach in Church. Even Cardinal Nicholas Wiseman, of whom it was said that he "subordinated the laity to the clergy in all matters in which religion was concerned, including education and politics,"[11] reported laymen preaching from the pulpits of churches in Rome in the middle of the nineteenth century.[12]

## Freedom and Its Presence and Absence in Catholic History

### The Middle Ages and the Early Modern Period

To carry out their tasks properly, Catholics must live in an atmosphere of freedom, freedom to search out the truth and speak it, regardless of the embarrassment it may cause. This also is true when Catholics are looking at the history of the Church. It has been noted that no less a person than Pope Leo XIII said that this was the right and duty of the student of history. Unfortunately, such has not always been the attitude of all Catholic Church authorities. The problem of freedom has long been an issue of concern in the Catholic Church. It certainly was not missing even in the earliest days of Christianity. But it was particularly sharpened during the latter part of the so-called Dark Ages and the Middle Ages as the Church and the State became more closely wedded. This marriage was especially pregnant with mischief for Christian freedom: as witness the essentially new Christian phenomenon of burning heretics at the stake, as witness the Inquisition and all its torturous horrors, under the threat of the torch.

Still, there was a great deal of liberty within Christendom — within certain limits — and in some ways this liberty was in practice expanded at the time of the Renaissance, only partly because the papacy suffered formidable blows against its authority and prestige with the rise of the national monarchies, the Avignon papacy, the Western Schism, and Conciliarism. Unfortunately these events, and others, helped to prepare the ground for the Reformation that was long overdue. Also unfortunately the reforms effected by Luther, Calvin, and others did not produce a unified reformed Christian Church, as they had hoped. Rather, it divided Christianity into warring camps which proceeded to close ranks, to whip their citizenry into phalanxes prepared for total war. Thus the Protestant Reformation exacerbated the problem of freedom — at least for Catholics.

In the latter half of the seventeenth and the eighteenth centuries there was a certain relaxation of this closed-rank, vigilant attitude among Catholics, if only because of weariness, the inroads of the Enlightenment and rationalism, and the attacks upon the authoritarianism of the Church by the

French *Philosophes* and others: witness the dissolution of the Jesuits and the rise of Gallicanism, Febronianism, and Josephinism.[13]

## The Post-Enlightenment Period

But it is in the nineteenth century — the century of freedom and liberalism — that we witness an extraordinary rolling back of Christian freedom, an extraordinary growth of archconservative authoritarianism, of Catholic ghettoism.

This is the century that saw the condemnation by Pope Gregory XVI of the perfectly orthodox Félicité Lamennais, who had attempted to foster a rapprochement between Catholicism and liberal thought. This was also the century which witnessed the pontificate of the longest reigning pope in the history of the Catholic Church, Pius IX. It was he who, on the strength of the papacy, declared the doctrine of the Immaculate Conception; it was also he who issued the infamous *Syllabus of Errors* in 1864 in which he stated that it was erroneous for anyone to say that "the Roman Pontiff can and should reconcile and align himself with progress, liberalism, and modern civilization." All this reached a climax with the declaration of papal infallibility in 1870 and the forbidding of all Italian Catholics to participate in Italian politics or to even vote, because of the loss of the Papal States to the newly unified Italian national state. Thus in a way all liberalism, all democracy, all science, all contact with the non-Catholic and modern world was condemned as being at best a waste of time and highly dangerous.

However, the reaction on the part of Catholics — perhaps best exemplified on the civil scene by Count Joseph de Maistre (1753–1821) and his insistence on the reestablishment of those two pillars of society, the pope and the executioner — is by no means historically and psychologically unintelligible.

Already during the Enlightenment, the Catholic Church was attacked from many sides under the banner of liberty. During the French Revolution, with its slogan of *liberté, égalité, fraternité,* the Church was tremendously ravaged — and not merely on the physical level. Priests and religious were persecuted, exiled, and murdered. Church property was desecrated, some being rededicated to the "Goddess of Reason," and confiscated all over France and Central Europe. The situation was only somewhat ameliorated by Napoleon — the same Napoleon who kidnapped and browbeat Pope Pius VII. But the Church's troubles were only just starting. The movement of democratic liberalism in its wider nineteenth-century sense cut away at the very foundation of the authoritarian, hierarchical structure of the Church and of society in general. This was followed by the seemingly more perverse movement of socialism, which would destroy the very basis of society — and hence the Church — that is, private property. And as if this were not enough, there then came the presumed satanic development of communism — the embodiment of materialism and atheism. Add to this the fact that the period between 1815 and 1870 was constantly filled with revolutions all over Europe and North and South America, the development of anarchism, scientism, evolutionism, and Protestant "liberal theology" with its debunking of the Bible as a Jesus myth foisted upon humanity by a dozen or so Jewish fishermen, and one will begin to see why so many nineteenth-century Christians were in a panic.

Nothing seemed certain. Nothing seemed stable anymore. Everything appeared to be washed away in the deluge of revolution and "isms" that swept across nineteenth-century Europe. In terror people frantically searched for something stable. Many Catholics found it in an authoritarian Church with its structured-from-above hierarchy and the papacy at its apex. The cry among many seemed to be, "To Peter, to the rock!" An impenetrable bastion was built around the rock fortress, and the condemned world was shut out. Until better times would come, only invectives and sallies were to come forth from the rock.

Those loyal Catholics of the nineteenth century who saw no incompatibility between the legitimate claims of liberalism and Catholic principles, between modern historical research and science in general on the one hand and the advancement of the Catholic faith on the other, unfortunately received short shrift. Lord Acton and his colleagues were a dramatic example; there were many others not so dramatic. For several years in the 1850s and 1860s Acton was one of the editors of an English Catholic quarterly, the *Rambler;* the articles published were on a high intellectual plane — by far the best in Catholic England. But because the *Rambler* exulted in the variety and freedom of Catholic thought in all areas beyond matters of faith, because it affirmed its right to speak on all matters not defined by the Church and to proclaim the truth regardless of the inconvenience that might be caused or the reputations that might be impugned, it came to be regarded by the hierarchy, ever fearful of anything that might disrupt the delicate balance of English Catholicism, as an *enfant terrible.* The pressures on Acton to say nothing controversial, to conform in the name of the faith, became almost overpowering. Acton, however, spoke out many times for intellectual freedom. On one such occasion he said:

> Solicitude for religion is merely a pretext for opposition to the free course of scientific research, which threatens, not the authority of the Church, but the precarious influence of individuals. The growth of knowledge cannot in the long run be detrimental to religion but it renders impossible the usurpation of authority by teachers who defend their own false opinions under pretense of defending the faith.... They want to shelter their own ignorance by preserving that of others. But religion is not served by denying facts! or by denouncing those who proclaim them.[14]

Nevertheless, Acton and his friends were eventually forced out of Catholic journalism through the pressures of the English hierarchy and the Vatican.[15]

In fact, Acton's whole scholarly life was pretty well ruined by the stifling restrictions present in Catholic England. He never produced his *magnum opus*, a history of freedom, for which he had huge bundles of notes.

The conservatives were dominant during the rest of the pontificate of Pius IX and on into the time of Leo XIII, although here they were gradually restricted and held back. Leo, for example, gave the cardinal's hat to the aged and almost broken John Henry Newman; many of the Vatican archives were thrown open to all scholars; the relatively revolutionary social encyclical *Rerum novarum* was written. There was the beginning of a renaissance, an upsurge of Catholic freedom; Catholic historical and biblical studies began to catch up with the rest of the world; there was even a beginning of a flowering of a Catholic lay movement in this country.

### The Twentieth Century

But this seemed to be only a hiatus, for soon after Pius X came to the papal throne in 1903 a terrible purge took place under the guise of rooting out the heresy of "modernism." Doubtless there were nonorthodox elements in the ideas of several so-called modernists. But unfortunately these elements were used as an excuse for the conservatives to conduct a campaign of terror, driving practically all of the Catholic Church's best scholars into silence, for example, Père Marie-Joseph Lagrange, the founder of modern Catholic biblical scholarship. Vigilance committees were ordered to be set up in every diocese throughout the world; these were to meet periodically — in secret — to report on any alleged modernist tendencies noted among the priests or their writings and take appropriate measures to stamp them out. The censors worked overtime; Catholic scholarship was relegated to mouthing outdated, and hence ineffective, formulas.

Only after many years did the fervor of the heresy hunt abate. But the restrictions on Catholic freedom remained very severe. Gradually, in slow, piecemeal fashion Catholic scholars pushed forward in various areas — but no one will ever know the number of books that never saw the light of day because of lack of ecclesiastical permission. Not that all of the books would have been good or that none of them would have contained nonorthodox ideas; but given the human condition humans must be permitted to make errors in the search for truth. There is no alternative.

Those who would "protect" the Church by chaining freedom were, and are, always there insisting that certain problems are not open for discussion (such as the ordination of women priests), that certain aspects ought not to be publicized, or at best that they should not be brought out into the open now. One Catholic, however, defended himself thus:

> One's obligation to historical truth does not admit of half-way measures, and facing up to this obligation has time and again proved to be the best way of serving one's cause. Certainly, in times of open or concealed ideological conflict

every impartial statement and every unbiased argument can be misused like a poisoned arrow. But anyone who considers a word of critical reflection within the Church to be opportune only when it could not be turned against her by an enemy would have to wait to the end of time. It is part of the conditions of existence for the Church that at no time does she lack enemies lying in wait for her....

Rather, it can only be a question of faithfully reporting what actually happened and of getting at the root of the mistakes that were made at that time. That is the easiest way to learn lessons and draw conclusions applicable to the present and to the future.[16]

Gradually the so-called *nouvelle théologie,* "new theology," developed, almost in underground fashion. At any rate the impression was given by the conservatives, who held most of the key positions of power, that this "new theology" was at best very dangerous and most likely contained large heretical elements. Those who had "liberal" ideas in the Catholic Church were made to feel that they were a very small minority, with very suspect ideas, who were kicking against the goad of the majority. All of the liberals apparently believed this; whether or not from their ecclesiastical vantage points the conservatives also sincerely believed it is difficult to say. Judging, however, from their very negative reaction to Pope John XXIII's suggestion that a Council be convened — and the dogged resistance on the part of some, notably in the Curia — the conservatives either knew that they were a minority overruling a majority, or at least had a terrible fear — a justified one, it might be added — that this would prove to be so.

## Vatican Council II

The liberals all strove mightily before Vatican Council II in a sort of desperate hope that a breakthrough in progress and liberty could be made. For the most part they were not optimistic — at least not in public and not in print. Hans Küng's book on reform and the Council, which came out in German in the middle of 1960,[17] was mildly optimistic, but mostly urgent in its plea that everything be done to make the Council a success. But two years later, shortly before the Council opened, his articles on the Council indicated a growing pessimism. It was not only the liberals who were striving mightily to promote their cause at the Council. The conservatives were diligently at work, too. Moreover, they seemed to have all the advantages. They surrounded Pope John and influenced him in many ways, as witness the papal statement *Veterum sapientia* in 1962, legislating greater insistence on the use of the Latin language in the Church. Pope John, who by his own admission never could speak Latin with any facility, certainly did not think of this himself. Probably even more important, the conservatives held most of the chairmanships and other key positions on the various commissions that worked to prepare the draft material to be discussed by the Council Fathers. The conservatives were all set to push through the Council their rather polemic, nineteenth-century scholastically phrased schemas with a minimum of discussion.

But then that which the conservatives most feared, and the liberals most hoped for, happened. A number of liberal cardinals spearheaded a resistance against the conservatives' attempt to make the Council a rubber-stamp affair. For the first time in a century the Catholic episcopate began to learn to know one another. The liberals found to their surprise and joy that they were not some small suspect minority, but that they formed a large part of the Church; and before the first session of the Council was over, they formed an overwhelming majority on many issues. Doubtless all those who voted for the reform schemas did not go to the Council as liberals. But the liberals appeared to be the ones with the most dynamic ideas. Moreover, those very theologians who had been constantly plagued with restrictions and censorship were at the Council, and increasingly were asked to address various national groups of bishops: men like Hans Küng, Karl Rahner, Yves Congar, John Courtney Murray, Godfrey Diekmann, Jean Daniélou. The influence of these theologians and the contact with liberal bishops, and particularly the more freewheeling missionary bishops, wrought amazing changes in many bishops — including American bishops. A spirit of ecumenism and freedom reigned, as it had not for a long, long time in the Catholic Church.

The conservatives, however, were by no means completely displaced or cowed, as was indicated by the Catholic University affair in the spring of 1963. This affair, however, marked not only a new high point in the intransigence of the conservatives, but also a turning point in the history of freedom in the Catholic Church in America. There had been some very forward-looking American bishops at the end of the last century who promoted a lay revival and a progressive attitude in the Church in general: men like Archbishop John Ireland, Bishop Martin Spalding, and Cardinal James Gibbons. But in many ways the open spirit of these and like-minded men dried up in the reaction against the phantom heresy of Americanism at the turn of the century and the modernist hunt shortly thereafter. The Catholic press was usually quite conservative, the diocesan newspapers being official organs for the hierarchy. *Commonweal*, founded in the middle 1920s by a group of Catholic laymen,[18] often provided a single beacon light. But here, too, in America the climate changed — very, very slowly. The influence of the "new theology" made itself slowly felt among the American clergy and educated laity.

If the first session of Vatican II can be said to mark the wedding anew of the Catholic Church and freedom, the Catholic University affair of the spring of 1963 was its consummation. A list of potential speakers for a Lenten series of lectures to be sponsored by the university was submitted by the appropriate committee of graduate students. The rector of the university then struck from the list the names of Gustave Weigel, John Courtney

Murray, Godfrey Diekmann, and Hans Küng, four of the most respected theologians of the Catholic Church. This was all to remain private — in the usual fashion. But it didn't. The student newspaper bravely protested. *Time* magazine picked up the story, and so did a few Catholic diocesan newspapers. In the past such a situation would probably never have developed even that far. But if it had, the most that would have been forthcoming would have been a few scattered remarks and then silence.

But the old days were gone. Dozens of Catholic newspapers carried the story week after week. Many of them courageously criticized the administration of Catholic University — whose board of trustees was composed of all the American cardinals, a number of bishops, and a few laymen. Several of the faculties of the Catholic University, including the theology faculty and the canon law faculty, publicly censured the administration for. its actions. Other Catholic University faculties also raised objections. As the protests spread and grew, evidence of a practice of past suppression came out. Monsignor John Tracy Ellis, a most highly respected American Catholic church historian, stated openly that similar suppression had been going on for at least the past ten years — with specifics given. An article was published by a Pittsburgh priest, in the Steubenville, Ohio, Catholic newspaper, criticizing openly the Apostolic Delegate, Archbishop Egidio Vagnozzi, in Washington, D.C., for having manipulated the whole suppression.

In the midst of all this Hans Küng, the celebrated — and banned at Catholic University — Swiss theologian arrived in America for his previously scheduled lecture tour. Several other places had forbidden him to lecture, notably Philadelphia and Los Angeles. But wherever he did speak, the hall was jammed to overflowing; his audiences ran as high as five and six thousand. When he arrived at Duquesne University in Pittsburgh, for example, he spoke in an auditorium which normally holds one thousand persons. Chairs were put everywhere, including two hundred on the stage, so that sixteen hundred could be packed in. For days ahead of time it was announced that people were not to come if they didn't have tickets. Still there were an additional two hundred who sat in the cafeteria to hear by loud speaker his speech entitled "Freedom and the Church." Hans Küng had suddenly become the symbol of the new freedom of the Catholic Church. Without the first session of Vatican II all this would have been impossible. But since it happened, the Catholic Church could never be the same again.

Indeed, this spirit of freedom continued to make new advances. Pope John XXIII followed his epoch-making encyclical on the social question, *Mater et magistra,* by his even more epoch-making encyclical, *Pacem in terris,* in which amid a wealth of wisdom he pointed out that even though error itself has no right to exist, those persons who may be erroneous are the bearers of rights; one may not force a conscience for any reason. This was a landmark for freedom in papal statements, as was also the Vatican II decree on religious liberty in conciliar statements.

Of course, the vision of Vatican II was not immediately accomplished, nor is it yet; there is much yet to be accomplished in the area of freedom. Still, the spiritual, moral, and intellectual developments in Catholicism during and after Vatican II have already transformed it so that that superauthoritarian of Vatican Council I, Cardinal Manning (who also so fearfully harassed the great nineteenth-century theologian John Henry Newman), would hardly recognize parts of it. Many avenues of thought have borne prodigious fruit, opening up areas that a hundred years ago were thought closed — Teilhard de Chardin's whole world of evolution, for example — or were not even dreamed of. And the key insight in so many of these new developments is found in the sense of history.

# 7

# Religious Freedom and Religious Dialogue

## Relationship Between Religious Freedom and Religious Dialogue

Earlier it was stated that "to be really humanly free, men and women must be liberated from any and everything that restricts their openness to, their knowledge of, their love of, the other." It will perhaps be helpful to reflect somewhat further on the free person's need to be open to the other, particularly in that most intimate and ultimate sphere of human life, the religious. As was noted above, it is ironic that our Christian religion, which ought to lead us to love and be open to all men and women, has most often been a powerful restrictive force, a great wall of unfreedom which has shut us off from them in a lack of love, or has even been the excuse for our attacking them, indirectly or directly, in a great outpouring of hatred. This has meant a gross disregard for the human, religious freedom of the other, and in the enslaving of the other, Christians, Catholics, also imprisoned themselves within the walls of their own egos — individual or communal — for thereby they have cut themselves off from the goodness, truth, beauty, and unity that can be found only in the unique other — again, individual or communal.

Our Catholic faith ought, in reality, to lead us not to dominate other persons and other faiths, but rather in a real way to serve them, or in other words, to be open to them and to respond to their values and their needs. Catholics must come to other persons and other religions in humility to learn something more of God and God's will for humanity and the world; they must meet the other in openness and in dialogue. If Christians are going to be receptive to the truth, they must shut off no possible avenue of its approach; they must be open to truth (God) everywhere and follow it when it is found, even when that means a modifying or abandoning of earlier presumably unchangeable positions (e.g., the complete reversal of the papacy on religious freedom, from Gregory XVI in 1832 to John XXIII in 1963).

If Catholics are going to be involved in dialogue, they must listen to the other person. But if they are really listening to other persons, they must be open to the possibility of being persuaded by them. If they are not, they are not really listening, but are just preparing to answer. In Christian religious language: if the Spirit is in some way speaking through the other person or religion, Catholics will not hear the Spirit — and of what greater sin can a Christian be convicted than refusing to hearken to the Spirit?

It is proper, therefore, to look at the persons and religious communities around us with whom it would be natural for us to be in dialogue. The closest potential religious conversation partner is Protestantism in its various forms; it is the closest geographically, culturally, and theologically. The next closest community would probably be the Eastern Orthodox Christians, then the Jews, other non-Christians, and nonbelievers. In a full treatment of religious dialogue one would have to be quite precise and detailed about a complete listing and about associations and relationships within the listing, but such a complete ecumenical discussion is not the aim here.[1] The main focus here is the relationship between religious freedom and religious dialogue.

Those who wish to attain and retain freedom must at least to some extent be concerned about the freedom of others, for a truly free person cannot be a tyrant. If others are free, one's own freedom will also be safe. But if others are unfree, are subject to tyranny of one form of other, one's freedom may one day also be threatened by their tyrants and tyrannies. Hence it is healthful for Catholics to be concerned about the freedom of Protestants and Orthodox (and vice versa).

Perhaps Catholics should first of all learn what frightful limitations on, and violations of, religious freedom Catholics have visited upon Protestants and Orthodox in the past — and in the present, as particularly against that portion of Eastern Christianity which is in union with Rome, the Uniates, who from the beginning have been badgered and bludgeoned into all kinds of culturally unnatural acts, including that liturgical transvestism known as Latinization.

But in the vendetta against the freedom of Protestantism, Catholics also suffered a severe loss of freedom: for centuries Catholics were not allowed to use the vernacular in the liturgy; they were denied free access to the Bible; proper responsibility of the laity in the Church was greatly restricted — all because such aspects were condemned as Protestant. Thus did Catholics chain their own freedom. Protestants, of course, did the same: by decree and social dictate they were often not allowed a full use of sacramental, symbolic, or aesthetic expression, nor were they allowed a nonprovincial worldwide Church structure, for that smacked of popery; the vaunted Protestant freedom for long could not burst these bonds. Eastern and Western Christianity have, of course, thrown each other into geographical and cultural prisons. Both sides have consequently incurred grave limitations, so that no Church is fully universal (catholic), or right in its thinking (orthodox), or true to the Christian gospel of sisterly/brotherly love and unity in freedom (evangelical).

## Vatican Council I

It is no accident that freedom and dialogue are associated in so many ways and in so many places. The First Vatican Council offers a very enlightening negative example, particularly in view of what happened at Vatican II. Vatican I was not a Council of freedom or dialogue with non-Catholics. It was the exact opposite, for it stressed time and again the full "power," the complete "jurisdiction," the papacy had over all Christians, and that if anyone were audacious enough to disbelieve that — let him go to hell! *Anathema sit!* In many of the speeches and drafts of schemata at the Council, the Protestants were frequently blamed for most of the evils of Christendom, either directly or indirectly.

Then in the thirty-first session, one of the strongest proponents of greater openness within the Catholic Church, and therefore an opponent of a declaration on papal infallibility, Archbishop Joseph Strossmayer of Bosnia, rose to speak about the laying of blame for everything evil at the feet of the Protestants in the schema at hand. Strossmayer had long worked for unity with the Orthodox and dialogue with Protestants. He was a close friend of the great Orthodox ecumenist Vladimir Soloviev, and, combining dialogue with freedom, strove vigorously to gain greater freedom, culturally and politically, for the southern Slavs in the Austro-Hungarian Empire.

Strossmayer said that the rationalism which the schema was blaming Protestantism for actually had its roots in the preceding era of the Renaissance and that it was exactly what Protestantism was protesting against most vigorously, and that, moreover, when rationalism rose to its full crescendo in the eighteenth century it did so in the Catholic land of France under the leadership of Voltaire and the Encyclopedists, mostly Catholics or former Catholics.

Strossmayer went on to recall that there were many good Protestants who also strove against the errors of the times; he mentioned the names of two, Leibnitz and Guizot. The official stenographic record of Vatican I says that at this point there were "murmurs" from the bishops.[2] Lord Acton, who was at Rome and had many sources of information about the debate's events, stated that there were "loud cries of 'Oh! Oh!' President Cardinal de Angelis rang the bell and said, '*Non est hicce locus laudandi Protestantes.*' [This is not the place to praise Protestants.]"[3]

Strossmayer continued for another sentence and then paraphrased St. Augustine by saying of the Protestants, "They err, but they err in good faith." Here again the official transcript in Mansi records that there were "murmurs," and Acton says, "Here there was a long interruption and ringing of the bell, with cries of 'Shame! Shame!' 'Down with the heretic!'"

President Cardinal de Angelis asked Strossmayer to abstain from words that caused scandal to some Fathers. Strossmayer again began to speak only to be interrupted again, this time by another president, Cardinal Capalti, who made the interesting distinction between Protestants and Protestantism and assured the archbishop that the former would not be insulted by the schema's laying of all the evils of modern times at the foot of the latter.

## Antidialogue: The Shouting Down of Archbishop Strossmayer

The following is the translation from the *official* verbatim Latin transcript (Mansi):

> *Strossmayer:* I thank Your Eminence for this instruction, but your argument does not convince me....
>
> (*Murmur*)
>
> *Capalti:*...So I ask you to please desist from this kind of speech, which I candidly confess, offends the ears of many bishops.

Strossmayer said he would conclude and spoke another two sentences, only to be cut off again by Capalti, who argued with him for four sentences.

Then Strossmayer said he would conclude with a remark on only one of the points Capalti had made, whereupon Capalti tried to take the floor away again, only to be drowned out by shouts from the bishops against Strossmayer.

Although the official stenographers confessed they could not make out Strossmayer's next words, they still politely referred to the bishops' tumult as "murmur." *Ob nimium indignationis murmur vix percipi verba omnia potuerunt* ["Because of many murmurs of indignation all of the words could hardly be understood"].

After a few more lines Strossmayer was again drowned out by episcopal shouts. Again, direct translation from the official transcript (Mansi):

> *Capalti:* This does not belong to the present discussion.
>
> *The Fathers vehemently [vehementer] applauded the interruption and assertion; the most reverend speaker attempted to continue and respond but most of the Fathers repeatedly shouted him down. They almost raged and many demanded that the speaker come down.*
>
> *Strossmayer:* Your Eminence surely must pardon me. I respect the rights of the Presidents... [these ellipses points in the official transcript doubtless mean the shouts obliterated the speaker's words] I certainly, if that former eternal and immutable rule of a morally unanimous consent... morally to all unani...
>
> *The voice of the speaker is drowned out by the uproar of indignation. Nevertheless he continued.*
>
> *Strossmayer:* I protest against every interruption, I...
>
> *Fathers standing up shouted:* We protest against you!

*Again Strossmayer:* I protest against every interruption!

*The first President rang his bell again and again.*

*The Fathers unanimously:* Enough! Let him come down! Let him come down!

*Strossmayer:* I protest against...

*The speaker stepped down and the indignant Fathers left their seats, each muttering different things to themselves.*

*Some said:* These people don't want the infallibility of the pope. Is this man infallible himself?

*Others:* This man is Lucifer! Anathema! Anathema!

*Still others:* He is another Luther! Let him be thrown out!

*Everyone however shouted:* Come down! Come down!

*But the speaker kept saying:* I protest! I protest!

*And he came down.*

Comment on this scene is almost superfluous. Suffice it to say that neither freedom nor dialogue and openness to others flourished there. But it is instructive for us to note that the uproar which crushed freedom of speech centered around the question of the Catholic's openness to the goodness in Protestants: freedom and dialogue were very closely related. It is also worth recalling that in the next few days what Strossmayer was willing to suffer the slings and arrows of outrageous bishops for was accomplished: the text was suitably amended and the direct insults to Protestants were eliminated.

## Prodialogue: Vatican Council II

Vatican II was quite different. Not that there were no moments of excitement and tension, though nothing even faintly approaching the Strossmayer affair occurred; there were many exciting moments. But the sides were reversed. The minority at Vatican II was ultraconservative and was not composed of recognized scholars, whereas Vatican I's minority was liberal and was made up of many of the Church's most renowned scholars and leading churchmen.

It is interesting to consider how freedom and dialogue fared in the two Councils under reverse conditions. In Vatican I the liberal minority, which was proportionately much larger than the conservative minority at Vatican II, was so driven to the wall that their only honorable alternative was a withdrawal from the Council. At Vatican II the tiny conservative minority time and again was placated by the majority, and more often by Paul VI, despite their incredible obstructionist and often boldly unethical and immoral tactics, such as unwarranted changing of committee-approved schema texts while they were at the Roman printer.[4] Vatican I stressed power and authority, to a crushing extent; Vatican II promoted freedom and responsibility.

Where Vatican I insulted non-Catholics and fumed at and abominated the contemporary world, Vatican II opened its arms to non-Catholics, brought them into its midst, and devoted its lengthiest document to the openness the Church must have toward the modern world.

The connection between freedom and dialogue was emphasized in a positive manner at Vatican II, just as it was stressed negatively at Vatican I. The connection was made so close at Vatican II that what eventually became the Declaration on Religious Freedom started as chapter 5 of the schema on religious dialogue, on ecumenism. In the declaration the inviolability of the individual conscience, particularly in religious matters, the overriding need for persons and institutions to guard and cherish religious freedom was thoroughly detailed and acclaimed.

Unfortunately this great concern for freedom in religious matters was directed at institutions other than the Church; however, the seeds for future development in an inward direction were liberally planted here. Father John Courtney Murray, who had so much to do with the writing of the document, said,

> The conciliar affirmation of the principle of freedom was narrowly limited — in the text. But the text itself was flung into a pool whose shores are wide as the universal Church. The ripples will run far.... The children of God, who receive this freedom as a gift from their Father through Christ in the Holy Spirit, assert it within the Church as well as within the world, always for the sake of the world and the Church.... Undoubtedly, however, it [the declaration] will be a stimulus for the articulation of a full theology of Christian freedom in its relation to the doctrinal and disciplinary authority of the Church.[5]

To attempt to work out a full theology of Christian freedom here would be both out of place and impossible. But I believe it would be in order to ponder this declaration to see how a document that is completely ordered toward freedom for the other does bear within itself impulses toward freedom for the initiator. While it is quite true that the Council Fathers thought of the statements in the declaration in terms of the relationship of the Christian to secular government, it is nevertheless also true that many of the statements would be applicable in other areas, as, for example, *within* the Church. Others would have at least some applicability and should stimulate thought about what adaptations would have to be made. It is well, therefore, to quote a few of the statements from the declaration, thinking of them not in terms of the individual Christian within general society, but in terms of the individual within a portion of that society, the Church, to see how much of the thought about the larger also applies to the smaller.

## Religious Freedom Within the Catholic Church

The declaration begins with a statement which describes freedom much like inertia — it just keeps going unless something limits it — or like innocence, which is presumed unless disproved; freedom is the presumption until other factors limit it.

> This Vatican Synod... proposes to declare them [the following "desires in the minds of men"] to be greatly in accord with truth and justice.... That men should act on their own judgment, enjoying and making use of a responsible freedom... that constitutional limits should be set to the powers of government,
>
> [*Might we not legitimately substitute here "Church government?"*]
>
> in order that there may be no encroachment on the rightful freedom of the person
>
> [*Could we possibly admit that Christians should have less freedom in the Church than U.S. citizens have in American society? But lay people almost do not exist in canon law, except to have obligations and be subject to punishments; women are in an even worse condition, for they are classified with children and insane persons,*[6] *priests have no effective recourse against an oppressive bishop — and the Doctrinal Congregation still operates as a star chamber, with its rules of procedure sui generis, unpublished and, therefore, arbitrary.*]
>
> and of associations."[7]

The Council also asserted on its own the right to religious freedom and stated what it understood by that phrase. It deserves to be read again — *within* the Church.

> This Vatican Synod declares that the human person has a right to religious freedom. This freedom means that all men are to be immune from coercion on the part of individuals
>
> [*Pope? bishop? pastor?*]
>
> or social groups
>
> [*Curia? hierarchy? clergy? males?*]
>
> and of any human power,
>
> [*This would obviously include the Church insofar as it has anything to do with human beings.*]
>
> in such wise that in matters religious
>
> [*That would include beliefs and practices.*]
>
> no one is to be forced to act in a manner contrary to his own beliefs.
>
> [*Contraception?*]
>
> Nor is anyone to be restrained from acting in accordance with his own beliefs, whether privately or publicly, whether alone or in association with others, within due limits.

The declaration went on to insist on the avoidance of all coercion in religion, and even detailed two major types of such coercion to be avoided. Again, think of the Catholic Church when reading the following:

It is therefore completely in accord with the nature of faith that in matters religious *every manner of coercion* [italics added] on the part of men

[*And God does not use coercion, but grace, which is a free gift.*]

should be excluded.... Men cannot discharge these obligations

[*To seek, adhere to, and live by truth.*]

in a manner in keeping with their own nature unless they enjoy immunity from external coercion

[*A repudiation of the Inquisition, and all its successors into the twentieth century.*]

as well as psychological freedom

[*This is a crucial phrase, for it would cut at the last, and terrible, weapon that can be used vindictively by a Church authority based on power rather than service; it could limit, e.g., punishments like suspension and excommunication almost entirely to self-imposed suspensions and excommunications.*]

Further statements were made about humanity being a truthseeker and about how the seeking of the truth is to be conducted. But since no individual person or any aggregate of persons has ever comprehended all truth, the rules for searching out the truth apply to the Church's members as well, for they too are human.

Truth, however, is to be sought in a manner proper to the dignity of the human person and his social nature. The inquiry is to be free,

[*No question then can be forbidden and no authority is above being tested (St. Paul admonished Christians to test all things); this would include the clergy, bishops, popes, tradition, and Bible, as well as the customs and claims of the world, to see what there is of truth in them.*]

carried on with the aid of teaching or instruction,

[*The teaching office, or magisterium, obviously has an important function, but note, it is to aid, not demand, overwhelm, or induce silence.*]

communication, and dialogue.

[*These two words clearly indicate that the search for truth is to be conducted on a two-way street so that men and women in the Church may come to a greater unity with (comm-unication) one another to a "consensus fidelium," but this can be arrived at only if all elements in the Church talk with, dialogue with, each other.*]

In the course of these dialogues, men explain to one another the truth they have discovered, or think they have discovered,

[*Within the Church, as outside it; this would mean that women and men would be expected to err in the free inquiry — and the free inquiry would go on. It would*]

*not be suspended, suppressed, or inhibited; otherwise it would cease to be free, which would be unbecoming "to the dignity of the human person," in the words of the declaration.*]

in order thus to assist one another in the quest for truth.

[*Again, all Church members are to be assisted by others, e.g., popes by laity, and vice versa — "Humanae vitae" and William F. Buckley's response to Pope John XXIII's encyclical, "Mater si, magistra no," are negative examples of the former and latter respectively.*]

Moreover, as the truth is discovered, it is by a personal assent

[*Not simply because the "authority" insists, but because the person is persuaded. Of course, each person must sincerely search to understand, and the import of each authority must be taken proportionately seriously, but ultimately the individual "person" carries the responsibility of giving assent if it makes more sense to grant it than to withhold it.*]

that men are to adhere to it.

Every freedom, however, connaturally carries with it a corresponding responsibility, for "no man is an island," and every freedom or right places a responsibility on all others to respect it in a manner that will promote the greatest good for all.

The right to religious freedom is exercised in human society; hence its exercise is subject to certain regulatory norms.... These norms arise out of the need for

[1] effective safeguard of the rights of *all* citizens [italics added],

[*This of course would include the rights of popes, Curia, bishops, and priests, but also those of lay people, and women in general, as well; and it is the latter two, or three, who today most need safeguarding.*]

[2] care of genuine public peace,

[*This we largely lack today, not because of rebellion, but because of tyranny, not because lay people, and priests, are protesting, but because they have to protest — the alternative is often silent acquiescence in immorality.*]

...[3] proper guardianship of public morality.

[*Churchmen have railed against "realpolitik" and governance by "raison d'état" in the secular sphere, and rightly so — although usually not at their own country and its policies and wars; public morality in the Church should then also include informing the public of the real reasons for policy decisions, avoiding attempts at censorship, avoiding a de facto support of racial inequality, paying its employees a living wage.*]

...Religious freedom, therefore, ought to have this further purpose and aim, namely, that men may come to act with greater responsibility

[*Acting with responsibility is a great good, presumably always desired in subjects on the part of all superiors — but no one can act responsibly who is not free. Hence, by stressing the need for responsibility the declaration automatically and correspondingly*

*stresses a proportionate need for freedom. However, it is clear that many author-*
*ities really do not want either responsible or free persons, but rather, subjects who*
*will be blindly obedient robots: the authority will carry all the responsibility — and*
*freedom.*]

in fulfilling their duties in community life.

[*It must be frankly admitted that many Catholics are unwilling to take up their*
*duties in the Church; this, of course, increases the temptation to usurpation for the*
*authority; but then it must likewise frankly be admitted that this intellectual and*
*moral laziness has often been fostered and abetted by the authorities — perhaps be-*
*cause they thought of themselves as pastors of sheep rather than as leaders of men and*
*women.*]

In the midst of this section pointing out the need for norms to regulate the exercise of religious freedom, the declaration inserted the following
*cautio:*

However, government [*Church?*] is not to act in arbitrary fashion

[*The history of the Church's arbitrary action is long and replete, including not only*
*that rule of the Inquisition whereby two anonymous denouncers of a third person's*
*orthodoxy were sufficient for conviction of heresy (which implied the stake), but also*
*the twentieth-century regulation that "secret" vigilance committees be set up in every*
*diocese to check on suspected heresy and the peremptory moving, or removing, of*
*priests who appear troublesome one way or another.*]

or in an unfair partisanship. Its action is to be controlled by juridical norms
which are in conformity with the objective moral order.

[*If there is one thing the West has learned in its political experience of the last*
*few hundred years it is the absolute necessity, for the safeguarding of freedom, of*
*the separation of powers. When the same person or group is at once the accuser,*
*judge, and executioner, tyranny is bound to result. The 1968 debacle of the fifty-four*
*Washington priests who publicly criticized* Humanae vitae, *versus Cardinal Patrick*
*O'Boyle (and were arbitrarily dismissed from the priesthood without any due process)*
*is only a more concentrated and publicized example of the standard fare of Catholic*
*canonical procedure. Catholic Church authorities consequently often literally are a*
*scandal (scandal literally means "stumbling block") to the world. "Woe to them by*
*whom scandal comes! It were better for them that a millstone be tied around their*
*necks...."*]

...For the rest

[*Other than following the three norms enumerated above.*]

the usages of society [*again the Church?*] are to be the usages of freedom in
their full range.

[*Here it is repeated unambiguously: freedom is presumed to be in possession.*]

These require that the freedom of [*Christian?*] men be respected as far as
possible, and curtailed only when and in so far as necessary.

[*In a footnote on this point Father John Courtney Murray, S.J., commented, "Freedom is the political method par excellence whereby the other goals of society are reached."*]

Let this suffice for an initial probing. Although the statements of the Declaration on Religious Freedom cannot be applied in mechanical fashion to freedom of religious life within the Church, it should be clear that this document implies that much concerning freedom in the Church is awry and must be set aright; openness to, and concern for the freedom of, the other does have far-reaching implications for the freedom of the initiator. Dialogue is inseparably linked with freedom and reform or renewal.

Although the Declaration on Religious Freedom was originally part of the Decree on Ecumenism, it by no means monopolized the concern for freedom when it became a separate document. Even in the decree on ecumenical dialogue per se, the need for freedom was recognized, and recognized explicitly, as needed *within* the Church. "Let all members of the Church...preserve a proper freedom in...spiritual life and discipline,...liturgical rites, and even in the elaborations of revealed truth." While this sentence is not a detailed program of the key areas where there ought to be freedom — the clear implication for greater freedom within the Church being that there is not a sufficient degree at present — it does mention many. The reason such a statement is in a decree on ecumenism, of course, is that one could not possibly enter a true dialogue, which by definition includes an openness to one another on the part of the participants, if one were not a responsible person, and this can be only to the degree one is free. At the same time it would also be impossible for Catholic Church authorities to think they were seriously engaged in ecumenical dialogue, with unity as a goal, if freedom for adjustment in matters that can be adjusted (and they are many more than many think) were not allowed.

## Inner-Church Reform, Freedom, and Dialogue Interrelated

Of course, it is not only interchurch dialogue that promotes Catholic freedom. Intrachurch dialogue also does so; in fact, it is one of the constitutive elements of Catholic freedom. And the aim of such internal dialogue is, naturally, change, or in the words of the decree, renewal and reform. It is hoped that this renewal and reform within the Catholic Church will then lead to a more effective interchurch dialogue; all three — freedom, intrachurch dialogue, and interchurch dialogue — are bound together very intimately. When one suffers, they all suffer. The decree makes the link quite explicit when it states:

In ecumenical work Catholics must assuredly be concerned for their separated brethren.... But their primary duty

[*Both words, "primary" and "duty," are very important. What follows is not what just some Catholics in high Church positions could engage in if they were so inclined. "Catholics"—no limiting adjective is used—are to undertake the described renewal as their first and most pressing obligation.*]

is to make an honest

[*It is interesting that the writers of the decree felt it necessary to include this adjective.*]

and careful appraisal of whatever needs to be renewed and achieved in the Catholic household itself.

[*Again, nothing is indicated as being not in need of reappraisal and renewal—not priestly ministry, not episcopacy, not papacy.*]

The sweeping character of the need for freedom and reform within the Catholic Church, as both a prerequisite and a concomitant of ecumenical dialogue, is indicated by the fact that the decree reiterates the need in enumerating the activities involved in the ecumenical movement:

Finally, all

[*Here again it is the masses of the faithful who are given this mandate, not just the various leaders.*]

are led to examine...and wherever necessary [*no limitations!*] undertake with vigor [*!*] the task of renewal and reform.

[*It does not seem possible to be clearer or more urgent than the decree is here. Even the previously allergic word "reform" is endorsed. And although the word "freedom" is not used here, it is clearly implied; how could one have renewal and reform without internal dialogue and freedom?*]

The sweeping character of the need for freedom and reform is further attested to in the second chapter of the decree as well as the first:

Deficiencies in conduct, in Church discipline,

[*Lack of an optional and free celibacy in the priesthood?*]

or even the formulation of doctrine...should be appropriately rectified.

The sweeping character in terms of time is also underscored in the decree:

Christ summons the Church, as she goes her pilgrim way,

[*This manner of describing the Church was not typical in ecclesiastical documents in the many past triumphalistic centuries; it does much to strike at the root of the image of an authoritarian, and hence, antifreedom Church.*]

to that *continual reformation* [italics added]

[*That terrible word is used again, and in a manner that clearly implies that the Protestant reformers could not have been entirely in the wrong in their attempts to reform the Church.*]

of which she always has need.

[*"Ecclesia semper reformanda" — thoroughly approved.*]

In a rather explicit reference to the Orthodox schism and the Protestant Reformation, the decree says that,

men of both sides were to blame.

[*This is quite an advance over the late 1940s, when German Catholics were informed by the Vatican that such a position was unacceptable, and the early 1950s, when Father Joseph Lortz was told by Rome that it would be better if his two-volume* Die Reformation in Deutschland *were not translated — the work clearly admitted the Catholic Church's many faults.*]

The writers of the decree sum up their contention that renewal and, of course, freedom, are vital to the ecumenical dialogue, and also justify their many references to freedom, renewal, and reform, when they note:

Church renewal therefore has notable ecumenical importance.

This should be sufficient indication that the reverse is also true: ecumenical dialogue has notable importance for renewal and freedom. It also should be clear that Catholics should not be working for the conversion of Protestants and Orthodox to Catholicism, not only because it is now recognized that such conversions can never heal the ecclesiastical breaches, but also because piecemeal conversion, or even premature corporate union, would stop the ongoing Catholic renewal and development of freedom. Without dialogue, freedom would not come to a full flowering in the Church, and the Church, and the world, would be cheated as a result.

# 8

# Religious Freedom and Catholic Church-State Relations

## From Illicit Religion to Union of Church and State

While freedom is one of humanity's central characteristics, another most intimate characteristic is religiousness. The Christian Scriptures and Tradition are full of references to both of these key notions, but it was only in 1965 that the Catholic Church put the two together in a solemn public espousal — in the Declaration on Religious Liberty of the Second Vatican Council. It took almost two thousand years for this fusion to take place in the Catholic Church. Why?

The Christian religion began with no recognition whatsoever by the State; in its first years it was viewed merely as a Jewish sect. After it was distinguished from Judaism, it led a checkered career in its relations to the State, sometimes being tolerated, sometimes being persecuted. But by the end of the fourth century the Christian Church had become the established religion. In the Eastern Roman Empire there developed a caesaro-papism, while in the West the situation — much more anarchic than in the East — evolved toward a papal-caesarism.

The apogee along this line of Church-State relations was reached in the infamous two-sword theory, which was put forth in its greatest clarity and vigor by Pope Boniface VIII in his Bull *Unam sanctam* (1302), directed against Philip the Fair of France.

> The gospel teaches us that there are two swords in the hands of this shepherd (namely, Christ and His vicar the Pope): the spiritual and the temporal sword. For indeed, when the apostles said, "Behold there are two swords here" (Luke 22: 38), that is, in the Church, the Lord did not reply, "It is too much," but on the contrary, "It is enough." He who would dare to deny that the temporal sword is in the hands of Peter would pay little attention to the words, "Put your sword into its scabbard" (Mat 26: 52). The two swords, the spiritual and the temporal sword, then, are in the power of the Church, the first is used by the Church, the second for the Church; the first by the priests, the second by kings and soldiers, but only for as long as the priest wills and suffers it [*ad nutum et patientiam sacerdotis*]. Therefore, one of those swords must be subject to the other. The temporal power must bow before the spiritual power.[1]

57

One need look no further than the now accepted bulwark of orthodoxy, Thomas Aquinas, to see how far the prevalent assumptions about the compenetration of religion and politics, with the presumed supremacy of the former, extended at that time. In treating of heretics Thomas views them as common criminals. Their crime is even greater than that of counterfeiters, for "it is much more grievous to corrupt the faith... than to falsify money." Therefore, heretics "may not only be excommunicated, but may justly be killed." The Church should properly tolerate their existence for a while, so long as there is some reasonable hope of conversion, but when that is gone, then heretics "must be cut out like rotten flesh," as Jerome says. They should be handed over "to the secular judge to be exterminated from the world through death."[2]

Though the overweening power ambitions of the popes and their supporters called forth violent reactions that greatly weakened the papacy and rent the Church asunder in the fourteenth and fifteen centuries — most dramatically exemplified in the succession of the Avignon papacy, the Western Schism, Conciliarism, and culminating in the sixteenth-century Reformation — the chief claim that received papal support, at least in practice wherever possible, was that of the ideal of an intimate union of Church and State, with the Church always ultimately supreme.

Thus the Church-State problem developed through the Counter-Reformation and into the eighteenth century. The theory and ideal never changed. It was challenged vigorously, even viciously, by the French Revolution, but the theory was only reinforced. Chief nineteenth-century lay expositor of the absolute supremacy of the papacy was Count Joseph de Maistre, who would have made the pope the political arbiter of all the world.

## "Liberal Catholicism" and Papal Reaction

But at long last, at the end of the eighteenth century and the early part of the nineteenth century, there appeared Catholics who urged that Church and State should be separate (Abbé Henri Gregoire, 1750–1831), that there should be "a free church in a free state"; this was said first by Count Charles de Montalembert (1810–70) and his friend Abbé Félicité Robert de Lamennais (1782–1854) in the early 1830s, long before Count Camillo Benso di Cavour (1810–61) ever used it in a somewhat questionable fashion as a weapon in the battle for a united nation of Italy, the *Risorgimento*. Unfortunately their position was rejected out of hand by Pope Gregory XVI (pope 1830–46) in his 1832 encyclical *Mirari vos:* (1) The idea that liberty of conscience ought to be assured was called sheer madness; whoever said that religion has something to gain from this pernicious error was said to be extremely impudent. (2) Freedom of the press was referred to as execrable and detestable. (3) Separation of Church and State was disapproved, and the princes, "Our dearest sons in Jesus Christ," were said to have been given their authority not only for temporal government but chiefly for the defense of the Church.[3]

The following are the pertinent portions of the encyclical:

> We come now to a source which is, alas! all too productive of the deplorable evils afflicting the Church today. We have in mind *indifferentism*, that is, the fatal opinion everywhere spread abroad by the deceit of wicked men, that the eternal salvation of the soul can be won by the profession of any faith at all. provided that conduct conforms to the norms of justice and probity.

To live a life of goodness was obviously not enough for the pope. Yet, he went further:

> From this poisonous spring of indifferentism flows *the false and absurd, or rather the mad principle* [*deliramentum*] *that we must secure and guarantee to each one liberty of conscience* [italics added]; this is one of the most contagious of errors; it smooths the way for that absolute and unbridled freedom of thought, which, to the ruin of Church and State, is now spreading everywhere, and which certain men, with outrageous impudence, do not fear to represent as advantageous to religion. But what more fatal blow to the life of the soul than freedom of error, says St. Augustine. As we thus see lifted from the shoulders of men the reins that alone can keep them in the way of truth, dragged as they already are by their natural inclination to evil to the very brink of eternal loss, it is in truth that we say that there now lie open before them the jaws of the abyss, of which St. John spoke.

After freedom of conscience and religion, freedom of the press is likewise utterly condemned as a modern horror.

> To this [error] is attached *liberty of the press, the most dangerous liberty, an execrable liberty, which can never inspire sufficient horror* [italics added], and which some men [nevertheless] very noisily and insistently demand [and attempt] to spread everywhere....

Then with perhaps the greatest fear of all, the pope denounced the separation of Church and State — which, as noted above, in my judgment is precisely an essential key to the almost unlimited advances of Christendom-become-Western-Civilization-becom*ing*-World-Civilization.

> We cannot foresee any happier results for religion and the civil power from the desires of those who so warmly advocate the separation of Church and State and the rupture of the agreement between clergy and Empire. For it is a well-known fact that all the most ardent lovers of liberty fear more than anything else this concord that has always been as salutary and as fortunate for the Church as it has been for the State.[4]

Count Montalembert and his colleague Père Henri Dominique Lacordaire (1802–61) submitted and remained within the Catholic Church, promoting their liberalism as well as they could in those unfavorable times. Abbé Lamennais unfortunately became perhaps the greatest loss to Catholicism in the nineteenth century — one might almost say perhaps the greatest loss to European civilization, for his fertile and penetrative mind seemed to fly off at a tangent once loosed from its natural roots. In absolute terror of the break-up of the Papal States under the impact of the modern ideas of liberty, the papacy clamped Catholics in the vise of the union of Church and State wherever it could.[5] Where it could not, it merely tolerated the inevitable.

When Pius IX came to the papal throne (this very term is a reflection of the medieval and baroque papacy which gives some insight into the conception of the role of the pope prevalent until John XXIII, who by his actions refurbished the ancient papal title the "servant of the servants of God") in 1846 he determined to do something about improving the government of the Papal States, which had been described at that time as an open scandal to all Europe. (The Great Powers had earlier insisted that the pope clean up his corrupt, incredibly inefficient government, or they would do it for him; his lands were breeding grounds of discontent and rebellion.) Pius IX vigorously undertook this task, but he had come to the papacy too late. Before anything substantive could really be accomplished, he was caught up in the maelstrom of the Europe-wide revolutions of 1848. His minister, Pellegrino Rossi, who was quite able, was assassinated, and Pius himself had to flee from the insurgents, able to return only behind French bayonets. Needless to say, any "liberal" ideas Pius IX may have had passed from his mind after his 1848 experience with the *Risorgimento* Italian nationalist leaders Mazzini and Garibaldi.[6]

Before discussing the strong imprint Pius IX put on Catholic Church-State theory, one should take further note of the activity of Count Charles Montalembert, who never lost his love for the principles of '89 or his dream of reconciling Catholic thought and practice to them. He gained further supporters after the century passed the half-way mark, finding his staunchest and most brilliant help in Félix Dupanloup (1802–78), bishop of Orleans. In 1863 Montalembert was invited to address a great Catholic conference held at Malines, Belgium. He was a magnificent orator and took this occasion to present his principles in a unified and effective fashion before a world audience. He quoted Bishop Dupanloup:

> We accept, we invoke the principles and liberties proclaimed in '89.... You made the Revolution of 1789 without us and against us, but for us, God wishing it in spite of you.

The great purpose, said Montalembert, was to Christianize democracy.

> The more one is a democrat the more it is necessary to be a Christian, the fervent practical cult of God-made-Man is the indispensable counterbalance to that perpetual tendency of democracy to establish the cult of Man believing himself God.

Nowhere, he argued, was true Catholicism less practiced than in so-called wholly Catholic countries. Naples and Spain, "those paradises of religious absolutism," had become "the scandal and despair of all Catholic hearts."[7]

Montalembert's speeches were enthusiastically received at Malines — but not so at Rome. He was sent a private message from Rome ominously reminding him of the condemnation of Lamennais. Similar and even more vigorous repressive measures were taken about the same time against Ignaz Döllinger (1799–1890), a Catholic church historian at the University of Munich. Döllinger also delivered an address at a great Catholic conference held that same year, 1863. His plea was not for a political liberalism on the part of the Church, but rather a freedom for Catholic scholars to pursue their disciplines without having to check with ecclesiastical authorities, except where matters of defined faith were involved — a pedestrian enough thought for non-Catholic Westerners of a century ago. However, Pius IX was not of a mind to allow this. He issued a letter to the bishop of Munich in which he insisted that Catholic scholars were bound to subordinate all their work to the ecclesiastical authorities. It was finally also because of this letter that Döllinger's avid disciple Lord Acton (John Emerich Edward Dalberg, 1834–1902) discontinued publishing *The Rambler.*

## Pope Pius IX and His *Syllabus of Errors*

The following year, 1864, the encyclical *Quanta cura* and the *Syllabus of Errors* were issued by Pius IX.[8]

Almost one hundred years later John XXIII wrote on the first page of his encyclical *Pacem in terris:*

> But what emerges first and foremost from the progress of science and the inventions of technology is the infinite greatness of God himself, who created both man and the universe.[9]

In language somewhat less conciliatory toward the world Pius IX wrote on the first page of his Bull *Quanta cura:*

> Wherefore those our predecessors have with apostolic fortitude continually resisted the nefarious attempts of unjust men, of those who, like raging waves of the sea, foaming forth their own confusion and promising liberty while they are the slaves of corruption, endeavored by their false opinions and most pernicious writings to overthrow the foundations of the Catholic religion and of civil society, to abolish all virtue and justice, to deprave the souls and minds of all men, and especially to pervert inexperienced youth from uprightness of morals, to corrupt them miserably, to lead them into snares of error, and finally to tear them from the bosom of the Catholic Church.[10]

He then referred to the chief errors of the time, which he had enumerated to some extent in earlier writings. The first error he specifically mentioned was that of a separation of Church and State; then he castigated freedom of conscience.

> These false and perverse opinions are so much the more detestable by how much they have chiefly for their object to hinder and banish that salutary influence which the Catholic Church, by the institution and command of her divine Author, ought freely to exercise, even to the consummation of the world — not only over individual men, but over nations and sovereigns — and to abolish that mutual cooperation and agreement of counsels between the priesthood and governments which has always been propitious and conducive to the welfare both of Church and State (Gregory XVI, Encyclical, August 13, 1832 [*Mirari vos*]) . . . Contrary to the teaching of the holy Scriptures, of the Church, and of the holy Fathers, these persons do not hesitate to assert, that "the best condition of human society is that wherein no duty is recognized by the Government of correcting by enacted penalties the violators of the Catholic religion, except when the maintenance of the public peace requires it."
>
> From this totally false notion of social government they fear not to uphold that erroneous opinion most pernicious to the Catholic Church, and to the salvation of souls, which was called by our predecessor Gregory XVI (lately quoted) the *insanity* (Encycl. August 13, 1832), namely, that "liberty of conscience and of worship is the right of every man; and that this right ought, in every well governed State, to be proclaimed and asserted by the law."[11]

Toward the end of the encyclical he quoted two previous popes' statements on Church-State relations with approval:

> And do not omit to teach "that the royal power has been established not only to exercise the government of the world, but, above all, for the protection of the Church" (St. Leo, *Epist.*, 156) . . . as our most wise and courageous predecessor, St. Felix, wrote to the Emperor Zeno. "It is certain that it is advantageous for Sovereigns, when the cause of God is in question, to submit their royal will according to his ordinance, to the priests of Jesus Christ, and not to prefer it before them" (Pius VII, Epist. Encycl., *Diu satis*, May 15, 1800).[12]

A syllabus was appended to the encyclical, a list of eighty of the most prominent errors of the time, statements about which were culled from the earlier writings of Pius IX. Many were strictly theological and caused no surprise, as, for example, the condemnation of pantheism. Several were very clumsily phrased so that confusion about their meaning abounded. But the last few appeared to have an incredibly general sweep. He condemned the following statements as erroneous:

> 77. In the present day it is no longer necessary that the Catholic religion shall be held as the only religion of the State, to the exclusion of all other modes of worship.
>
> 78. Whence it has been wisely provided by the law, in some countries called Catholic, that persons coming to reside therein shall enjoy the free exercise of their own worship.
>
> 79. Moreover it is false that the civil liberty of every mode of worship and the full power given to all of overtly and publicly manifesting their opinions

and their ideas conduce more easily to corrupt the morals and minds of the people, and to the propagation of the pest of indifferentism.

80. The Roman Pontiff can, and ought to, reconcile himself to, and agree with, progress, liberalism, and modern civilization.[13]

The root of the whole reactionary regime of Pius IX can be detected in the political coloring of the two prior statements that were declared false:

75. The children of the Christian and Catholic Church are not agreed upon the compatibility of the temporal with the spiritual power.

76. The abolition of the temporal power of which the Apostolic See is possessed would contribute in the greatest degree to the liberty and prosperity of the Church.

N.B. — Besides these errors, explicitly noted, very many others are rebuked by the certain doctrine which all Catholics are bound most firmly to hold touching the temporal sovereignty of the Roman Pontiff. These doctrines are clearly stated in the Allocutions *Quantis quantumque*, April 20th, 1859, and *Si semper antea*, May 20th, 1850; Letters Apost. *Quam Catholica Ecclesia*, March 26th, 1860; Allocutions *Novas*, September 28th, 1860, *Jamdudum*, March 18th, 1861, and *Maxima quidem*, June 9th, 1862.[14]

The non-Catholic world, and most of the Catholic world, was stunned. It looked as if the pope had set himself, and all Catholicism, squarely against all progress and civilization and was insisting on all Catholics everywhere working ceaselessly for the State establishment of Catholicism and the subsequent abrogation of freedom of conscience. In fact, this impression was somewhat of an illusion fostered by the incredible ineptness of the pope and his advisers. First of all, the errors listed, as mentioned, were all taken from earlier documents and could be understood only in the original context.

For example, the final statement — that the pope cannot reconcile himself to progress, liberalism, and modern civilization — was taken from the allocution *Jamdudum cernimus*, March 18, 1861, which was directed against the confiscatory actions of the Piedmontese government under the leadership of Cavour — which justified its actions by saying that the pope would just have to accept these confiscations of church property and reconcile himself to progress, liberalism, and modern civilization. In this context the statement was simply a refusal to accept the highhanded actions of the Cavour government. But it is a tribute to the isolated, ghettoized kind of life the Vatican was able to forge for itself that it was able to simply lift that phrase as it was and place it before the world for reflective meditation. Public relations sensitivity had not yet invaded the Vatican.

## "Thesis-Hypothesis"

But there were still the questions of the insistence on the union of Church and State and the elimination of freedom of conscience. Was the position of the Ultramontanists,[15] whom Pius IX greatly favored, the one the pope really meant to espouse? The organ of the Spanish Traditionalists — echoed by the principal journal of the French Ultramontanists, *Le Monde* — wrote: "Our unique faith is henceforth to stigmatize liberalism, progress, and modern civilization as anti-Catholic. We condemn as anti-Catholic these abortions of hell."[16] If this really was Pius IX's position, anarchy, apostasy, and bloodshed would surely result. At this moment Bishop Dupanloup leapt into the breach with an *explication du texte* that brought sighs of relief all around the world. In fact, Pius himself, who was in turn stunned and horror-stricken at the violent reaction of the whole world to the *Syllabus*, wrote Dupanloup that he had given the "true explanation" and told him "you have understood well."[17]

Dupanloup had issued a pamphlet in which he explained the *Syllabus* in terms of thesis and hypothesis: the thesis, which was condemned, was the notion that a variety of religious beliefs was ultimately and ideally desirable. But no "hypothesis" could be fairly deduced from that that it was undesirable to allow a variety of religious practices, or even in certain cases a separation of Church and State here and now. The pope was not concerned with denouncing such varieties as might happen to exist in various countries. He was only concerned with asserting that such varieties should not be introduced everywhere else. He did not anathematize; he merely bade people reflect. *Notantur* was the word that he used.[18]

Which meaning did Pius really intend? Perhaps no one can be completely certain, but his inclinations were certainly in the direction of Louis Veuillot, the French leader of the Ultramontanists, who said in no sense can a Catholic be or call himself a liberal.[19] Nevertheless, the interpretation given by Dupanloup was given approbation and hence "saved" many Catholics. Some liberal Catholics later accused Dupanloup of emptying the pope's words of their intended meaning. Perhaps this is so, but at the time his intervention was a desperately needed political move. Of course, it was *not* a matter of infallible statements; this is acknowledged not only by all Catholic theologians today, but was also acknowledged by the best ones, such as Newman, at that time. Doubtless many, perhaps most, ordinary Catholics at that time thought they were irrevocably bound by the papal statements. Indeed, such a sophisticated twentieth-century Protestant scholar as James Hastings Nichols wrote in 1956, "... but, infallible or not, the *Syllabus* is binding on all Catholics and requires their internal assent."[20] It is with good reason that Nichols made such a statement, for this is what many Ultramontane theologians had put into the theology manuals since 1870, but that is not what Vatican I said, as has been amply demonstrated in more recent years.[21]

After 1864, the thesis-hypothesis interpretation was the main line of Catholic thought. Pope Leo XIII was much more flexible in his diplomacy than his predecessor had been. But he still held to the theoretical position that the ideal State is the Catholic State, one where the State protects and fosters the Catholic religion alone.

A later example of this position can be found in the article "Church and

State" in *The Catholic Encyclopedia,* published in 1912 in the United States. Although granting the need to live peaceably in a mixed society, the author insisted that the desirability of separation of Church and State in a Catholic State does not exist. "Such a separation for a Catholic State would be criminal, as ignoring the sacred obligations of the State." And in speaking of alternate theories of Church-State relations, none of which, he insisted, are acceptable to Catholics, he spoke only of an extreme aggressive atheistic regime, a caesaro-papist regime, and the "moderate liberalism" of the new Italian State — no mention was made of Montalembert's position or of any other liberal Catholic's. In speaking of the "moderate liberalism" position he sounded very much like the Muslim Fundamentalists of the 1990s. He said:

> The axiom of this newer Liberalism is "a free Church in a free State," which in point of fact means an emasculated Church with no more freedom than the shifting politics, internal and external, of a state chose to give, which in the event, as was to be foreseen, amounted to servitude.

## The Liberals Continue the Struggle

In America there was hardly much possibility of opposition to the Ultramontane position in the time of Pius IX since the Church was so relatively small and made up of new immigrants. Still one of the leaders of the opposition to the doctrine of papal infallibility at Vatican I was Archbishop Peter Kenrick (1806–93), originally from Ireland but then archbishop of St. Louis,[22] and of the two negative votes at Vatican I on papal infallibility one came from Edward Fitzgerald, bishop of Little Rock, Arkansas (in fact, because many bishops left Rome in protest, only 535 out of the potential 1054 — just 50.76 percent — voted for the doctrine of papal infallibility).

After the brilliant lights of Archbishop John Carroll and Bishop John England of the first half of the nineteenth century went out — more on them below — liberal and democratic thought once again began to show itself vigorously toward the end of the nineteenth century in the actions of Archbishop John Ireland of St. Paul, Minnesota, and others who saw a great advantage in the American system of separation of Church and State. They even preached its efficacy abroad. However the condemnation of the so-called heresy of "Americanism" at the end of the century and the reign of terror during the "modernist" heresy hunt in the years just before World War I scotched that burgeoning development.

The tradition of insisting on the medieval ideal State as *the* ideal was continued by a group of conservative theologians centered at the Catholic University of America in Washington, D.C., into Vatican Council II itself. They were referred to by one Catholic scholar as "the canonists," a not inapt appellative. They insisted that in a pluralist society one would have to separate Church and State, but when a vast Catholic majority was reached, as in Spain, the State had an obligation to render God public homage as State, i.e., it would have to promote the Catholic liturgy and forbid the public, not private, worship of all other citizens.[23]

This was challenged by Father John Courtney Murray, S.J., who in the 1940s began to argue that this was not the only possible Catholic position, that, in fact, a truer line could be found expounded in John of Paris,[24] among others, and that this truer line held that liberty of conscience was a human right which could not be invaded. He then also argued that when Leo XIII and other popes wrote in favor of Church-State union, they were naturally writing against the background of the conditions of their time. But conditions have changed; therefore the same rules cannot be univocally applied. Separation of Church and State can be seen as being a positive good for our time, though it may not have been so in the past.

In 1953 Cardinal Ottaviani, Secretary of the Holy Office, entered the fray with an article in the *American Ecclesiastical Review* upholding the position of the "canonists."[25] After that Murray was silent for many years. One Catholic scholar wrote that it is rumored that Murray was silenced.[26] Rather, it was an open secret that he was silenced.

Another Catholic thinker in this area, Father Albert Dondeyne, at the beginning of Vatican II when it was still risky, maintained a similar historical position in his book *Faith and the World.* Being a Lowlander and not a Jesuit, however, may have had something to do with his not having been silenced. He wrote:

> We have already remarked that the concept "ideal" is something relative and that it leads to useless misunderstanding when it is used in season or out of season. What may have been useful for Church and State in the Middle Ages would be a calamity for both in modern society. Moreover, one and the same juridical relationship can have various meanings according to the society in which it is adopted. Thus Catholics as well as non-Catholics in the U.S.A. consider, and not without reason, the complete separation of Church and State the best guarantee for a sound life of the State and a free Church. The same separation also exists behind the Iron Curtain, but there it has a totally different meaning.[27]

This statement of Dondeyne was courageous for that time, but I would suggest that the medieval Church-State structure may have been the ideal for the time, but just because it so existed does not mean it *necessarily* was the best.

Likewise, concerning the ultimate ideal, a distinction has to be made between the Church and the State that usually has not been made and that is of vital importance in the matter. The Church is, as far as humans are concerned, essentially a voluntary institution. People belong because they choose to. For practically all men and women this is *not* so with the State. Everyone must for all practical purposes live in a State. People can move from one State to another perhaps, but they cannot secede from the human race, from all states, and still live a human life. Therefore the State, which women and men *must* belong to, may not perform, as State, acts which are essentially voluntary for men and women. Even if all citizens at one moment happen to be believing Catholics, the State as State should not perform religious liturgies, since this would tend to *force* all the citizens to remain Catholics, and this they should do only voluntarily. Thus every union of Church and State is basically inimical to human nature and the nature of religion, and therefore also basically anti-Christian. If one *must* use the terms "thesis" and "hypothesis" — which, to say the least, is not necessary — then separation of Church and State is the thesis, and their union is the evil to be tolerated under some circumstances, e.g., the medieval.

It should be noted at this point that there is no problem in asserting that the Catholic Church has seen and proclaimed less than the full truth on this matter in the past. Perhaps its could not have done better, given the state of knowledge and experience of the past. We have learned more with the passage of time and hence are better able now in this situation to give a better description of what the Christian position on this problem should be.

This is exactly what happened at Vatican II when two huge steps were taken which vindicated the position of Fathers Murray and Dondeyne and, in fact, extended their position. Pope John XXIII in his encyclical *Pacem in terris* stated flatly that although error itself had no right to exist, persons who might be erroneous were the bearers of rights. No reason whatsoever justifies forcing a conscience.

The second step, of course, was the Declaration on Religious Freedom, which had such a tortuous history at Vatican II. The Council Fathers declared:

> The exercise of religion, of its very nature, consists before all else in those internal, voluntary, and free acts whereby man sets the course of his life directly toward God. *No merely human power can either command or prohibit acts of this kind* [italics added]. . . . Government . . . would clearly transgress the limits set to its power, were it to presume to *command or inhibit acts that are religious* [italics added].

Thus the Constantinian age and the Church-State theories and the condemnation of religious freedom that went with them in the Catholic Church were finally sloughed off.

# 9

# Doctrinal Authority and Freedom in the Church

## Scripture-Tradition-Magisterium

Men and women are free and responsible creatures, not only in regard to choice of action, but also choice of belief. They can assent to believe something only if they can be persuaded that it makes more sense to say yes rather than to say no or to say nothing. To go through the motions of giving assent without having been freely persuaded would hardly be a rational, human action. Hence, one can say that the preservation of proper human freedom in determining what should be believed is of the utmost importance, particularly for an institution which maintains that the whole purpose of human life is love of God and neighbor — something that can only be done freely.

The Catholic Church, then, ought to not only do everything it can to make its message as persuasive as possible, but at the same time guard vigilantly against all types of coercion, overt or covert: better and more pleasing to God by far a freely committed Jew or Hindu or humanist than a coerced Catholic. Such concern for both persuasiveness and avoidance of force has not always been easy to put into action. But behind that concern there lies another concern — or perhaps it is the same concern looked at from another point of view — that needs to be investigated first, namely, how does one know what a Christian should believe?

At the time of the Reformation, choices seemed to be between either Scripture alone or Scripture and Tradition (in the sense that not everything that Jesus said and instituted was written down, but was merely handed on orally). However, later the choices were complicated, for certain dogmas were declared by the Catholic Church to be of the essence of the Christian faith, dogmas which had no apparent scriptural basis and for which the "second" source, Tradition, also offered questionable support, e.g., the Assumption of the Blessed Virgin Mary. In this case the "Tradition" does not appear until several centuries (the fifth century) after the Apostles had died. This would mean that the earliest Christians who were eyewitnesses, or who heard from eyewitnesses, passed on this tradition of the Assumption orally for centuries without mentioning it in their writings or causing others to do so — a rather large supposition upon which to base one's faith.

Then one would be faced with the possibility of choices, not only between one or two sources of Christian belief, but among three sources. The third source is the living magisterium, the teaching office of the Church. The Fathers of the First Vatican Council, of course, maintained that the gift of papal infallibility, "which was the same as that which Christ willed to the Church," did not allow the pope to declare a new doctrine. But if the doctrine is not to be new, then it must be old; this would seem to mean that the basis for it is found somewhere in the past beliefs of Christians, namely, in the Scriptures or in Tradition — the latter here taken in the broader sense of the beliefs and practices of the Christian community through the ages — or in both Scripture and Tradition.

But if a doctrine can be declared to be essential to Christian faith on the basis of a tradition first found in the *fifth* century, then there seems to be no reason why a doctrine could not be declared on the basis of a tradition found at a later time, e.g., the sixth century, the sixteenth century, the twentieth century, the *twenty-sixth* century.

The possible choices, therefore, require additional consideration. For example, can the Church's magisterium, under the guidance of the Holy Spirit, express truths not found in Scripture? George Tavard and other like-minded Catholic theologians have said no, that all dogmas *must* be in Scripture somehow. Yet, traditionalists claim that Catholics cannot reject the infallible teaching of the Church, the magisterium; Catholics must, they insist, believe, pray, and work so that someday they will be able to see *how* such dogmas, like the Assumption of Mary, are in Scripture.

## Emergence of the Magisterium

Professor Albert Outler of Southern Methodist University has produced evidence showing that the Ante-Nicene Church (pre-325 c.e.) always judged heretics on the grounds of whether or not they interpreted Scripture in keeping with the Tradition as it had been received up to that time.[1] If they did not interpret it thus, they were judged to be without the Holy Spirit and, therefore, were really not even reading Scripture. This conclusion was arrived at by reasoning that the Scriptures were God's message to humanity and this message could be communicated to humanity only under the guidance and inspiration of the Holy Spirit — "No one can call on the Father except that the Spirit prompt him" — and this was tested by matching past and present Church teaching, the magisterium, with the newly proposed doctrine, which, if not congruent, was held not to be in Scripture.

If it is true that there was major agreement on the content of the Christian message, then the first centuries might well be an acceptable common ground for most Christians seeking unity. But what about the period after the divisions between Eastern and Western Christianity and those resulting from the Reformation and its aftermath? Where is the Church tradition, the magisterium which is the measure of orthodox scriptural interpretations? Either one Church, one magisterium has remained completely true, as both Rome and Constantinople claim for themselves, or none has remained completely true. This latter position would be acceptable to some Protestants, but not official Catholicism or Orthodoxy. Hence the central problem became no longer so much who can interpret Scripture, since most agreed it must be the Church (magisterium), but whether the magisterium has made (or in the future will make) any essential errors. Protestants said that the magisterium could make, has made, and will in the future make essential errors, whereas traditional Catholics and Orthodox have agreed in denying this, but have disagreed on where the loyal magisterium is lodged, in Catholicism or in Orthodoxy.

The need to maintain the doctrine of the "indefectibility" of the Church would make it difficult for Rome to accept the Protestant position of the possibility and reality of essential errors on the part of the magisterium.

The problem is a genuine one; it must not be understood *merely* as representative of a rigid conservative position trying to retain its power. For complete relativism is an abyss that must be avoided. If we cannot maintain *some* sort of continuity, then Christian faith has no objective basis, but is merely subjective, constantly remolded to fit the individual's fancy. Theologically the Holy Spirit clearly, then, could not be said to be the Spirit of the Church. Obviously an essential continuity of the Church, an essential connection of the present with what the Church claims was God's redeeming action of the past under the guidance of the Spirit must be maintained. But in what does this essential continuity consist? For the traditional Catholic this continuity has meant that the Church, under the guidance of the Holy Spirit, has not committed itself definitively to any doctrinal error.

One possible solution, or at least a partial one, would attempt to deal primarily with problems like those raised by the solemn declaration of the Assumption, which, although apparently without real scriptural basis or early traditional basis, has nevertheless been declared by the magisterium to be a Christian truth. The problem posed is that since this doctrine is not found in Scripture or even in the earliest tradition, it cannot correctly be declared a Christian truth, otherwise the door would be opened for any newly constructed doctrine to be declared *de fide* in the future: and this would be the abyss of relativism.

Therefore, it might be suggested that it would be helpful to distinguish between truths that are essential for salvation and those that are not. It is obviously concerning the former that Christians must have certainty, and it is therefore in their regard alone that the Church, the magisterium, needs and has the assurance of the guidance of the Holy Spirit. It is these essential truths that are subject to infallible doctrinal definition in the sense that the magisterium will be preserved from error concerning them. Concerning other nonessential "truths," the magisterium does not need, and therefore does not have, the assurance of the guidance of the Holy Spirit. These "truths" would not be fit subjects for infallible doctrinal definitions.

The argument would then run that it appears that the bodily assumption of Mary into heaven (whatever that exactly means) is in no way an essential part of the Christian message, as is, for example, the historical reality of Jesus. Therefore, it is not a fit subject for an infallible doctrinal definition. Hence the "error" involved would not be one that destroyed the infallibility of the magisterium, but rather a sort of point-of-order error in thinking this "truth" could be infallibly defined.

One major difficulty with this line of reasoning lies in the problem of who decides what is essential to salvation and what is not. Some would argue that the power of decision must be in the hands of the magisterium, the "Church teaching" (*Ecclesia docens*), otherwise any doctrine could be rejected by the "Church learning" (*Ecclesia discens*). It is, of course, true that such a nonmagisterium body could theoretically decide to declare any doctrine nonessential, but then, theoretically, so could the magisterium. What would prevent the magisterium from so acting that could not also equally prevent the nonmagisterium? Wisdom?

Surely popes and bishops make no claim necessarily to be wiser than other groups of people: popes have been murderers, adulterers, thieves, warmongers, heretics; bishops, too, have not always been models of virtue. Can the magisterium claim that it has a special grace of office from God that will guide it infallibly in deciding what is essential and what is not? But, of course, that is the point that is disputed by the argument. Ultimately, the question is: Can humans, who, as all know from experience and also from Scriptures, are contingent, ambivalent, incomplete, finite beings, possibly expect to attain a basically necessary, univalent, complete, infinite knowledge? Surely not by an act of reason. By an act of faith in what a necessary, univalent, complete, infinite God has spoken? But would not such act of faith humanly have to be based on a contingent, ambivalent, incomplete, and finite human act, a judgment that God has spoken here?

Such a line of reasoning, at any rate, though fraught with many obvious problems, might possibly be of some help in a matter which concerns an issue that clearly is not central to the Christian message, that is, does not really make a great deal of difference in how women and men understand the meaning of life. It is truly ironic that the one time a pope apparently claims to have used the charism of infallibility since it was defined in 1870 was on a teaching, the "Bodily Assumption of Mary into Heaven," that clearly does not *centrally* contribute to the understanding of human life; it can say something to this matter only by a great deal of indirect reasoning — all based on a lack of historical evidence! Perhaps, however, this event will turn out to be a *felix culpa* which will lead to a salutary reassessment of authority and infallibility. But what about issues which are central to Christianity and to the meaning of human life? Has there always been clarity in these? It would seem not, as is becoming more and more painfully apparent in recent years.

After the issuance of Pope Paul VI's 1968 encyclical on birth control, *Humanae vitae* (referred to by one wag as "Paul's Epistle to the Fallopians"), the dissent by Catholic hierarchy, theologians, clergy, and laity mounted rapidly. As a consequence many Catholics were shocked; many traditionalists argued that a Catholic may not reverse a papal condemnation; this apparently was also the thinking of those advisers who counseled Paul VI that he had to reiterate the 1935 stand on birth control taken by Pius XI in *Casti connubii.*

## Papal Teaching Not Developed but Reversed

However, the historical evidence does not warrant such an attitude. Fully authoritative papal condemnations have often been reversed. And it is appropriate to use here the word "reversed" rather than "developed." Perhaps most of the time development will most accurately describe the changes in doctrinal positions that constantly take place within the Catholic Church, or in any other institution. But there are times when not evolution, but revolution, takes place, when positions are not just expanded, modified, or supplemented, but are clearly rejected.

It may be illuminating to review how this has happened in some other key moral issues in the Church's history. One does not, of course, have to delve into ancient church history to find such evidence (as, for example, when in the eighth century Pope Gregory II solemnly authorized bigamy[2]). Some very bitterly fought examples have occurred in the recent past concerning religious and other personal freedoms. In fact, the reversals were definitively declared, as recently as in 1965.

As was noted earlier, in 1832 Pope Gregory XVI issued the encyclical *Mirari vos* in which he made some vigorous condemnatory statements. For the sake of comparison it will be helpful to repeat some of the key phrases of that document:

1. We come now to . . . the fatal opinion everywhere spread abroad by the deceit of wicked men, that the eternal salvation of the soul can be won by the profession of any faith, provided a man's morals are good and decent.

2. Now from this evil-smelling spring of *indifferentism* flows the erroneous and absurd opinion, or rather madness, that freedom of conscience must be asserted and vindicated for everyone.

3. To this is attached liberty of the press, the most dangerous liberty, an execrable liberty, which can never inspire sufficient horror.

Here we have freedom of religion, freedom of conscience, and freedom of the press condemned quite definitively and in unequivocal terms. As also noted above, a little over thirty years later, Gregory XVI's successor, Pius IX, issued another encyclical and syllabus of the principal errors of the time (*Quanta cura,* 1864) with equally condemnatory utterances:

4. These persons do not hesitate to assert that "the best condition of human society is that wherein no duty is recognized by the Government of correcting by enacted penalties the violators of the Catholic religion, except when the maintenance of the public peace requires it." From this totally false notion of social government, they fear not to uphold that erroneous opinion most pernicious to the Catholic Church, and to the salvation of souls, which was called by our predecessor Gregory XVI, "madness," namely, that "liberty of conscience and of worship is the right of every man, and that this right ought, in every well governed state, to be proclaimed and asserted by the law. . . . "

### [Condemned as Erroneous]

5a. Every man is free to embrace and profess the religion he shall believe true, guided by the light of reason.

5b. Men may in any religion find the way to eternal salvation, and obtain eternal salvation.

5c. In the present day it is no longer necessary that the Catholic religion shall be held as the only religion of the State, to the exclusion of all other modes of worship.

5d. Whence it has been wisely provided by the law, in some countries called Catholic, that persons coming to reside therein shall enjoy the free exercise of their own worship.

5e. Moreover it is false that the civil liberty of every mode of worship and the full power given to all of overtly and publicly manifesting their opinions and their ideas conduce more easily to corrupt the morals and minds of the people, and to the propagation of the pest of indifferentism.

5f. The Roman Pontiff can, and ought to, reconcile himself to and agree with, progress, liberalism, and modern civilization.

Pius IX apparently also had trouble with theologians who did not automatically accept in silence everything stated in encyclicals, for he added:

6. Neither can we pass over in silence the audacity of those who, not enduring sound doctrine, assert that "the judgments and decrees of the Holy See the object of which is declared to concern the general welfare of the Church, its rights, and its discipline, do not claim acquiescence and obedience under pain of sin and loss of the Catholic profession, if they do not treat of the dogmas of faith and morals." How contrary is this doctrine to the Catholic dogma of the plenary power divinely conferred on the Sovereign Pontiff by our Lord Jesus Christ, to guide, to supervise, and govern the Universal Church, no one can fail to see and understand clearly and evidently.

To make certain it was clear he was exercising his *full condemnatory powers* on the errors mentioned in this document, he stated:

7.   Therefore do we, by our apostolic authority, reprobate, denounce and condemn generally and particularly all the evil opinions and doctrines specially mentioned in this letter, and we wish and command that they be held as reprobated, denounced, and condemned by all the children of the Catholic Church.

After such thoroughgoing condemnations of liberty of religion, conscience, and the press by these two popes, it would have seemed that such notions and practices were forever forbidden to Catholics.

It is difficult to grasp why these papal statements of Gregory XVI and Pius IX should not qualify as an *ex cathedra* infallible teaching. They would certainly seem to fulfill the obvious requirements — the pope solemnly teaching the universal Church on a matter of faith or morals — as perhaps the majority of Catholics thought until relatively recently. But of what use to the Church is an infallible teaching office when only a tiny number of superexperts can know with any kind of assurance, and perhaps only after much debate and a long passage of time, that a particular papal statement is infallibly true? Then the Church is dependent on the superexperts! Who are they? How are they designated? How does the Church know them? Could they be mistaken, or are they too infallible — but then we have several popes instead of just one. Shades of the fourteenth century's Western Schism!

And yet how many American Catholics even before Vatican II would have thought freedom of religion, conscience, and the press forbidden to them? Millions of Catholics in the last century, and in this, took such freedoms for granted, and for the generation of the middle of the twentieth century John Courtney Murray, S.J., among others, provided the scholarly bases for such Catholic assumptions — although he endured years of silencing as a result of his efforts. But perhaps most enlightening would be a comparison of the above condemnations with some statements by Popes John XXIII and Paul VI. In *Pacem in terris* (1963) John XXIII wrote:

Man has a right to freedom in investigating the truth, and — provided no harm is done to the moral order or the common good — to be accurately informed about public events.

Compare with statements (3, 5e) where freedom of public expression of opinion and freedom of the press were condemned as most dangerous, execrable, and corrupting.

If there could have been any doubt remaining that Popes Gregory XVI and Pius IX had been fully *reversed,* Paul VI and the vast majority of the Catholic bishops of the world laid that doubt to rest when they stated at Vatican II in the Declaration on the Relationship of the Church to Non-Christian Religions the following:

The Catholic Church...looks with sincere respect upon the ways of conduct and life, these rules and teachings [of religions other than Roman Catholic] which, though differing in many particulars from what she holds and sets forth, nevertheless often reflect a ray of that Truth which enlightens all men....The

Church therefore has this exhortation for all her sons: prudently and lovingly, through dialogue and collaboration with the followers of other religions, and in witness of Christian faith and life, acknowledge, preserve, and promote the spiritual and moral goods found among these men, as well as the spiritual values of their society and culture.

Compare with statements (1, 2, 4, 5a, 5b) above. While this may not be a literal reversal of the words of *Mirari vos, Quanta cura,* and the *Syllabus of Errors,* it is a reversal of their clear intent and spirit of denigrating all religions other than the Catholic as false paths to salvation.

Then in very clear rejection of Pope Gregory XVI's and Pope Pius IX's condemnation of religious freedom (statements 2, 4, 5a, 5d, 5e), Pope Paul VI with the Council Fathers, as noted earlier, in the Declaration on Religious Freedom said:

The human person has a right to religious freedom. This freedom means that all men are to be immune from coercion...in such wise that no one is to be forced to act in a manner contrary to his beliefs.

Still maintaining the 180-degree turn away from Gregory XVI and Pius IX, Paul VI and Vatican II rejected their statements condemning the notion that religious freedom was "to be proclaimed and asserted by the law" (statement 4) when they said:

This right of the human person to religious freedom is to be recognized in the constitutional law whereby society is governed.

Pope Paul VI and the Council continued to follow the lead of Pope John when they again opposed the positions of Popes Gregory XVI and Pius IX wherein they forbade public worship to non-Catholics (statements 4, 5d):

Injury, therefore, is done to the human person...if the free exercise of religion is denied *in society* [italics added].... [G]overnment...would clearly transgress the limits set to its power were it to presume to direct or inhibit acts that are religious.

In the face of Gregory XVI's and Pius IX's condemnation of the freedom of opinion, speech, and the press (statements 3, 5e), Pope Paul VI, and the Council Fathers, stood with Pope John XXIII and contradicted completely the previously firm papal position:

The inquiry [the search for truth] is to be free, carried on with the aid of teaching or instruction, communication, and dialogue. In the course of these, men explain to one another that truth they have discovered, or think they have discovered.... It follows that man is not to be forced to act in a manner contrary to his conscience...especially in religious matters.

Let this comparative listing suffice to make the point that is centrally vital: in moral issues popes have made statements as unequivocally and solemnly definitive — and apparently "infallible" — as possible which have quite quickly been totally reversed as a result of dissent in the Church.

## Ecumenical Councils Not Developed but Reversed

The problem of the reversals of solemn magisterial statements, seemingly in-fallible, is not limited to papal statements. Ecumenical councils have reversed popes, as shown in the instances above and in others, such as the famous case of Pope Honorius, who was declared heretical and anathematized by the Sixth Ecumenical Council, Constantinople III (680–83). Councils have also, as demonstrated on the basis of historical evidence, contradicted previous councils. For example, Vatican I stated quite clearly that:

> All the faithful of Christ are bound to believe that the holy apostolic See and the Roman pontiff have the primacy over the whole world,... that the judg-ment of the apostolic See, whose authority has no superior, can be reviewed by none, and that no one is allowed to judge its judgments. Those, therefore, stray from the straight way of truth who affirm that it is lawful to appeal from the judgments of the Roman pontiffs to an ecumenical council — as to an authority superior to the Roman pontiff.

However, in the decrees of the Sixteenth Ecumenical Council, Constance (1414–18), there is the following statement:

> This synod declares first that, being legitimately convoked in the Holy Spirit, forming a general council and representing the universal Church, it has imme-diate power from Christ, which every state and dignity, even if it be the papal dignity, must obey in what concerns faith, the eradication of the mentioned schism [there were three popes at that time, the so-called "Western Schism"], and the reformation of the said Church in head and members.
>
> Likewise, it declares that whoever of whatever condition, state, dignity, even the papal one, refused persistently to obey the mandate, statutes and orders of prescripts of this sacred synod and of any other general council legitimately convened, above set out, or what pertains to them as done or to be done, will be penalized and duly punished with recourse if necessary to other means of law.[3]

The conciliarists, that is, those who argued for the supremacy of a council over a pope, who composed a majority in the Council of Constance, refused to allow Pope Martin V (who, after the Council deposed the then three si-multaneous popes and elected Martin V as the only valid pope) to give an official papal endorsement to the Council decrees, for they felt that would implicitly recognize papal supremacy over a council. However, Martin V did, during the last session of the Council, April 22, 1418, declare that he held, approved, and ratified everything in matters of faith (*in materiis fidei*) that the Council had decided upon in conciliar fashion (*conciliariter* as opposed to *nationaliter*, that is, those things decided by certain nations or sections of the Council rather than in joint fashion). Moreover, it would seem difficult for Martin V to have done other than accept the authenticity and binding force of the decisions of the Council of Constance, for it was this same Coun-cil which either persuaded the three other popes to renounce their claims to the papal office or deposed them, and then proceeded to elect Martin V the new pope. Still, with a sufficient passage of time a minuscule majority (less than 51 percent of the bishops of the world) of the Council Fathers at Vatican I (1870) were able to decide that because the Constance decrees were not "officially" endorsed by Pope Martin V, they were not dogmatically binding. Dogma triumphed (?) over history once again in the Catholic Church.[4]

But then which of the two ecumenical conciliar statements does one accept? Always the later one? If so, could one not perhaps have a still later one which will contradict Vatican I in this matter and follow it? After all, the Council Fathers of Constance must have been as confident of the binding power of their decisions (as apparently was also Pope Martin V, who accepted the papacy on the strength of them) as were the Fathers of Vatican 1. *Ab esse ad posse:* if it happened once it can happen again — and we are looking right down the tunnel of complete relativism. Or are we?

## A Problem for Catholics: Doctrine and History

We Catholics have a special problem in this area. To ignore or play with historical data would seem unworthy of humans, therefore, of Christians. Yet, this apparently is what the magisterium has done time and again in an attempt to maintain some sort of rigid notion of infallibility, of always being right. It is strange that the magisterium and its supporters have gone to all lengths to insist and "demonstrate" that they have always kept the purity of the teaching of doctrine in the inner sanctum of theologians and churchmen, and yet for decades and even centuries have been massively deficient where it matters to persons (and it is supposedly "persons" Jesus Christ came to save, rather than abstractions or organizations). For example, much of the Middle Ages and the Counter-Reformation period was a vast liturgical wasteland wherein almost all the people were effectively mistaught in word and deed about much of the central meaning of the Eucharist: it became a spectacle to be viewed from afar rather than a communal meal of spiritual nourishment. *That* is something that would have been worth avoiding, if possible, rather than having the magisterium declare that Mary was bodily assumed into heaven (whatever exactly that means and for whatever reason it was important).

Of course, the teaching of doctrine is important, but its primary importance is whether it effectively leads women and men to lead a more (w)holy life, and not in some sort of abstraction which has little significance for the meaning of human life. St. Paul said that everything that is written (meaning the manifold story of God's dealing with humanity) is written for our "upbuilding." Perhaps the magisterium, and theologians in general, should take more seriously Paul's remark: if something does not significantly build up, does not significantly lead men and women to live more human, Christian, lives (Immaculate Conception, Assumption?), then don't write it; obversely, the magisterium and theologians should search out that which will help women and men lead more human, Christian lives and write about it (e.g., religious freedom, about which Vatican II wrote magnificently, even though it refused to recognize that its action was a historic reversal of a previous magisterial stance).

## A Distinction Between the Contingent and Continuous

For the Catholics who feel they must take history seriously in this area of solemn conciliar and papal documents, another avenue of thought suggests itself. For quite some years now Scripture scholars have habitually made distinctions in scriptural texts between the timebound language, concepts, myths, and values of the periods, which the biblical writers necessarily used, and the essential religious, and the later, specifically Christian, message contained in those vehicles. This has been true of Catholic Scripture scholars as well as Protestant, particularly since the time of the Magna Carta of Catholic biblical studies, the encyclical *Divino afflante Spiritu* in 1943. Even in his retrenching encyclical *Humani generis* in 1950, Pope Pius XII stated that, although it is clear that the Genesis account of creation was not meant to be taken literally, it did to some extent have some sort of historical basis.

Such a distinction between the passing and the permanent elements in the Bible is, of course, also applied regularly in the crucial area of social and moral values. The principle of an eye for an eye was advocated in the Hebrew Scriptures, and polygamy was condoned there too. The New Testament Pauline material categorically stated that women must keep their heads covered in church (1 Cor. 11:5–17), keep silent in church (1 Tim. 2:11–12), not braid their hair or wear gold or pearls (1 Tim. 2:9); and, in a number of places (notably the deutero-Pauline materials) it showed that women were felt to be inferior to men. Paul also apparently accepted the morality of slavery, for on several occasions he admonished slaves to be obedient to their masters (Eph. 6:5; Col. 3:22; 1 Tim. 6:1).

Yet, there is hardly a Catholic theologian or churchman today who would support, theoretically at any rate, the *lex talionis*, or the morality of slavery; following Western civilization in general, many of them are now advocating the equality of women. The contrary moral values expressed in the Scriptures are usually regarded by such theologians and churchmen as reflections of the moral and social values of the then current stage of cultural, social, and moral development.

If it is legitimate to make such distinctions in the "inspired" word of Scripture, is it not, *a fortiori*, legitimate to make similar distinctions in the noninspired words of ecclesiastical documents, conciliar and papal, since they presumably are of less weight than the Bible? Might it not be argued, for instance, that the bishops of Vatican I were mostly very conservative politically (most were monarchists), lived in dreadful fear of the upsurge of bourgeois, nationalist, and proletarian revolutions, and that consequently their almost limitless stress on the hierarchical (opposed to the laity or proletariat), monarchical (opposed to the bourgeois or priests), and even imperial (opposed to the nationalists or Gallicans) primacy of the papacy was more a reflection of the social and moral values of their time and class than the permanent religious, Christian message?

Almost all of those bishops were in their sixties, seventies, or eighties, and consequently were over forty when the deluge of revolution broke across all of Europe in 1848 and 1849. That revolution so deeply scarred Pius IX, for example, that his "liberal" period of 1846–48 was followed by one of the most severe periods of reaction in the history of the Papal States and the Church in general. Could such men have produced anything but a very authoritarian document? It would seem not, for they, like all men, were children of their time. If the inspiration of the Spirit was not such that it prevented time-conditioned social and moral judgments from entering into the Scriptures in crucial matters, is there any reason to think it would have prevented it in ecclesiastical documents? To insist on an affirmative answer would seem to border on the sin of presumption, on unwarrantedly expecting a special act of God outside the normal laws of cause and effect.

But if it is possible to make distinctions to discern passing social and moral values in ecclesiastical documents, as it is in the Bible, then, as the social and moral climate within which the Church lives changes, certain social and moral positions adopted earlier by the Church might, and in some instances, perhaps, ought to, change (e.g., the attitude toward slavery). Starting from such a principle, would not, as one example, the rise of democracy suggest that perhaps some, or much, of Vatican I was culturally conditioned, and hence could, maybe should, change? But more of that below.

## No "Universal Pope" in Catholic History

Since Vatican II Catholic theologians and thinkers in general have begun to face the problem of magisterial authority and freedom more squarely. In his highly respected book *The Church*, Hans Küng had a number of concrete suggestions to make about this problem. In the process of leading up to a key issue, he referred to Pope Gregory the Great (590–604), who, instead of always being the superpapalist one might have thought him to have been, regarded the two Apostolic sees of the East, Alexandria and Antioch, as being on the same level as the Roman see (since there is New Testament evidence that Peter was at Jerusalem and even Antioch long before he supposedly went to Rome and so one wonders why the bishop of Jerusalem or Antioch is not the pope — but more of this below). Küng also pointed out that it is curious that when speaking of the primacy and complete power of jurisdiction of the Roman See, Vatican I referred to the pope as "the supreme and universal pastor" and then quoted Gregory: "My honor is the honor of the whole

Church. My honor is the firm strength of my brethren. I am truly honored when to each of them is not denied the honor due to him." But in the letter quoted from Gregory to Patriarch Eulogius of Alexandria, Gregory rejected the title of "Universal Pope"[5] and in the same paragraph stated:

> ...you say to me: You command thus. I wish to have that word command ["*jussio,*" which comes from the root "*jus, juris,*" as does also "*juris-dictio* "] removed from my hearing for I know who I am and who you are. For by location [in another *Apostolic* see] you are a brother to me, and by your customs you are a father. Therefore, I have not commanded, but have taken care to point out those things which seem to be of use....I do not consider that an honor which I know robs my brothers of their honor.

*Then* follows the section quoted by Vatican I: "My honor is the honor of the whole Church...." which is again followed by a further rejection of the title "Universal Pope": "But away with this. Away with words which inflate vanity and wound love."[6]

The apparently deliberate choice of a pope who did not insist on the imperial supremacy of the Roman papacy and, even more so, the choice of a letter of his in which he explicitly and vigorously rejected the notion of universal Roman jurisdiction as leading to the chief sin, pride, and the injuring of the essence of Christianity, love, to quote in the same breath with the claim to universal papal power and jurisdiction would seem to suggest a purposeful, and perhaps ironical, flouting of historical evidence — perhaps brought forth by some opponent of papal power. At any rate, this small point again illustrates Vatican I's lack of a sense of or respect for the realities of history.

The way back to the primacy of service, as opposed to the primacy of power, in the Petrine office, Küng suggested, is by the voluntary renunciation of spiritual power (jurisdictional and doctrinal) by the papacy, as temporal power was renounced — but it was renounced only under force. Küng admitted that this is not likely to happen easily. It seems to me that the history of the papal renunciation of temporal power bears a lesson for those who wish to see a renunciation, at least partial, of papal spiritual power. Papal spiritual power will be renounced only when, and to the extent that, something else takes its place. Papal supporters, because they are in possession of power, will be impervious to all theoretical arguments against papal power; this is not to accuse them of being evil men — only of being men. Hence, the best researched and best thought out arguments cannot expect much in the way of results from this quarter. But de facto the papal power is not the only power in the Church, as is always the case with every power, which exists only at the sufferance, most often unconscious, of the "powered," the dominated. It is from this quarter that truly persuasive arguments can hope for results, and hence are decidedly worth the effort.

This may sound like a call to revolution. Perhaps it is — depending on the notion of revolution that is used.

## Evolution and Revolution

For those concerned about freedom — and everyone is today — one of the most serious questions to be faced is how it is to be attained, or limited, depending upon one's position. That question, then, very quickly brings one to the issue of revolution. In recent decades, in fact, the word, and reality, of revolution has been in the air, and in the streets. The Catholic Church is not immune to it; many of its prominent members have been helping to lead and inspire it both within and without the Church. Hence revolution and its ramifications are factors that must be reflected upon, and then acted upon, by all serious Christians. Reflection comes first.

The term "revolution," in a general sense, means a turning around. In human social affairs, it usually means a drastic change in the order of the relationships of one person to another, of groups, classes, or offices to one another. The term is also often used in distinction to evolution and therefore also implies that the change takes place not gradually, but rather suddenly. There is, however, something slightly deceptive about this aspect of revolution. Revolutions in human society rarely, if ever, take place quite as suddenly as is often thought and portrayed in some history books. The so-called "Industrial Revolution," for example, really developed gradually in a long period preceding the latter part of the eighteenth century, as did also the "Scientific Revolution" of the seventeenth century. What had happened was that a rather slow concatenation of events eventually began to interact in a way that resembles an atomic chain reaction.

There is another aspect of human revolution that is of vast concern, and that is the destruction it causes. There is no doubt that all revolutions include some sort of destruction. In fact the very essence of revolution is the "destructuring" of something, to be followed by a "restructuring" of it. The same phenomenon, of course, happens in evolution as well. But because it happens slowly, the destruction and reconstruction are not so noticeable at the time. From the standpoint of a human community, obviously not all destruction and reconstruction are harmful, for as Newman put it: to live is to change and to be perfect is to have changed often. Or as Jesus said: If the seed does not die, it will remain alone and not bear fruit. Life and growth demand the passing of some structures and the developing of others.

But at the same time not all destruction is beneficial; it can be quite wasteful and harmful to a human community. The point is not to avoid all "destruction" (or change, to use a term less loaded with pejorative connotations), for that would be both harmful and impossible, but to promote beneficial change and avoid harmful change. The primary issue is not whether to opt for evolution or revolution, but rather to determine the way to engender the most beneficial change with the least amount of wasteful destruction. This determination at any one juncture in the history of a human community will decide whether one should take a more evolutionary or revolutionary path.

The great advantage of the evolutionary path is that there is more time to try one approach out and adjust it or reject it, without investing too much human energy in an untested idea. Of course, this advantage will operate only so long as the situation is not critical and demanding of quick action.

Revolutionary change, of course, has its own particular advantage. Oftentimes an idea is made up of several essential parts, the absence of any one of which would destroy the effectiveness of the whole idea. A revolutionary change often has the advantage of allowing the full trial of a complete idea. Naturally, then, the investment of human energies is heavy, and failure and retrenchment will be costly (e.g., the Communist experiment in the USSR and Eastern Europe).

In the final analysis the decision of whether an evolutionary or a revolutionary path, or something in between, will be more beneficial will rest upon a reading of the "signs of the times." In other words, it will depend on whether we are good politicians or not. The good politician will opt for evolutionary beneficial change whenever possible, but will also be aware that in human history adequate evolutionary change is often blocked by those in power, with the result that a revolutionary situation is created.

Once a revolutionary movement has been released, the good politician attempts to sense its mood and lead it to beneficial change. The making of the right moves at the right times may promote sufficient beneficial evolutionary changes to avoid the building up of a dangerous revolutionary crisis. But it is also true that, if a revolutionary situation is present, it is very important to perceive it rightly so that its great advantage of sweeping reform can be utilized to the maximum and its parallel disadvantage of a proportionately great danger of disastrous change and destruction can be lessened.

The history of humankind has been the story of periodic revolutions of the more or less violent attempts of dominated groups to gain certain rights. It is possible for groups in positions of power to maintain their positions for extended lengths of time but not indefinitely, and certainly not without ever expanding evolutionary changes, if nothing else at least the kind of changes that will allow the potential leaders of the dominated groups to move into the established structures of power. If this kind of a change is not permitted, then a change within the dominated groups will occur which will be like the backing up of a river behind a dam whose sluices are jammed shut. The changes that must come in human life, instead of being channeled through creative, energy-producing sluices, will come in the form of a devastating flood. "You can dominate some of the people all of the time, and all of the people some of the time, but you can't dominate all of the people all of the time."

Although the task of the leaders of any organization or society, if they have the welfare and growth of that society at heart, is not to prevent change, but to direct it into nondestructive, creative efforts, persons in positions of power will often resist sharing their power. Hence, the leaders of a society cannot hope to avoid the periodic welling up of the forces of grievance in the dominated groups. Their task is to have the wisdom to read the signs of the times early enough to foresee the building of a potential revolution and move to enact sufficient changes in the dominant groups to allow the building forces in the dominated groups to flow creatively into new positions of power, thereby avoiding the harmfully destructive revolution and advancing the welfare of the society in general.

To carry out their task adequately, the leaders of a society must avoid several rather traditional failures. They must avoid the social myopia which prevents them from seeing the potential revolutions building. This failure will most easily happen if the leaders identify solely with the dominant groups, extending at most a paternalistic attitude toward the dominated groups. A second source of failure is that, although the potential revolution has been discerned in time, the leaders may be at a loss as to how to bring about the necessary changes in the dominant groups. But perhaps the failure most difficult to avoid can be described as tokenism, that is, fobbing off the dominated groups with mere token changes. Such action will deceive the leaders into thinking the revolution has stopped building; but once the dominated groups realize they have been duped, the agitation for radical change will probably become more insistent than ever.

It is true that once a certain point is reached, violence is probably more or less inevitable, in the same way that, as Father Joseph Lortz long ago stated, by 1517 a Reformation had become "historically necessary." But the limited historical necessity of the Reformation did not make its violent aspects any less destructive of the welfare of all Christians — and non-Christians, who by Christian division were robbed of the sign and service of reconciliation which all the world always so desperately needs.

In sum: revolutions, which are too often almost entirely harmful and destructive and uncreative, are up to a point *not* inevitable and, in any case, witness to a failure on the part of the leaders of a society.

If these reflections on revolutions in human communities have any validity, they will also be applicable to the Christian community in general, the Catholic Church included. As members of that community, Catholics have to ask themselves whether in general they are in a period of evolutionary or revolutionary change. I believe it is clear that they are in a period of general revolutionary change, perhaps even comparable to that of the sixteenth century. Consequently what Catholics need to do today is do discern the route of beneficial changes and then bend every effort toward moving the Church as far down it as possible, for if far-reaching beneficial changes are not enacted rapidly enough, great harmful changes will occur, perhaps by schism, but more likely be even more disastrous irrelevance.

# 10

# The Turn Toward
# Inner-Church Reform

Within the Vatican II Copernican turn toward inner self-reform a key notion was "collegiality." It primarily referred to the governance of the Church by all the bishops acting together as a College of Bishops. However, it is obvious that acting in a collegial manner at the top of the hierarchical ladder was bound to have its effect on all the lower levels as well. In order to understand what a significant move the lifting up of collegiality was, and is, it is important to see it against the backdrop of the historical development.

## The Development of Authority Structures
## in the History of the Catholic Church

### The Early Church and Christendom

An important shift in terminology occurred between the 1917 and the 1983 Codes of Canon Law: the former spoke of the supreme "power" and the latter of supreme "authority." The shift is a major one of reconceptualization whereby, as Pope John Paul II stressed in promulgating the 1983 Code, authority in the Church is to be considered as service.

In the primitive Church power and function were identical. However, with disputes over unworthy ministers (the third-century Donatist controversy) a distinction between the power and the person exercising it began to emerge. Here was the source of the notion that the sacraments are effective of themselves (*ex opere operato*) and not dependent on the worthiness of the celebrant (*ex opere operantis*).

After the Emperor Constantine (274[?]–337) freed and favored the Christian Church, effectively initiating "Christendom" by largely uniting Church and State, the theory of the two "powers" began to be formed. The State exercised secular power (*potestas laicalis*) and the Church spiritual power (*potestas spiritualis*). Because spiritual power had Christ as its source and was exercised by various "vicars," bishops were known as "Vicars of Christ," while the pope was known as the "Vicar of Peter."

## The Middle Ages

The distinction between the exercise of power and the one exercising it increased in the West during the Middle Ages. This was largely as a result of the struggle for power between the Church and the secular authorities, which reached a first climax in the "Investiture Controversy" at the end of the eleventh century between Pope Gregory VII (Hildebrand, pope 1073–85) and Henry IV, Emperor of the Holy Roman Empire: who was going to "invest" the new bishop, who was also a civil "prince," with his symbols of office — the State or the Church? The distinction was further emphasized by the rise in the twelfth and thirteenth centuries of religious priests not locally bound, e.g., those of the new religious orders, Norbertines, Franciscans, Dominicans. As already with the Benedictine monk of the Cluniac reform movement, Hildebrand-become-Pope Gregory VII, reform movements often went the route of appealing to the Church's central authority, thereby increasing Rome's power. This centralization climaxed in the thirteenth century under Pope Innocent III (pope, 1198–1216) in two significant steps: (1) he established "absolute" ordinations, that is, ordinations to the priesthood as such, thereby granting spiritual power which was not necessarily locally tied; (2) he changed the title of "Vicar of Christ" from one applying to all bishops to one reserved for the pope.

Religious theories of power within the Church moved from thinking of power as being single (in the early Church) to being dual (in the medieval Church). One is the power of orders coming from ordination and the second is the power of jurisdiction coming from the pope's granting of a "canonical mission." After Innocent III, the pope as the "Vicar of Christ" was claimed to be the conduit of all jurisdictional power; all other jurisdictional power derived from him. According to Innocent III and several of his successors, even secular power derived from the pope. Innocent III issued such statements as: "No king can reign rightly unless he devoutly serve Christ's vicar."[1]

His successor later in the thirteenth century, Pope Boniface VIII (pope, 1296–1302), reached the apogee in such absolute claims of power in his 1302 Bull *Unam sanctam*, issued against King Philip the Fair of France, as partially noted above:

> The two swords, the spiritual and the temporal swords, then, are in the power of the Church, the first is used by the Church, the second for the Church; the first by the priests, the second by kings and soldiers, but only for as long as the priest wills and suffers it [*ad nutum et patientiam sacerdotis*]. Therefore, one of those swords must be subject to the other. The temporal power must bow before the spiritual power....
>
> Consequently we declare, state, define and pronounce that it is altogether necessary to salvation for every human creature to be subject to the Roman Pontiff [Why would this not also qualify as an *ex cathedra* "infallible" statement — and yet, no Catholic theologian, or pope, would affirm it today?].[2]

After Boniface VIII the status of the papacy declined significantly and rather regularly through the decades-long "Babylonian Captivity" of the Avignon papacy (the period 1309–77, when the popes lived in Avignon in France) into the morass of the late fourteenth- and early fifteenth-century "Western Schism," wherein there were for still more decades simultaneously two, and even three popes. As recalled, this disaster was resolved finally by the Ecumenical Council of Constance (1414–18) which accepted and confirmed the resignation of two of the popes and deposed the third, and then elected a new pope, Martin V (pope, 1417–31).

There had already been since the beginning of the thirteenth century, and increasingly so in the following two centuries, a great deal of canonical and theological argumentation in opposition to the idea of supreme papal power in favor of the notion of the supreme power of the ecumenical council. This "conciliarist" movement reached its high point with the Council of Constance, which on April 6, 1415, issued its famous decree *Sacrosancta,* declaring the Council to be superior to the pope: "A General Council...has immediate power from Christ, which every state and dignity, even if it be the papal dignity, must obey in what concerns faith."

Three years later on October 9, 1417, the Council issued its equally famous decree *Frequens,* solemnly declaring the regular calling of an ecumenical council every ten years mandatory, thereby placing the power of the pope within the College of Bishops in ecumenical council:

> We enact, decree and order by this perpetual edict that henceforth General Councils shall be...always held from decade to decade...if no such action shall have been taken by the Pope, the Council itself shall do so. So that with this continuity a Council will always be either in session or it will be awaited at the end of a certain current period.[3]

## The Reformation and into Modernity

The Protestant Reformers called for a truly spiritual Church, freed from the trappings of secular power; the State was to resolve the problems of Church structure — not unlike the approach Josephinism took within Catholicism over two centuries later. The Catholic response was to stress the visible dimension of the Church, which they said was as visible as any civil society. The claim now was that the Church, like the State, is a "perfect society," one which had all the powers it needed to fulfill its function. This was in contrast to an "imperfect or dependent society," such as the family, which depended on others to fulfill some of its functions. Against the claims of the Protestant Reformers and secular leaders, the claim was that the Church as a visible society had its own "proper jurisdiction" and this was a power as proper to the Church in the spiritual realm as the power natural to civil governments were proper in the secular sphere.

In the wake of the reforms of the Council of Trent (1545–63), the so-called Counter-Reformation, a centralized papacy was resurgent on into the middle of the eighteenth century and the Enlightenment. Then the forces of the Enlightenment began to melt away to some extent the centralized fortress of the papacy, especially through the movements of Gallicanism, Febronianism, Josephinism, and Aufklärung Catholicism.[4] As noted above, the situation reverted back to the Counter-Reformation mentality under the popes Gregory XVI (1830–46) and Pius IX (1846–78).

### Vatican Council I

Under Pope Pius IX papal jurisdictional supremacy was formally declared once again, along with the more notorious papal doctrinal infallibility. Vatican Council I (1869–70) intended also to spell out the relationship between the papacy and the body of bishops, but that goal was frustrated by the proroguing of the Council with the invasion of the Papal States by the *Risorgimento* forces shaping the modern nation-state of Italy. The German bishops, who as a group had been most resistant to the papal claims of infallibility and primacy, issued a public clarification after the Council in 1875 (which received the explicit approbation of Pope Pius IX[5]) insisting that bishops were not the agents of the pope, but authentically pastors in their own right within their dioceses. Nevertheless, the lack of a conciliar document stating that in practice pretty well left the field to the ultrapapalist elements, with the result that the centralizing forces in the Church continued apace until Vatican Council II (1962–65).

## Vatican II and Subsequent Interpretations of Collegiality

### Constitution on the Church: Lumen gentium

As noted above, the notion of collegiality, of the leadership of the Church being in the hands of the College of Bishops, including its head bishop, the pope, came to the fore at Vatican II. Officially Vatican I was closed and Vatican II was opened in 1962. This pair of moves provided an appropriate opportunity for the Council Fathers, all the bishops of the world (a number approaching twenty-five hundred), to take up the unfinished task of Vatican I, namely, to spell out the function of the College of Bishops and its relationship with the pope and the Church at large.

The first important step that was taken in this connection was the changing of the order of the document dealing with the Church from the one suggested by Cardinal Ottaviani's Preparatory Commission, which started with the pope on down through the hierarchy, as if the term meant "higher-archy" rather than the "rule of the sacred" (*hierous*, sacred, set apart; *arche*, rule). The first element the new order of the document (*Lumen gentium*) dealt with was "The People of God," within which and for whose service the hierarchy existed.

The second important step the Council took was to declare the College of Bishops likewise the subject of supreme, full power of the whole Church, just as is the pope. However, the College of Bishops must always act in communion with its head, the pope.

### Interpretations of Collegiality[6]

There are three main interpretations of collegiality. The most papalist one claims that no act of supreme authority can take place without the involvement of the pope. If the College of Bishops attempted to do anything without him, even in an ecumenical council, it would be null and void. Only the pope is the subject of supreme authority; when he associates other bishops with him, it is only for the sake of solemnity, for appearances. In brief: there really is no episcopal collegiality.[7]

A second view is different, but not by much. It is the position expressed by the "Explanatory Note" of the conciliar committee responsible for the shaping of *Lumen gentium*. It holds that the pope can act on his own, or he can act in concert with the College of Bishops; both are subjects of supreme power in the Church, but they are not "adequately distinct." Some would critically remark that this is a distinction without a difference, but what is clear is that here an attempt is made to affirm on the one hand the total papalist position expressed in Vatican I, and on the other to claim that the College of Bishops is also supremely powerful. The attempt patently fails.

A third attempt at understanding the notion of the College of Bishops (always in union with its head the pope) and the pope each being the subject of supreme power in the Church locates the subject of supreme power in the College of Bishops alone. The pope does not function as an independent agency but as Peter's successor, that is, as head of the College of Bishops. It is as such that he is enabled to act on his own, that is, always assumedly in union with the College of Bishops. The difficulty with this interpretation is that it is also the pope who determines that he is in fact acting in union with the College of Bishops; no one, including all the other bishops together even gathered in an ecumenical council, can authoritatively do anything but ultimately yield to his authority.

### Collegiality Blunted

Without directly challenging the extreme papalist positions expressed in Vatican I, Vatican II attempted with modest success to emphasize the episcopal collegial approach — which of course has an even much more honored history in the Catholic Church going back to the early centuries before the rise of the centralized feudal papacy well after the first millennium of Christian history. However, even that modest progress was even further restricted during the pontificate of Pope John Paul II, as can be seen among other places in the 1983 Code of Canon Law. The fine words of Vatican II are repeated:

> The College of Bishops, whose head is the Supreme Pontiff and whose members are the bishops...together with its head, and never without its head, is also the subject of supreme and full power over the universal Church. (Canon 336)

> The College of Bishops exercises power over the universal Church in a solemn manner in an ecumenical council. (Canon 337 §1)

However, repeatedly any power the College of Bishops might appear to be granted is always checkmated by wording such as:

> Decrees of an ecumenical council do not have obligatory force unless they are approved by the Roman Pontiff....(Canon 341 § 1)

> For decrees which the College of Bishops issues to have obligatory force this same confirmation and promulgation is needed, when the College takes collegial action in another manner, initiated or freely accepted by the Roman Pontiff. (§ 2)

What was even more discouraging was what happened to the international Synod of Bishops that Vatican II conceived and approved and was put into action on a regular basis under Pope Paul VI. The Synod of Bishops was conceived of as an instrument by which the universal College of Bishops would exercise its collegiality. However, Pope John Paul II in the 1983 Code turned it around to an instrument of papal power:

> A synod of bishops is directly under the authority of the Roman Pontiff whose role is to:
>
> 1. convoke a synod as often as he deems it opportune and to designate the place where its sessions are to be held;
>
> 2. ratify the election of those members who are to be elected in accord with the norm of special law and to designate and name its other members;
>
> 3. determine topics for discussion...
>
> 4. determine the agenda;
>
> 5. preside over the synod in person or through others;
>
> 6. conclude, transfer, suspend and dissolve the synod. (Canon 344)

This conceptualization and terminology is far distant from that of the 1414–18 *Ecumenical* Council of Constance, which restored the papacy and upon which the papacy's validity today depends:

A General Council...has immediate power from Christ, which every state and dignity, even if it be the papal dignity, must obey in what concerns faith. (*Sacrosancta*)

General Councils shall be...always held from decade to decade...if no such action shall have been taken by the pope, the Council itself shall do so. So that with this continuity a Council will always be either in session or it will be awaited at the end of a certain current period. (*Frequens*)

# 11

# Church Reform:
# Vatican II and Aftermath

## Mandate for Church Renewal

"Christ summons the Church, as she goes her pilgrim way, to that *continual reformation of which she always has need.*" Those are not the words of Luther, Calvin, or some other sixteenth-century Reformer, but those of all the Catholic bishops of the world, including the pope, at Vatican Council II. Indeed, the pope and bishops were even more insistent when they said: "All are led . . . *wherever necessary*, to undertake with vigor the task of renewal and reform." Notice, the pope and bishops did not say all bishops, all priests, all religious, but simply, "all," that is, all those to whom that decree was addressed, namely, all the Catholic faithful.

Moreover, this mandate to renewal and reform was not conceived as a luxury for those Catholics who have nothing else to do. Rather, it is a *duty* that is incumbent on all Catholics, as the pope and bishops made clear: "Catholics' . . . *primary duty* is to make a careful and honest appraisal of whatever needs to be renewed and done in the Catholic household" (all three citations from Vatican II Decree on Ecumenism, sections 4 and 5; italics added).

Many in the Catholic laity, religious, clergy, and even hierarchy responded positively to the charge to renew and reform the Church to make it relevant to today's world. (Pope John XXIII spoke of *aggiornamento*, that is, "bringing up to date," when he explained the need to call the Second Vatican Council.) Renewal moved ahead with great elan for the first few years after the end of the Council in 1965.

## First Slowing of Reform

Renewal received its first major setback in 1968, however, with Paul VI's encyclical against birth control, *Humanae vitae.*

Another heavy blow came by way of omission in connection with the recommendation to change the electors of the pope from the papal-appointed cardinals to delegates elected by the national bishops' councils around the world. This decree sat on Pope Paul's desk already in 1970, but he was dissuaded from signing it by conservative Curial elements who seemed to have whispered in his ear the prediction of a catastrophe that would result if he did sign it. The only catastrophe, of course, would have been for certain Church power-holders. Had he made this momentous decision, the whole subsequent history of Catholic church renewal would have been radically different. Every new pope would necessarily have had a sense of responsibility to, and more collegiality with, his "constituents," the representatives of the world Church. But most importantly, this structural change at the top would have released an irresistible movement for bishops in some substantial way to be elected by their "constituents," and then also for pastors in turn to be elected.

As the Church moved further into the 1970s Pope Paul became increasingly indecisive, wanting on the one hand to carry out the Vatican II mandate of renewal and reform, while on the other fearing the specter of error and anarchy that was constantly whispered in his ear. Then came Pope Paul's death in 1978 and his replacement first by the briefly reigning John Paul I and then the long-reigning John Paul II, beginning late in 1978.

## Pope John Paul II and Restorationism

It was a bad year, 1979. It had started bad — and was ending worse. Three a.m. on December 18, my phone rang insistently, and I eventually answered it, groggily. An American theologian-journalist in Rome, Ed Grace, said breathlessly: "The Vatican just condemned Hans Küng!" Obviously shortly after John Paul II took power the headhunters at the Holy Office ("of the Inquisition" had been struck from the title earlier in the century, but apparently not from the reality) had been quickly unleashed, for the following sequence of events occurred:

1. Already in the spring of 1979 the French theologian Jacques Pohier was silenced for his book *When I Speak of God;*[1]

2. in July the book on sexuality by a team of four American theologians of the Catholic Theology Society of America was condemned;

3. in September the Jesuit General in Rome, Father Pedro Arrupe, was forced to send a letter to all Jesuits warning them that they could not publicly dissent from any papal position;

4. all autumn severe accusations of heresy against Edward Schillebeeckx were recurrently issued in drum-beat fashion; December 13–15 Schillebeeckx was "interrogated" by the Holy Office in Rome;[2]

5. that same month writings of Brazilian liberation theologian Leonardo Boff were "condemned" (he was later silenced — and still later left the Franciscans and the priesthood);[3]

6. then on December 18 — at exactly the same time Pope John Paul II said, "Truth is the power of peace. . . . What should one say of the practice of combatting or silencing those who do not share the same views?" (*Washington Post,* December 19, 1979) — the Holy Office issued a declaration on Hans Küng saying he "can no longer be considered a Catholic theologian."

A few hours later I was on the phone with Father Charles Curran of Catholic University and Father David Tracy of the University of Chicago — the former one of the foremost American Catholic moral theologians (and later given the same inquisitorial treatment as Küng), and the latter clearly the most creative American Catholic systematic theologian.

We moved quickly to issue a press statement by U.S. Catholic theologians stating that "Küng was indeed a Catholic theologian." We decided to resist Rome with earlier Roman tactics, and took a leaf from Caesar's writings: "All Gaul [America] is divided into three parts" (*Omnis America in tres partes divisa est*). For the next twenty-four hours each of us got on the phone to our third of America. As I spoke with people, time and again the refrain recurred: This can't go on! Who will be next? We cannot allow Rome simply to continue to "Divide and conquer!" (*Divide et impera!*) We have got to organize!

## Founding of the Association for the Rights of Catholics in the Church — ARCC

In the following days I drew up a proposal to organize what became the Association for the Rights of Catholics in the Church (ARCC) and sent it around to all interested contacts. The response was overwhelmingly positive, and on March 7–9, 1980, the Founding Convention of ARCC was held in Milwaukee, with thirty delegates from nine cities, with organizing groups from another eight cities indicating support without sending a delegate.

The Association for the Rights of Catholics in the Church was thus founded in 1980, "to institutionalize a collegial understanding of Church in which decision-making is shared and accountability is realized among Catholics of every kind and condition. It affirms that there are *fundamental rights* which are rooted in the humanity and baptism of all Catholics." It sees its particular contribution to the Church and world in the area of the rights of Catholics in the Church. This is in keeping with the urging of the 1971 International Synod of Bishops, which stated that "within the Church rights must be preserved. No one should be deprived of his ordinary rights because he is associated with the Church."

ARCC rejects all divisive dualisms in Christian life, whether they take the form of dividing Church and world, men and women, clergy and laity, or others. This is in line with the Charter of the Rights of Catholics in the Church issued by ARCC in 1983, after worldwide consultation, and with

Canon 208 of the 1983 Code of Canon Law, which states that "there exists among all the Christian faithful, in virtue of their rebirth in Christ, a true equality," and likewise with a widespread sense among the majority of the Catholic laity. All these pairs, springing from one source and seeking ultimately one goal, must mutually interpenetrate and cooperate. On this unity the rights of all Catholics are based: "The rights of Catholics in the Church derive both from our basic humanity as persons and from our baptism as Christians" (Preamble, *Charter*).

## Restorationism Continues

The subsequent years of the pontificate of Pope John Paul II have been characterized by an extraordinary *Wanderlust* on the part of the pope, which allowed him, among other things, to stress the implementation of human rights in the secular sphere. In this he has been indefatigable. At the same time, however, he also used his world travels as an instrument of massive centralization of power within the Church, simultaneous with what must be described as an insistent repression of rights within the Church — projecting in the world a credibility-damaging image (and reality) of an ethical double-standard.

There has been an alternating rhythm of severe repression, as in 1979–80, followed by a certain relenting in the face of mounting protest and resistance. All during this period Pope John Paul has been appointing conservative and ultraconservative bishops and launching one conservative or reactionary project after another, such as the loyalty-oath and the world catechism, in moves to consolidate his centralizing conservative power.

# 12

# The Maturation of
# American Catholicism

However, all this "Restoration" activity has had less than the desired result, especially in American Catholicism, as far as the Neo-Integrists (reactionary Catholics) are concerned — and this is most encouraging. The profile of American Catholicism that emerged from the Gallup survey taken in the summer of 1987 just before the pope's September 1987 visit to the U.S. portrayed a rapidly maturing Church.

Sunday church attendance had dropped from a pre-*Humanae vitae* (1968) 65 percent to 50 percent by 1975, but has remained steady ever since. Before Vatican II American Catholics were characterized by a stress on doctrinal orthodoxy, ritual regularity, and obedience to clerical authorities.[1]

That docility has dramatically diminished. Now 70 percent of American Catholics surveyed think one can be a good Catholic and not necessarily go to church every Sunday. In a 1987 survey 79 percent of American Catholics opposed the Vatican prohibition on artificial birth control, and by 1992 that disagreement percentage reached 87 percent. In 1992, 74 percent of American Catholics believed divorced and remarried Catholics should be able to remain Catholics in good standing.

In 1971, 49 percent of American Catholics were in favor of married priests; by 1983, the percentage reached 58 percent and remained stable through 1987, but by five years later the figure leaped to 70 percent.

A very clear connection between power and sex can be seen in the fact that statistics consistently show that every time the Vatican publicly condemns the idea of women priests the percentage of support for it among American Catholics rises. Record keeping started with the 29 percent of American Catholics recorded being in favor of ordaining women priests at the time of the Vatican declaration against women priests in 1977 (*Inter insignores*)[2] to 36 percent shortly after the Vatican prohibition, to 40 percent in 1979, 44 percent in 1982, 47 percent in 1985, and then a sharp jump to 60 percent in 1987, and 67 percent in 1992 (in 1992, 80 percent also favored ordaining women deacons). Perhaps even more interesting is the fact that of American Catholics under thirty-five in 1992, 80 percent are in favor of ordaining women priests.

Ninety percent of American Catholics said that a person could dissent from Church doctrine and remain a good Catholic; and only 26 percent thought belief in papal infallibility was necessary to be a good Catholic.

But American Catholics have not abandoned the Church in large numbers, as the drop in docility might suggest would happen. Rather, they are staying in. As sociologist Teresa A. Sullivan says, "There is something American Catholics find in Catholicism that is deep and nurturing and doesn't have very much to do with the Vatican and the bishops and all the rest."[3] At the same time, sociologist Ruth A. Wallace notes that the Gallup survey finds among American Catholics an "eagerness with which the laity seem to want to participate in a lot of policy questions, no matter what age or level of education."[4] The survey further strengthens what Joseph Fichter, S.J., found a decade earlier:

> The church is being modernized in spite of itself. It appears that the changes are occurring at the bottom of the structure. American Catholicism is experiencing adaptation at the grass roots. The most significant aspect of this change is the switch of emphasis in the basis of moral and religious guidance. Dependence on legislation from above has largely switched to dependence on the conscience of the people.[5]

Even more interesting in the Gallup survey figures are those reflecting the attitudes of the large bulge in the American population, the so-called "baby-boomers," those born between 1948 and 1957. They represent not only a disproportionately large segment of the American population, but because the Catholic "baby-boom" was even larger than the general American one, they are really the trend-setters for the future of the American Catholic Church. And they are much more liberal than the average, much more prodemocracy, proreform in the Church. The same is also true of educated Catholics: the more educated the Catholics, the greater the likelihood of their being liberal, prorenewal and reform, more mature — and American Catholics are rapidly becoming increasingly more educated.

ARCC is by no means the only grassroots Catholic church-renewal organization to spring up in the United States since Vatican II. Many have emerged, and continue to emerge with each passing year. What is even more interesting is that many of these renewal movements have begun to coalesce and coordinate. In the fall of 1991 an initial grouping of them formed an umbrella coordinating organization entitled "Catholics Organizing Renewal" (COR). COR is a coalition of grassroots Catholic organizations working on various aspects of renewal in the Church which are banding together to reinforce each other's compatible renewal efforts, and when appropriate launch joint projects.

At present COR has thirty-one organizations of various goals and sizes. The national-level ones include, besides ARCC, the following:

- Catholics Speak Out: founded in 1987, concerned with democracy in the Church.

- New Ways Ministry: concerned with ministry to homosexuals.

- Call to Action: concerned with general church renewal, grew out of the 1976 National Conference of Catholic Bishops' "Call to Action."

- Catholics for Free Choice: concerned with reproductive issues.

- CORPUS: concerned with married priests.

- Dignity: organization of Catholic homosexuals.

- NETWORK: a national political lobby.

- Federation of Christian Ministries: focused on diverse faith communities and alternative ministries.

- Women's Ordination Conference: concerned with equality for Catholic women.

- Coalition of Concerned Canadian Catholics: a national level organization concerned with general Church renewal.[6]

This burgeoning cooperation on the national level of grassroots Catholic church-renewal organizations is another sign on the national level — simply mirroring what is happening on the grassroots level — of the maturation of American Catholicism. American Catholics are increasingly deciding that Catholicism is not only their nostalgic childhood home, but also their adult home — and they are more and more going about the task of making it into a home not just for children, intellectually and spiritually, but also for adults.

# 13

# European Church
# Renewal Movements

The rise of grassroots Catholic Church renewal movements in Europe easily matches, if not surpasses, that of North America. The December 18, 1979, Vatican attack on Hans Küng served as a galvanizing event for Catholics in Europe just as in the United States. In its immediate aftermath two organizations concerned with rights *inside* the Church were formed, one in Germany, Christenrechte in der Kirche, and one in France, Droits et Libertés dans les Eglises. Those two organizations have continued to be active and have in the following years been joined by other Catholic rights-in-the-Church organizations, so that now there are eight such national organizations that have banded together in the European Conference for Human Rights in the Church. One major reason there are different national organizations is the plurality of languages, but of course even just the existence of separate national states provides its own momentum for separate organizations.

## Holland

In addition to these organizations which focus specifically on rights in the Catholic Church, there is also a plethora of other grassroots Catholic Church renewal organizations in several European countries. For example, Holland has redeveloped in recent years a strong and broad-based grassroots Catholic Church renewal movement known as the Eighth of May Movement. It was inadvertently launched in 1985 by Pope John Paul II when he refused to meet with a number of progressive Dutch Catholic organizations during his visit to Holland. The response to his refusal was to set up a demonstration in eleven tents, which drew some thirteen thousand people. Although it was supposed to be a one-time affair, it was quickly decided to hold the demonstration annually.

ARCC National Board member Terry Dosh attended the May 8, 1989, demonstration and after a lengthy interview with leaders and participants described one aspect of it as follows:

98

People can speak [at the annual demonstration] only if a special committee says OK; this applies to bishops too. Theme for '89: Women and Men in the Image of God. There were more gray hairs the first two years; many young people (in their 20s and 30s) in the last three years; they have programs for children. Much bonding occurs. Many of the groups create huge banners; the process begins the previous November and the banner becomes a symbol of commitment and an occasion for regular bonding.[1]

Further, according to Dosh, at that 1989 demonstration 104 groups, including all seven diocesan pastoral councils, the Catholic Women of the Netherlands (30,000 members), the married priests' group, and the organization of Gay Pastors (100) participated. "One comes as a member of a group, which is the Dutch way. This time 15,000 (out of 6 million Dutch Catholics — which would be the equivalent of 140,000 in the U.S.) came." The numbers participating in the annual demonstration continue to stay high; in 1992 11,000 participated, in 1993 12,000, and in 1994 10,000.

The Eighth of May Movement in fact immediately became a year-round organization with a national Coordinator and series of ongoing projects pursued through nine standing committees. These include "International Affairs," "Inequality Between Men and Women," "Human Rights in the Church," and "Democracy in the Church." It likewise puts out regular publications, including an English-language newsletter.[2]

## Germany

In just the Germanic-speaking lands there is a growing networking of organizations, e.g., Switzerland has an umbrella organization, Aufbruch-Bewegung (The Breaking Forth Movement), which coordinates a large number of member grassroots Catholic Church renewal organizations.[3] Austria likewise has an umbrella organization — also called Aufbruch — which loosely coordinates at least eight regional grassroots Catholic Church renewal organizations.[4]

In Germany many of the grassroots Catholic Church renewal groups, but by no means all, coordinate some of their activities through the umbrella organization Initiative Kirche von unten (Movement of the Church from Below) which has forty-five member organizations throughout Germany.[5] Related but not identical is another German movement, Katholikentag von unten (The Catholic Congress from Below).

In the middle of the nineteenth century the German Catholic Church began the custom of sponsoring a huge (usually over 150,000 attendees) Katholikentag (Catholic Congress) every two years. The custom was reestablished after hiatuses during World Wars I and II; it is funded and organized by the official Catholic Church of Germany.

Starting in 1982 a group of progressive Catholics began to sponsor the Katholikentag von unten (Catholic Congress from Below), parallel to the

Katholikentag at the same location and time — at times drawing even larger audiences than the official congress. They have successfully continued this practice every two years to the present. Not only has the Congress from Below featured speakers who are more liberal than those at the official congress and dealt with subjects that were taboo there, but its continued success has also significantly affected the official congress's programs, moving them in a more progressive direction.

One dramatic manifestation of this renewal-oriented influence is the very extensive "Statement for Discussion" issued by the Central Committee of German Catholics (Zentralkomitee deutschen Katholiken, ZdK), the body responsible for the Katholikentag. This statement, issued in October 1991, was entitled "Dialogue Instead of the Avoidance of Dialogue: How Should We in the Church Deal with One Another?"[6] The statement, coming as it does from an official organ of the German Catholic Church, is extraordinarily strong, speaking very concretely of the need of dialogue within the Church and the elimination of clericalism, authoritarianism, and sexism. It was widely distributed and responses were solicited.

In all these movements throughout the Germanic-speaking nations of Europe many causes are promoted, such as liberation theology/social justice concerns, equality of women and men, peace activities, and ecumenism. But the theme which appears most often is the "Need for the Democratization of the Catholic Church." That idea and term surfaces time and again.

On April 24, 1994, the Plenary Assembly of the Bund der Deutschen Katholischen Jugend (BDKJ, Association of German Catholic Youth), an official organization of the Catholic Church in Germany with over a half million members, formulated and approved its "Plan to Promote Democracy in the Catholic Church." It too is very strong, laying out in detail the current dissatisfaction among many Catholics: "For a long time there has been an increase of voices — and even precisely of the committed Christians of the Catholic Church — which have been expressing their dissatisfaction with the still dominant clericalism, centralism, and patriarchalism and demand a change in the Church."[7] The plan goes on to claim:

> Instead of experiencing themselves as equally valuable and acknowledged partners in the Church, they time and again are treated as incompetent objects of clerical tutelage. Especially girls and women dramatically encounter the current ecclesiastical legal situation and practice in which they are confronted with an experience of structural and personal disparagement and injustice.
>
> Instead of trust in the liveliness of Christian groups, communities, and local churches, Christians most of the time experience the centralizing measures of an *angst*-filled Church, which more and more values uniformity rather than variety and is suspicious of every pluralism of opinion, expression, and form of life within the Church.

The concentration of power within the Church in the hands of the clergy excludes the laity in most questions (and precisely in those which affect them) from coresponsibility and decision. A decision which provides the laity with equal possibilities in decision-making is not foreseen, and in the best of cases would carry only nonbinding advisory weight.

These contradictions between Church and cultural-societal reality bring more and more Christians into personal difficulties and conflicts, make their personal witness of faith and their Christian involvement in society unnecessarily more difficult, and massively endangers the credibility of the Church in general.[8]

The document then produces a number of concrete demands, including the following:

In decision-making questions of Church life the laity can participate, if at all, only in an advisory capacity. The faithful, however, are to be taken seriously as subjects of their faith, as bearers of the Church's life as *Communio* with equal rights. This, therefore, is not accomplished with the possibilities of giving advice alone without real shared working and shaping plenary power. The BDKJ demands, therefore, access to and the creation of decision-making structures in which all — including the laity — can appropriately participate:

The calling to Church offices, the ordering to Church responsibility and the staffing of leadership bodies must result from votes by the Christians concerned, which may not be restricted by a veto power by a Church officer.... Decisions should take place only when those concerned have been heard and have participated in the decision-making process.... The BDKJ demands a participation of women in all Church functions. This demand of course includes — though not only — the office of Church ordination. This presumes that the Church sets in motion a discussion of the concept of office that has prevailed until now.... The BDKJ demands that women participate in the formation of priests.

The understanding of office which long has characterized the structure of the Church leads to a monopolizing in the hands of office holders of the powers of setting norms, making decisions and carrying them out. Church office is often law-giver, judge, and executive body all in one. This concentration of power burdens a dialogical collaboration of laity and clergy. In disputed issues a nonpartisan mediating and judging agency is lacking by way of both substantive differences and formal ambiguities. In such instances the laity lacks the possibility of calling upon an independent agency.... The BDKJ demands the establishment of independent arbitration and mediation agencies.[9]

The executive director of the BDKJ, Michael Kröselberg, in the spirit of that document took a vigorous part as a panelist on "A Constitution for the Catholic Church," along with Professor Norbert Greinacher of the Catholic theology faculty of the University of Tübingen, Germany. He responded to a paper on the topic by Leonard Swidler at the Katholikentag von unten, June 30, 1994, in Dresden, Germany.

## Western and Central Europe

In addition, there are more than fourteen other Catholic Church renewal organizations in as many European countries which have formed a federation under the German name Kirche im Aufbruch (The Church Breaking Forth).[10] Part of this European federation are the eight national Catholic Human Rights in the Church organizations that are banded together in the European Conference for Human Rights in the Church.

Kirche im Aufbruch held its fifth annual conference at the same time and place that the European Conference for Human Rights in the Church held its fourth annual conference on January 6–9, 1994, in Brussels. There were some fifty representatives at that conference, including a representative from ARCC in the U.S. (Leonard Swidler) and representatives of the base communities movement in Europe (which consists of scores of base communities in Western and Central Europe). At the conference the "Declaration of Human Rights in the Catholic Church" was issued by the European Conference for Human Rights in the Church, and a commitment was made to work together with ARCC in the U.S. on "a new constitution for the Catholic Church incorporating the spirit of the Gospel, and showing respect for human rights with an ecumenical dimension."[11]

The most recent, and perhaps telling, development in the grassroots movement for Church reform came in midyear 1995 in Austria. A handful of lay Catholics became so disgusted with the current situation that they planned to hold a short survey to gather signatures on a petition. In their wildest dreams they hoped to assemble a hundred thousand names.

Their petition called for five simple reforms:

1. The building of a Church of sisterly and brotherly love based on coresponsibility of laity and clergy, including the people's right to have a voice in choosing their bishops;

2. full, equal rights for women, including ordination;

3. free choice of a celibate or noncelibate way of life for priests and laity;

4. separation of the issues of birth control and abortion;

5. *Frohbotschaft statt Drohbotschaft!* "Good News Instead of Dread News!"

The response to the gathering of the petition was so positive that 1,500 volunteers came forth to work and $62,000 was voluntarily spent on the petition. The result was not 100,000 but over 500,000 signatures gathered between June 3 and June 25, 1995, and formally presented to the Austrian bishops. There are six million Catholics in Austria, so that the half million represents about 9 percent. However, since the signatures were overwhelmingly gathered at the churches and less than two million Austrian

Catholics are church-goers, the percentage represented more accurately is over 28 percent — a not insignificant percentage.[12]

Basically the same petition was taken up in Germany in fall 1995, resulting in a million and a half signatures! Plans are now well advanced for a similar petition to be taken up from mid-1996 to mid-1997 in the U.S.

# 14

# Call for a Catholic
# Constitutional Convention

Most recently an idea, whose time I believe has come, has surfaced, namely, the calling of a "Catholic Constitutional Convention." The countries of Eastern Europe, which most Westerners feared would not experience the inestimable advantages of democracy in our lifetime, have burst through to freedom and have either drastically restructured their constitutions, or, like Poland, the pope's homeland, formed them anew. Those who downgraded the human rights of freedom and democracy to secondary or tertiary human values have learned that the vast majority of humankind — whenever they have a chance to express themselves freely — places them at the primary level.

Catholics are no less human than the citizens of Poland, Hungary, Czechoslovakia, and the other recently freed countries in the valuing of and demand for human rights and democracy — within the Church. Conclusion: the time is right for Catholics too to work toward calling a "Catholic Constitutional Convention." To initiate that process all concerned Catholic organizations and individuals need to begin now to plan for the third millennium's "ecumenical council." In the language of the now predominant political reality, democracy, such an ecumenical council might well be called a "Catholic Constitutional Convention."

## "New Thinking"

What must be borne in mind when focusing on the development of the modern moves for democratization in the Catholic Church is that it takes place within what Pope Paul VI called "New Thinking."[1] (This was long before Mikhail Gorbachev in the late 1980s borrowed the phrase "New Thinking" to popularize his new approach to communism.) This "New Thinking" was characteristic of Vatican II and was likewise supposed to characterize the subsequent revision of church law, the 1917 Code of Canon Law.

Pope John Paul II described this resultant shift in thinking, this "New Thinking" of Vatican II, in the following manner when promulgating the new Code of Canon Law (1983) for the Latin Church:

1. the Church seen as the People of God,

2. hierarchical authority understood as service,

3. the Church viewed as a communion,

4. the participation by all members in the threefold *munera* [functions] of Christ [teaching, governing, making holy],

5. the common rights and obligations of all Catholics related to this, and

6. the Church's commitment to ecumenism.[2]

James Provost added further: "In addition to providing the basis for understanding the new canon law, these elements set an agenda for the church, an agenda which might be considered to form the basis for a kind of 'democratizing' of the church."[3]

## The Term "Democracy"

Something must be said about the words "constitutional" and "convention," because for many Catholics they have such a secular political, non-Catholic-Church tone about them. But even more troublesome for some Catholics is the term, and even the concept, "democracy," within whose framework "constitution" and "convention" fall. A recent book is even entitled: *The Tabu of Democracy within the Church.*[4] Talk of Catholic rights, human rights in the Church, and a "Catholic Bill of Rights" also all seem to disturb a number of intelligent, informed Catholics.

But none of that unease is warranted. In a number of instances no less a stalwart of tradition than Pope John Paul II has explicitly made that clear. Pope John Paul II has advocated (1) participation in making choices which affect the life of the community, (2) a role in the selection of leaders, (3) provision for the accountability of leaders, and (4) structures for effective participation and shared responsibilities.

> The Church values the democratic system inasmuch as it ensures the participation of citizens in making political choices, guarantees to the governed the possibilities both of electing and holding accountable those who govern them, and of replacing them through peaceful means when appropriate.... Authentic democracy...requires...structures of participation and shared responsibility.[5]

We Catholics should not shy away from contemporary democratic political terminology any more than our Catholic ancestors shied away from the imperial political terminology of their time: for an "Ecumenical (*Oikumenikos,* 'Universal') Council" is simply the imperial Greco-Roman political terminological equivalent of the modern democratic "Catholic (*Kat-holos,* 'Universal') Constitutional Convention." The Church did not hesitate to meet under the protection of the then predominant civil agency, the emperor;

indeed, the emperor, or empress(!), called the first seven ecumenical councils, i.e., Catholic Constitutional Conventions. Because a freely/responsibly deciding democracy is a more fully human political structure than an empire (and therefore more fully in keeping with humanity's being the "image of God," the *imago Dei*), *a fortiori* we Catholics should not hesitate to meet in the context of the verbal symbolic inspiration of constitutional democracy.

The strong Plan to Promote Democracy issued by the BDKJ (discussed above) should also lay to rest any remaining fears about the term and reality of democracy in the Church, especially when it is recalled that that Plan was passed by the five-hundred-thousand-strong official youth organizations of the German Catholic bishops.

## The Term "Convention"

Some have quivered with nervousness at the thought of using the more "political" term "convention" rather than the ecclesiastical one, "council" or "synod." The terms "council" and "synod" have been used largely interchangeably throughout Catholic history, both meaning a meeting of persons "gathered together." "Council" is simply the Latin form and literally means a "calling together" (*con-calare*), and "synod" is the Greek form, and literally means a "coming together" (*syn-hodos*). The term "convention" in fact is a more literal Latin translation of the earlier Greek "synod," for it also means a "coming together" (*con-ventio*). So, why not use the Latin cognate, "convention," which is closer to the earlier Greek? Vatican II itself does when referring to itself, terming itself a *"Conventus."*[6] Also, as will be detailed below, for twenty years the first bishop of Charleston, South Carolina, held annual "Conventions" of his diocese, which were mandated by his "Constitution."

## The Terms "Constitution" and "Bill of Rights" in Conciliar, Papal, and American Catholic Documents

The term "Constitution" does appear in church documents, most recently in the titles of several of the documents of Vatican II, e.g., the "Constitutions" on the Church, on Revelation, etc. The term "constitution" is used because the matter treated is "constitutive" of Christianity. The term "Bill of Rights" of course does not appear in ecclesiastical documents because it is a specifically English-language phrase, but its exact equivalent does appear from the pens of both Pope Paul VI and John Paul II and long before that from the American Catholic bishops.

During Vatican Council II, on November 20, 1965, Paul VI spoke of a "common and fundamental code containing the constitutive law [*Jus Constitutivum*] of the church" which was to underlie both the Eastern and

Western (Latin) codes of canon law. It was clearly what Americans refer to as a "Constitution."[7] Thus was born the modern idea of a "Constitution," a *Lex Ecclesiae Fundamentalis* (more about the *Lex* below). In his address to the Roman ecclesiastical high court, the Rota, just one month after the promulgation of the new Code of Canon Law (1983), Pope John Paul II called specific attention to the "Bill of Rights," *"Carta Fondamentale,"* in the Code:

> The Church has always affirmed and protected the rights of the faithful. In the new code, indeed, she has promulgated them as a *"Carta Fondamentale"* (confer canons 208–23). She thus offers opportune judicial guarantees for protecting and safeguarding adequately the desired reciprocity between the rights and duties inscribed in the dignity of the person of the "faithful Christian."[8]

American Catholics have a major precedent for the use of the terms "Constitution" and "Convention" in the outstanding Catholic bishop of Charleston, South Carolina, 1820–42, John England. He wrote a democratic "Constitution" with which his diocese was most creatively governed. He informed Rome, writing:

> The people desire to have the Constitution printed, so that they may have a standard by which they may be guided. I have learned by experience that the genius of this nation is to have written laws at hand, and to direct all their affairs according to them. If this be done, they are easily governed. If this be refused, a long and irremediable contention will ensue. By fixed laws and by reason much can be obtained, but they cannot be compelled to submit to authority which is not made manifest by law.

Following his "Constitution," every year a "Convention" was held to review matters and plan the coming year.[9]

Concerning the official Catholic use of the terms "Rights" and "Bills" or "Declarations of Rights," American Catholic history in the middle of this century needs to be recalled. In December of 1946, just a year and a few months after the end of the Second World War, the Administrative Board of the American Catholic Bishops' official agency, the National Catholic Welfare Conference (the Administrative Board was composed of ten bishops with Cardinals Samuel Stritch of Chicago and Francis Spellman of New York at the head), issued in the name of the American Catholic episcopate a declaration entitled "Man and Peace."

They argued that the fundamental problem of the postwar period was the understanding of what it meant to be human. They were critical of the practice of the victorious powers (mainly the USSR) of not releasing prisoners of war and of forced labor practices, and of the Western Allies for succumbing to the totalitarian pressure from the East to drive out millions of Germans from their homes. They called upon all the signatories of the United Nations Charter "to work together in the establishment and fostering of respect for human rights and the fundamental freedoms for all, without regard to race, language or religion." They ended with a ringing commitment: "For us... it is impossible to remain self-satisfied and actionless while our brothers in the human family groan under tyranny and are hindered in the free exercise of their human rights."

One specific action followed immediately. In January 1947, a committee made up of laity and bishops appointed by the National Catholic Welfare Conference issued nothing less than a Declaration of Human Rights,[10] almost two years before the United Nations proclaimed its Universal Declaration of Human Rights in December 1948. In fact, the American Catholic declaration was handed over to the Committee on Human Rights of the United Nations, the chair of which was Eleanor Roosevelt. A comparison of the American Catholic declaration (which with fifty articles is more detailed than the UN declaration with thirty articles) and that of the United Nations reveals amazing similarities, some passages of the latter being even verbatim versions of the former. The Catholic document speaks of human "personal dignity... being endowed with certain natural, inalienable rights.... The unity of the human race under God is not broken by geographical distance or by diversity of civilization, culture and economy."

After the General Preamble there are four major parts, the first of which being "The Rights of the Human Person" (eighteen articles): "The dignity of man, created in the image of God... is endowed as an individual and as a member of society with rights which are inalienable," which include life, liberty, religion, equal protection of the law regardless of sex, nationality, color or creed, information and communication, choice of state of life, education. The other parts are the rights pertaining to the family (nine articles), domestic rights of states (ten articles), and rights of states in the international community (thirteen articles).

Here is a chapter of American Catholic history that was almost forgotten. After its initial impact,[11] no one seemed to remember or record it, until 1990.[12] And yet this is a chapter of history that makes one proud of being an American Catholic. The American Catholic Church here took the lead in promoting human rights on a worldwide basis and probably had a significant influence in the drafting of the United Nations 1948 Universal Declaration of Human Rights.

Hence, there is ample precedent in church documents for using the terms "democracy," "rights," "bill of rights," "constitution," and "convention."

A third millennium international Catholic Constitutional Convention to decide on the fundamental constitutive structures of the Catholic Church is not a radical, new departure from tradition. Very much on the contrary. Though it is of the essence of Paul VI's and John Paul II's "New Thinking," it is also very much a return to our founding tradition, our First Millennium "Constitutional Conventions." Moreover, it should be recalled that those First Millennium Catholic Constitutional Conventions (Councils) not only had lay as well as clerical participants, but were even called by the then predominant lay political agency — the emperor, or empress — and were not accepted as official until promulgated by laity, the emperor/empress. Hence it is traditional and appropriate that the third millennium Constitutional Convention also have lay as well as clerical participants and be called by the now predominant lay political agency, the *Demos*, the People.

# 15

# Democracy in the Catholic Church

Democracy cannot be just a set of procedures, but must ultimately engender and depend on an attitude, a consciousness of life, which views human life both individually and communally as based on the central human characteristics of freedom and responsibility. A lack of such a consciousness cannot be simply replaced by a set of democratic procedures, any more than there can be a concrete being consisting of just "form" but no "content." At the same time, a democratic consciousness cannot effectively express itself except through a set of effective procedures. Further, it is only through the use of such procedures over time that a democratic consciousness can be fully developed.

Humankind has painfully developed through experience a number of democratic principles and procedures which have been found either essential or in some instances at least highly beneficial for the development and expression of a democratic consciousness of human nature, of freedom and responsibility. Among many, these include prominently:

1. participation in decision-making,

2. election of leaders,

3. limited term of office,

4. separation of powers,

5. open dialogue as essential to achieving mutual understanding and creative decisions,

6. equal access to positions of leadership,

7. accountability of leaders,

8. the principle of subsidiarity [i.e., a higher agency does not do what a lower can do],

9. the right to information, and

10. due process of law.

I will deal here only with the most prominent of these, and then just briefly, though obviously all of them, and those not listed here as well, need to be thoroughly presented, analyzed, discussed, and acted on eventually.

## Church Structures in Early Christianity

How was this freedom and responsibility, this democracy, first put into action in the history of the Church? From the earliest documentary evidence we have, the Christian Church operated with wide participation in decision-making. This was true not only of the more free-wheeling, charismatic churches related to Paul, but also the more "ordered" ones. Thus we find in the Acts of the Apostles that, for example, "the whole multitude elected Stephen" (Acts 6:5). Again, when a large number of people in Antioch was converted to Christianity, it was not just the Apostles or the Elders, but rather the *whole* Church at Jerusalem which sent Barnabas to Antioch (Acts 11:22). Still later in the Acts of the Apostles there is the statement: "Then it seemed good to the Apostles and Elders, with the whole Church, to choose men from among them and send them to Antioch with Paul and Barnabas" (Acts 15:22).

In Eusebius's *History of the Church* (323 C.E.), the major source of the postbiblical history of the Church, we find Peter not referred to as the leader or bishop of the Church at Rome, in either the first or subsequent centuries. Rather, Linus was said to be the first bishop of Rome.[1] Moreover, Peter *is* indirectly referred to by Eusebius as the first bishop of Antioch![2] (Does that mean that the "bishop of Antioch" should be the head of the Catholic Church rather than the "bishop of Rome"?) However, it should be noted that Ignatius of Antioch was said by Eusebius to be Peter's second successor as bishop of Antioch. Ignatius is the one who provides the earliest evidence of "monoepiscopacy," that is, one bishop as head of the Church in an area (a *diocese*, in imperial Rome's political terminology), which developed in some, but by no means all, areas of the Christian world at the beginning of the second century.

Ignatius does *not* refer to a bishop at Rome. Further, the *Shepherd of Hermas*, written during the second quarter of the second century, describes the leadership of the Church at Rome as a committee of presbyters. All other early documents — the New Testament Pastoral Epistles, *1 Clement*, *Didache*, *Kerygma of Peter*, *Apocalypse of Peter*, *Epistle of Barnabas*, and the *Epistle of Polycarp* — give no evidence of monoepiscopacy at Rome or anywhere else. Only Ignatius points to monoepiscopacy, and then only in Syria and Asia Minor.[3] It is only around the middle of the second century that we have clear evidence of monoepiscopacy at Rome.[4] Concerning Peter at Rome, then, there is evidence from early tradition (and the digging in recent decades under St. Peter's Basilica in Rome) that Peter died and was buried in Rome, but not that he was head of the Christian community, the Church, at Rome.

In sum, it is clear that from the earliest period of Christianity there were various forms of community structure, from the very charismatic Pauline community at Corinth to the more presbyterally ordered community at Jerusalem. Then later, through a long period of development, the monoepiscopal structure gradually arose and slowly spread, until by the end of the second century it was generally accepted and practiced. However, even the monoepiscopacy of that time and the following centuries was by no means the nearly absolutist authoritarian power center it later became. It operated much more like a limited monarchy, or just as accurately said, a limited democracy.

## Election of Leaders

The fundamental act of choice on the part of the Christian people from the initial period of monoepiscopacy and for many centuries thereafter was that of electing their own leaders, their own bishops — and priests and deacons. In this, of course, they were simply continuing the same primordial custom reflected in the New Testament documents. We find corroboration in two other first-century documents, the *Didache* and Clement of Rome's First Letter: "You must, then, elect for yourselves bishops and deacons...";[5] bishops should be chosen "with the consent of the whole Church."[6]

Early in the third century Hippolytus made it clear that it was an "apostolic tradition," which was still practiced, for the entire local community along with its leaders to choose its own deacons, presbyters, and bishop.[7] His testimony is closely followed by that of St. Cyprian of Carthage (d. 258 c.e.), who often referred to the election of bishops by the presbyters and people. He himself was so elected and consequently made it his rule never to administer ordination without first having consulted both the clergy and the laity about the candidates: "From Cyprian to the presbyterium, deacons, and all the people, greetings! In the ordaining of clerics, most beloved brethren, it is our custom to take your advice beforehand and with common deliberations weigh the character and qualifications of each individual."[8] Cyprian also reported a similar democratic custom prevailing in the Church of Rome: "Cornelius was made bishop by the ... testimony of almost all the people, who were then present, and by the assembly of ancient priests and good men."[9]

Cyprian also bore witness to the custom of the people having the right not only to elect, but also to reject and even recall bishops: "The people themselves most especially have the power to chose worthy bishops or to reject unworthy ones."[10] Optatus, a successor to Cyprian as bishop of Carthage, attests to the continuance of the practice of electing bishops into the fourth century when he reports: "Then Caecilianus was elected by the suffrage of all the people,"[11] and over in Asia Minor the Council of Ancyra (314) confirmed the right of election and rejection of bishops by the people.[12] Every Catholic schoolgirl and schoolboy knows the stories of the elections of St. Ambrose as bishop of Milan and St. Augustine as bishop of Hippo (fourth and fifth centuries) by the acclamation of the people: "We elect him!" ["Nos elegimus eum!"] A little later Pope St. Celestine (d. 432 C.E.) said: "No one is given the episcopate uninvited. The consent and desire of the clerics, the people and leadership are required."[13] That redoubtable Pope St. Leo the Great (d. 461 C.E.) who faced down Attila the Hun and saved Rome from the sack wrote: "Let him who will stand before all be elected by all."[14] These principles from the early centuries of Christian practice were reiterated in various synods until at least as late as the Council of Paris in 829 C.E.[15]

Basically the election of bishops by the clergy and people remained in effect until the twelfth century — over half the present span of Christianity. Even at the beginning of the United States of America, our first bishop, John Carroll, was, with the full approval of Rome, elected at least by all of the priests of the U.S.; he then proposed a similar election of all subsequent bishops in America — only to be blocked by Rome.[16]

### The American Heritage: John Carroll

The great Catholic "Americanists" of the end of the nineteenth century — Cardinal James Gibbons, Archbishop John Ireland, Bishops John Keane and Martin Spalding, etc. — were by no means the first "Americanists" in the Catholic Church. Already at the beginning of the new country there stood the initial "Americanist," the first American bishop, John Carroll. Carroll was born into a founding family of Maryland, the only English colony in the New World established by Catholics, and the first to declare and practice religious liberty. He became a Jesuit, was trained and taught for many years in Europe, until 1773, when the Jesuits were suppressed, and then returned home to America.

There he not only continued his priestly work, but also took an active part in the American Revolution (as an emissary along with Benjamin Franklin on a diplomatic mission to Catholic Canada in 1776) — much as did his cousin Charles Carroll, the only Catholic signer of the Declaration of Independence in 1776. The Carrolls, including John, were very much at home in America, and the latter set the new church on a course that paralleled and supported what he saw as the virtues of the new nation: religious liberty, democracy, optimism.

When Rome wanted to make him the first American bishop, he insisted that all the priests of the nation elect their bishop. Rome acceded, and John Carroll was in fact elected by them. Carroll clearly wanted this tradition to continue, as indicated in one of his letters to a fellow former Jesuit: "I wish sincerely, that Bishops may be elected, at this distance from Rome, by a select body of clergy, constituting, as it were, a Cathedral chapter."[17] Rome did subsequently grant his wish that his two coadjutor bishops be elected by all the priests of America. Unfortunately, that is where that happy practice — which of course was reflective of the ancient tradition of the Church and to some extent was still practiced then in certain European countries — was ended as far as America was concerned. Carroll had assumed it would of course continue, and made preparations accordingly, but it was blocked by Rome. Still, there the fact stands at the beginning of American history: the election of the bishop by and from among his future constituency.

### Trusteeism

One of the most difficult issues John Carroll had to contend with, starting even before he was made the first American bishop, was the controversy known as "trusteeism." The trustees were the laymen of a parish who corporately were responsible for the temporal matters of the congregation. The trustee issue raised not only the question of the election of the parish leaders, the pastors, but also that of serious participation in Church matters in general.

Coming from Europe, the Catholic immigrants naturally carried with them the customs of their home countries, and at the same time were influenced by the new environment. Both the old and the new pointed to the practice of the ancient principle: *cujus est dare, ejus est disponere,* that is, those who contribute should have a say in the disposition of their voluntary contributions.[18] The trustees of Holy Trinity Church in Philadelphia made the point about European customs clearly when in one of their petitions to the state legislature they wrote, "In many towns in Germany, the Catholic priests are elected or chosen by the authorities of such towns. So also in France, the bishops have not the sole and absolute right of appointing pastors, which belongs more to the civil authority."[19]

Of course those trustees were correct. One articulate trustee from Philadelphia had earlier noted that the historical tradition and canon law itself provided a foundation for some form of domestic nomination of bishops. Mathew Carey was surprised to learn that in canon law there were some things "almost unknown — certainly unnoticed" about the election of bishops, noting that the Code of Canon Law "most expressly declared, that no Bishop shall be appointed for a people unwilling to receive him — and even that those are not to be regarded as Bishops, who are not chosen by the clergy — or desired by the people."[20]

However, as the most knowledgeable scholar on trusteeism, Patrick W. Carey, has pointed out, "The new institution of the trustee system was a legitimate outgrowth of prior European Catholic customs and not a capitulation to the republican and Protestant values in American society." He went on to state that American Catholics did not simply borrow ideas and procedures from the host society, but reappropriated flexibly and creatively the European Catholic traditions in an American context, which was the lens through which they were viewed: "Thus, the new circumstances forced them not so much to create a new sense of lay participation as to nourish and democratize traditions of lay involvement which were already rooted in their European Catholic experiences. Democratization, however, was indeed a powerful new element."[21]

The difficulties were known not as the "trustee system," but as "trusteeism." It is extremely important to keep this distinction in mind because the vast majority of American Catholic parishes in the late eighteenth and early nineteenth centuries were incorporated under the trustee system, that is, the church buildings and properties were deeded to the trustees — but only a very few experienced any conflicts. It is that grouping of relatively few conflictual situations involving trustees that is known as "trusteeism." These conflicts almost always arose because of troublesome priests — frequently wandering immigrants — whom the congregation, or a portion of it, wished to dismiss. In other words, the congregation through its trustees claimed to have a voice in the selection and, if necessary, dismissal of their pastors.

The claims of the trustees were largely accepted during the first decades of the new nation, but the few prominent "trusteeism" conflicts eventually led to a strong resistance on the part of a growing number of bishops as the early years of the nineteenth century wore on, and the entire trustee system was eventually crushed, particularly under the leadership of the bishop of New York, John Hughes, "a forceful advocate and practitioner of episcopal absolutism," who "in the same sentence referred to the 'venerable Brethren of the clergy and the beloved Children of the laity.'"[22]

This development had a lasting traumatic effect on American Catholicism. It engendered a mentality of opposition to lay and clerical participation in the Church's administration, producing an American Catholic Church with few if any local checks on episcopal authority. Hostile memories "were passed on from generation to generation of American bishops and clergy, creating fears, even in some contemporary clergy, of recurrences of 'trusteeism.'... They greatly affected ... American Catholic structures and consciousness." However, in winning, the American bishops "merely ignored, submerged, or buried the ideological issues of the conflicts and therefore did not really solve the fundamental problem involved in trusteeism." This was to adapt a hierarchical Church "to a democratic political climate in such a way as to preserve the values of both within the Church. Thus, the problem of more widespread participation in the American church kept arising in the subsequent history of American Catholicism."[23]

What the more reflective and articulate trustees, both clerical and lay, attempted to do was to establish an ecclesiastical "quasi-democracy in American Catholicism that would acknowledge the lay trustees'... rights to elect pastors and bishops, and at the same time the clergy's canonical status and prerogatives. The trustees wanted to define constitutionally the relative rights and duties of people, priests, and prelates within the church."[24] In this they had significant support from the first American bishop, who even before he was bishop wrote to one group of trustees:

Whenever parishes are established no doubt, a proper regard, and such as is suitable to our Governments, will be had to the rights of the congregation in the mode of election and presentation; and even now I shall ever pay to their wishes every deference consistent with the general welfare of Religion.

A few months later he wrote to the pastor in question: "I know and respect the legal rights of the congregation. It's as repugnant to my duty and wish, as it exceeds my power to compel them to accept and support a Clergyman, who is disagreeable to them."[25] In another instance, as Bishop Carroll wrote to the trustees of Holy Trinity Church of Philadelphia: "Let the *election* of the pastor of your new church be so settled that every danger of a tumultuous appointment be avoided as much as possible."[26]

When after two decades the American Church was divided into several dioceses, Carroll in 1810 was made the archbishop of Baltimore. Already in 1791 he had summoned a national synod, and later as archbishop he laid plans for a national council in 1812. However, these plans were blocked by the War of 1812–14, shortly after which he died. It was clear, however, that his legacy included as a top priority governance by consensus, as befitted both the new American democracy and the ancient Church tradition. He wanted American Catholics to make their own decisions as much as possible. Already in 1785 while he was the American Prefect-Apostolic he wrote to the Vatican Secretary of State, Cardinal Giacomo Antonelli: "We desire...that whatever can with safety to religion be granted, shall be conceded to American Catholics in ecclesiastical affairs."[27]

America was most fortunate in having at its very beginning a giant of a leader who was fully committed to both the Catholic Church and the American nation, with its principles of democracy, religious liberty, and separation of Church and State. Perhaps it would have been expecting too much to have looked for many more bishops of his stature among his successors — though one wonders whether their *election* rather than *appointment* might not in fact have much better fulfilled that expectation.

In any case, as late as the beginning of the twentieth century less than half of the bishops of the world were directly named by the pope. Thus it is only in our century that the right of choosing our own bishops has been almost completely taken away from the priests and people — contrary to almost the whole history of the Catholic tradition and the beginning of the American Catholic Church.

## Participatory Decision-Making

In the ancient Church it was not only in the election of their deacons, priests, and bishops that the laity were involved in Church decision-making. Eusebius reports that already in the second century the *"faithful...examined the new doctrines and condemned the heresy."*[28] Cyprian in the third century noted that he himself often convoked councils: *"Concilio frequenter acto."*[29]

On the burning Church issues of the day he wrote to the laity: "This business should be examined in all its parts in your presence and with your counsel."[30] And again: "It is a subject which must be considered...with the whole body of the laity."[31] And again: "From the beginning of my episcopate I have been determined to undertake nothing...without gaining the assent of the people."[32] Furthermore, this custom of participatory decision-making was also prevalent in the Roman Church of the time, for the Roman clergy wrote: "Thus by the collaborative counsels of bishops, presbyters, deacons, confessors and likewise a substantial number of the laity...for no decree can be established which does not appear to be ratified by the consent of the plurality."[33]

Even outside the reach of the law-oriented culture of the Roman Empire the principle of participatory decision-making flourished in the ancient Christian Church. For example, in the East Syrian Church the Synod of Joseph (554 c.e.) stated that "the patriarch must do all that he does with the advice of the community. Whatever he arranged will have all the more authority the more it is submitted for examination."[34]

It was not only on the local and regional levels that the laity were actively involved in ecclesiastical decision-making; from the beginning that was also true on the Church universal level as well. In the fourth century the great worldwide ecumenical councils began, the first of course being held in 325 at Nicea — called and presided over by a layman, the Emperor Constantine. In fact, as noted before, all the ecumenical councils from the beginning until well into the Middle Ages were always, with one exception, called by the emperors. That one exception was Nicea II in the eighth century, which was called by the *Empress* Irene! Moreover, the emperors and empress called the councils on their own authority, not necessarily with prior consultation and approval of the papacy — not even, for that matter, necessarily with the subsequent approval of the papacy. That is, the decrees of the ecumenical councils were promulgated and published by the emperor without always waiting for the approbation of the papacy.

Laity were also present at the ecumenical councils, as well as the large regional councils, such as the ones at Cyprian's Carthage in the third century, the Council of Elvira in the fourth century, the Fourth Council of Toledo in the sixth century, and on down through the centuries, reaching a high point in some ways at the ecumenical councils of Constance and Basel in the first half of the fifteenth century. Even at the sixteenth-century Council of Trent, laity were present and active. Only with the First Vatican Council in 1870 did the participation of the laity in ecumenical councils shrivel to almost nothing.

## The American Heritage: John England, "Apostle to Democracy"

There was only one other giant church leader in America following upon John Carroll's demise in 1815 until the latter part of the nineteenth century when the subsequently "condemned" Americanists arrived on the scene. That giant was John England of Cork, Ireland, who, in 1820, was named by Rome bishop of Charleston, South Carolina. In the matter of a Catholic Constitution he merits special attention.

John England was called by his first biographer "Apostle to Democracy."[35] England was indeed a fervent admirer of democracy, but more importantly he was also a committed and skilled practitioner of democracy in all aspects of his life, and especially as bishop. In the matter of the selection of bishops he followed in the footsteps of his great predecessor John Carroll in his dissatisfaction with the cabalistic appointment of American bishops by Rome. He was so frustrated in the matter that at the point when both the important sees of Boston and New York were vacant and all sorts of power brokering was in process he took the extraordinary step of placing a notice in his weekly diocesan newspaper:

**To the Roman Catholic Clergy and Laity of the United States**

The Sees of Boston and New York are now vacant, or if Prelates have been appointed for them, I am not aware of who they are. They will both be filled before I shall probably address you upon the *necessity of having some permanent and known mode of having our Sees filled, not by faction, intrigue or accident — but in a manner more likely to be useful and satisfactory than that which is now in operation.*[36]

His plea is equally pertinent — and unfulfilled — today.

England took extraordinary steps in making his diocese a model of American, and Catholic, democracy, but to appreciate them fully they must be seen against the background of the chaos and near-schism that he walked into in the Charleston of 1820.

As noted above, American Catholic church historiography has been marred much more by the specter than the reality of "trusteeism," which ever since has been used by bishops as a club to keep laity in submission. Recall: the laws of the new nation required that church property be placed in the possession of a lay corporation; in the early American Catholic churches this corporation was known as the trustees, and it operated much as was already the case in French Canada at that time. It was true that for the great majority of cases this system worked very well, but in a small minority of cases, partly because of a few manipulative, malcontent Irish priests and partly because of some poor administrative tactics by several of the bishops, cases of serious open conflict between the bishop and the trustees of certain churches developed. In one case a young lawyer named Abraham Lincoln defended the trustees. Because of their notoriety these few cases attained more importance than they intrinsically merited, and the fumbling of the bishops only tended to exacerbate the problems.

Charleston of 1820 was the scene of one of the longest, bitterest of these trustee conflicts. One might have expected that this situation would have forced a vigorous young bishop from outside of America to make authoritarian kinds of moves. Nothing, however, could have been farther from the truth with Bishop John England. His initial, and subsequent, actions were the very epitome of toleration, democracy, and voluntaryism. "For England, the evils of trusteeism were the result of the failure of proper constitutional provisions in the original trustee charters.... England responded to the sources of these evils by creating his constitutional form of government."[37]

There were precedents even in American Catholic history preparing the way for Bishop England's idea of a Constitution for the Catholic Church. Already in 1783, just ten years after the Jesuit Society was suppressed by the pope, Father John Carroll, a former Jesuit, prompted initially by concern for the properties of the former Jesuit Society, formed a "Constitution for the Clergy," providing a number of checks and balances concerning the use of properties, reflecting republican ideals.[38]

In addition, among some of the more reflective, knowledgeable trustees there grew the notion that "clearly defined and published rights and duties within the church would avoid capriciousness in the exercise of ecclesiastical authority. Bishops and clergy...should govern by written law and by reason, not by will power."[39] Nevertheless few trustees actually put forward any concrete proposals for such written regulations or constitutions. The trustees of Norfolk, Virginia, were among those few. In 1817 they sent a delegate to Rome with a plan for a "Supreme Ecclesiastical Synodus" which should manage the affairs of the new diocese of Virginia. "The plan outlined in detail the rights and duties of people, priests, and bishop in the new diocese, giving lay trustees significant powers on the diocesan as well as congregational levels of ecclesiastical government."[40]

## The Constitution

As the first bishop of Charleston, however, John England was in a position not simply to propose, but to act, and he did just that. To begin with, he wrote a Constitution by which his vast mission diocese (comprised of the states of North and South Carolina and Georgia with perhaps only one thousand Catholics) was to be governed — a most extraordinary procedure, to say the least, especially in the time of the floodtide of Reaction after the ebbing of the French Revolution and the defeat of Napoleon. He wrote that he had carefully studied the American Constitution, as well as other writings on the subject, and the laws and tradition of the Catholic Church and was persuaded that his Constitution was in the best spirit of both American-

ism and Catholicism. Just two years after he arrived in America he wrote to
Cardinal Fontana in Rome when sending him a copy of his Constitution:

> Having paid great attention to the state of several Churches in America, and
> studied as deeply as I could the character of the government and the people,
> and the circumstances of my own flock, as well as the Canons and usages
> of the Roman Catholic Church, and having advised with religious men and
> Clergymen, and lawyers, I this day...published the Constitution by which
> the Roman Catholic Church under my charge is to be regulated, and I trust
> with the blessing of Heaven much disputation and Infidelity restrained. It was
> subscribed by the Clergy and by many well-disposed Laymen.[41]

Only a few weeks after his arrival in Charleston and a strenuous pastoral
journey through much of his mammoth diocese (twice the size of all Ireland),
he wrote in his first pastoral letter: "And we ourselves have for a long time
admired the excellence of your [American] Constitution."[42] Three years later,
in 1824, writing to Rome, he stressed the importance of written laws in
America and hence their importance for the healthy governance of American
Catholicism:

> But the people desire to have the Constitution printed, so that they may have
> a standard by which they may be guided. I have learned by experience that the
> genius of this nation is to have written laws at hand, and to direct all their
> affairs according to them. If this be done, they are easily governed. If this
> be refused, a long and irremediable contention will ensue. By fixed laws and
> by reason much can be obtained, but they cannot be compelled to submit to
> authority which is not made manifest by law.[43]

(It should be remembered that this published Constitution — in the English
vernacular — preceded by almost a hundred years the first publishing of a
Code of Canon Law, in 1917 — still in Latin.)

The Constitution laid out the rights and responsibilities of the several
parties involved in the diocese: the laity, the clergy, the bishop. Moreover,
the Constitution was not simply unilaterally declared in force by England.
Rather, it was submitted for acceptance to every priest and all the leading
laymen of the parishes for voluntary adoption; each new congregation, as it
was formed, adopted it voluntarily. In fact, St. Mary's Church, the oldest
church in the diocese and the one that had previously been involved in the
bitter trustee dispute with Archbishop Ambrose Maréchal of Baltimore, did
not accept the Constitution until 1829, at which time their representatives
at the annual Convention were warmly received. Until then, England was
careful to let them make up their own minds. Furthermore, the Constitution
itself included a procedure for amendment.

Although, with the single exception of St. Mary's, England's Constitution
quickly gained warm acceptance by his laity and clergy, it met with a very
cold response by the other American bishops. At the First American Provincial Council of Baltimore, in 1829, which all the American bishops attended,

it was rejected as unacceptable in the other dioceses, stating merely that, "by this decree we do not desire to interfere with the method which the bishop of Charleston now follows in his diocese."[44] Indeed, England's Constitution stood in the way of his being recommended for the much more populous and important sees of Boston or New York.

Bishop Patrick Kenrick of Philadelphia magnanimously wrote to Cardinal Cullen in Rome, in 1834, after the Second Provincial Council of Baltimore, that England was

> perfectly disgusted at the treatment he received at the last Council.... Besides, Charleston diocese is not a fit theatre for a man of his splendid talents... and I would at any moment resign my mitre to make place for him. This I authorize you to communicate to the Sacred Congr... I had proposed him for the administration of New York which most sadly needs an efficient Prelate, and in consequence of the entire unwillingness of Bp. Dubois I had offered my place in case I should be forced to put on the thorny crown of that diocese. The Archbishop had signified assent, provided the *Constitution* would be left behind; but now that hope vanishes.[45]

Somewhat earlier England and his Constitution had suffered the venom of the poison pen of Kenrick's predecessor, Bishop Henry Conwell of Philadelphia, who, Andrew Greeley in his brilliant book *The Catholic Experience* says, was "in the process of making a complete fool of himself." He nevertheless had time to warn the Holy See that "if this constitution or *democratic* method of ruling the Church be approved by the Holy See, it might become necessary to extend it to all the dioceses here; it would mean the quick collapse of the American Church."

Greeley added: "It never occurred to Conwell that such a democratic method might have saved his diocese from utter chaos. Later he wrote to Rome warning them once again that England was violating the most sacred of ecclesiastical traditions and was threatening the American Church with ruin."[46]

England was convinced that despite the trustees' difficulties, it was far better that the Church and its clergy depend primarily on the Catholic people at large rather than the government — as it still does in many European countries, e.g., Germany. According to his Constitution each congregation elected representatives who were to constitute a vestry. Then, also despite the trustee controversies, the Constitution provided that "the churches, cemeteries, lands, houses, funds, or other property belonging to any particular district [here meaning parish], shall be made the property of the Vestry of that district, in trust for the same." All money belonging to the congregation could be "expended only by authority of an act of the vestry of that district." At the same time the approval of the bishop was also required for the sale of any property. Thus, the key notions of the American Constitution of "election of representatives," "separation of powers," and "checks and balances" were here incorporated into England's Constitution. In addition, the salary of the parish priest was also to be raised by the vestry, but kept separate from the general funds so that no improper pressure could be levied on the pastor. The wisdom and practicality of this structure was demonstrated by the fact that it operated flawlessly for the twenty years of England's episcopacy.[47]

## Annual Convention

A second critical element of the Constitution was the provision for annual diocesan Conventions for all the clergy, and a proportional representation of the laity from each congregation elected by all the people. The Convention possessed certain decision-making powers parallel to those of each vestry, such as control of the General Diocesan Fund (used for the seminary, schools, hospitals — all of which England started — widows and orphans and similar concerns). The bishop was *required* to make a full report on the expending of all funds to the Convention; England in fact did an exemplary job of this at every Convention. In addition, he took the opportunity to present an overview of the Church in all America as well as in his diocese at each Convention. Consequently his twenty-six Convention Addresses give a history of the Catholic Church in America for those years. Most importantly, it was through the Convention that the scattered Catholic churches began to grow together with a sense of unity and belonging to a larger church, a "catholic" Church, which was *their* Church where they had both rights and responsibilities.

In the beginning years of his episcopate the Convention was legally incorporated in each of the three states and met accordingly. It was only in 1839 that the mission diocese had developed sufficiently to legally incorporate the Convention for all three states together so that there could be a single annual diocese-wide Convention (twenty-six state Conventions were held between 1823 and 1839). The first General Convention of the diocese lasted for seven days, with sixteen priests and thirty laymen present as delegates; in 1840 there were almost double that number. The third Convention was scheduled for late in 1841, but was delayed because of England's extended mission in Europe. Then, early in 1842, he died, and with him his Convention, Constitution, and mostly everything else, it seemed, that made him great, for the small leaders who came after him could not match the stride of his footsteps.

## American Councils

Dialogue and democracy on the national level were also major concerns of England from the very beginning of his time in America. Although Archbishop Carroll had scheduled a first national Provincial Council of all the American bishops already in 1812, he was, as noted above, prevented from carrying that plan out first by war and then death. His second successor, Ambrose Maréchal (Carroll's first successor, Ambrose Neale, outlived him only a little over a year), a French prelate, who perhaps somewhat understandably (remembering the French Revolution) was not enthusiastic about procedures which smacked of "democracy," did not see fit to call a Provincial Council. England wrote him often, urging the many good reasons for an immediate convocation of the Council — including the requirement by the Council of Trent that they be held every three years — but on the back of each of these letters of England's that are in the Baltimore archives there is the single word written in Maréchal's hand: "Negative."

Hence, it was only after Maréchal's demise that England was able to persuade his successor, James Whitfield, to call the first American Provincial Council in 1829. It is clear from records that England dominated this Council, and all the rest during his lifetime (four altogether). He was asked to write all the pastoral letters (five) coming out of each of the Councils, which he did with his customary talent.

For example, concerning the first pastoral letter, which was on the clergy (a second one was on the laity), the premier American Catholic church historian of the early twentieth century, Peter Guilday, wrote in 1923: "The *Pastoral* stands today, as it did then, as one of the clearest mirrors of priestly zeal and devotion in the English language."[48] Difficult though these Provincial Councils often were, they nevertheless did resolve many pressing problems of a growing American Church, whose population and geographical expanse were exploding, in effective collegial fashion, operating in a land that insisted on religious liberty, democracy, and separation of Church and State — all Catholic neuralgic issues during the time of Popes Gregory XVI (1831–46) and Pius XI (1846–78). Moreover, the work of these Councils, of which Bishop England has been called the "Father,"[49] had wide influence in world Catholicism. Theodore Maynard wrote that these Councils, "through their inclusion in the collection published at Maria Laach [1875], have had a remarkable influence on conciliar legislation and Catholic life throughout the world."[50] Just eight years after the death of England, Bishop Kenrick of Philadelphia wrote: "The Church in this country owes to Bishop England the celebration of the Provincial Councils, which have given form and consistency to the hierarchy and order to her internal economy."[51]

It was precisely England's strengths, however, that were his undoing with his fellow bishops. He could not get Archbishop Whitfield to call the second Council, but was able nevertheless to persuade Rome to insist on it to Whitfield — which fact doubtless galled the latter. After the Second Provincial Council, in 1834, Kenrick wrote to Cardinal Cullen:

> Little was done in consequence of the suspicion with which every measure emanating from Bishop England was viewed. The prelates for the most part second the archbishop who felt mortified that he had been obliged by the influence of Bishop England to call the council.... The talents, learning, fame, eloquence of Bishop England rendered him not an object of envy for I believe the good prelates superior to this narrow passion but fear for they dreaded

lest his active mind and liberal views might lead them into the adoption of measures which might weaken their authority and disturb the repose of the Church. To me they appeared to fear where there was no cause for fear. Their votes could always outweigh his arguments. Had they manifested a respect for his judgment, a disposition to hear his reasons, and to adopt his suggestions if found correct, had there been more personal courtesy, fraternal charity... the results of the council would have been more consolatory. We would have not seen... a young man having no experience of the ministry save that which he would have had within the college walls [Samuel Eccleston] raised to the office of coadjutor to the archbishop.[52]

Andrew Greeley commented that the bishops led by Archbishop Whitfield

were more eager to block John England than they were to govern the American Church, so eager in fact that they selected a thirty-one-year-old coadjutor for Whitfield, to lessen so far as they could the possibility that Rome might be remotely tempted to make England the Archbishop of Baltimore.[53]

What a different course American Catholic history might have taken had England had the personal ambition to circumvent the cabal to make the disastrously incompetent Eccleston the archbishop and had eventually ended there himself. Unfortunately for the Catholic Church he did not; he promptly rose at the Council and approved the nomination of Eccleston as coadjutor of Whitfield at Baltimore.


## Deliberation and Dissent

In many ways England made it abundantly clear that American Catholics felt — and he obviously agreed with them — that they ought to be consulted in all important matters, including Church matters. He wrote to Rome that "the American people are a law-abiding people, and the laws are respected so long as the voice of the people is heard in their making." He reported elsewhere that the American Catholic "will never be reconciled to the practice of the bishop, and oftentimes of the priest alone, giving orders without assigning reasons for the same." He told his 1827 Convention that he was searching for and training clergy who were "attached to our republican institutions."[54]

England recognized that there could still be disagreements with Church authorities and spoke of "dissent" in a letter to U.S. Secretary of State John Forsythe in 1841 wherein he wrote that if the American bishops had found in a papal Apostolic Letter "anything contrary to their judgment, respecting faith or morals, it would have been their duty to have respectfully sent their statement of such differences to the Holy See, together with their reasons for such dissent." He even went so far, when addressing a joint session of the U.S. President (John Quincy Adams), Supreme Court, Senate, and House of Representatives in 1826, as to say:

A political difficulty has been sometimes raised here. If this infallible tribunal which you [Catholics] profess yourselves bound to obey should command you to overturn our government, and to tell you that it is the will of God to have it modelled anew, will you be bound to obey it? And how then can we consider those men to be good citizens, who profess to owe obedience to a foreign authority, to an authority not recognized in our constitution, to an authority which has excommunicated and deposed sovereigns, and which has absolved subjects and citizens from their bond of allegiance?

Our answer to this is extremely simple and very plain; it is that we would not be bound to obey it, that we recognize no such authority. I would not allow to the Pope, or to any bishop of our church, outside this Union, the smallest interference with the humblest vote at our most insignificant balloting box. He has no rights to such interference.[55]

Strong words in such a public forum in a period when reaction, not liberty, was in vogue with the papacy, as, e.g., when Catholic Polish freedom-fighters were condemned and handed over to the tender mercies of the Orthodox czar by the Pope (1830), and again the Catholic Hungarians in 1848.

In summary, it is clear that for responsible dissent, for a Catholic Constitution, for democratic Catholic Conventions, for National Councils in the Catholic Church — in short, for the employment of participatory decision-making, of democracy as it flows from the American civil experience, in the life of the Catholic Church — Bishop John England of Charleston, South Carolina, provides a premier precedent.

The decades-long actions of the "Americanists" at the beginning of the nineteenth century were again vigorously articulated especially by the most prominent of the "Americanists" at the end of that century, Archbishop John Ireland of St. Paul, Minnesota:

This is an age of liberty, civil and political; it is the age of democracy!... The Catholic Church, I am sure, has no fear of democracy, this flowering of her own most sacred principles of the equality, fraternity, and liberty of all men, in Christ and through Christ. These principles are found upon every page of the gospel.... I say that the government of the people, by the people, and for the people, is, more than any other, the polity under which the Catholic Church, the church of the people, breathes air most congenial to her mind and heart.[56]

## Vatican II and Aftermath

### A Constitution of the Catholic Church

In very many ways the Second Vatican Council (1962–65) was a return to the spirit and form of the first "Constitutional Conventions" (Councils) of the early Church — even though the influence of the laity came only largely through the massive power of the free press.

Another of the democratizing moves Vatican Council II made was to inspire the total revision of the 1917 Code of Canon Law in the spirit of democracy and constitutionalism. Already on January 25, 1959, Pope John XXIII announced simultaneously the calling of the Second Vatican Council and the revision of the 1917 Code of Canon Law.[57] Even before Vatican II was completed, work was begun on the writing of this Catholic "Constitution of Fundamental Rights," the *Lex Ecclesiae Fundamentalis.* Father James Coriden, a coeditor of the 1985 magisterial 1150-page folio-size *The Code of Canon Law: A Text and Commentary* (commissioned by the Canon Law Society of America) and the Dean of the Catholic Theological Union of Washington, D.C., wrote that "the origins of the Code's bill of rights [the new 1983 Code of Canon Law eventually absorbed the fundamental 'rights' articles of the *Lex Ecclesiae Fundamentalis*] were not in a Constitutional Congress, but its history and development clearly reveal its truly constitutional character."[58]

As noted above, it was on November 20, 1965, that Pope Paul VI said to the Coetus Consultorum Specialis (Commission for the Revision of the Code of Canon Law) that the opportunity to provide a "Constitution" for the Church should be seized while the 1917 Code of Canon Law was being overhauled in the light of Vatican II. The Coetus was led by Cardinal Pericle Felici (an ultraconservative) and Msgr. William Onclin (a moderate) of Louvain University. Already by the middle of 1966 the Coetus had a draft prepared for discussion and a revised version the following year, 1967. That year the Coetus drew up and submitted to the International Synod of Bishops a set of ten "principles to guide the revision of the Code" (*Principia quae dirigant recognitionem Codicis*), which were overwhelmingly approved. Three more sessions of the Coetus followed and then a first formal draft was presented to the cardinals of the Coetus in 1969 and was relatively widely circulated, although officially still *sub secreto.* Then in 1971, the further revised draft (so-called *textus emendatus*) was sent to all the bishops, still *sub secreto.* However, it was leaked to the press and published on March 15, 1971, in the Bologna periodical *Il Regno* (the editors were all fired for their efforts).

Two things should be especially noted about the *Lex Ecclesiae Fundamentalis:* (1) It clearly was to serve as a "Constitution" in the sense that it was to provide the fundamental juridical framework within which all other church law was to be understood and applied. Like the American Constitution, if any subsequent law passed were found to be contrary to the *Lex Fundamentalis,* the subsequent law would be void. (2) The *Lex Fundamentalis* was to serve as a fundamental list of rights of the members of the Church, like the American "Bill of Rights."

Concerning the first point, the explanation (*Relatio*) by Msgr. Onclin that accompanied the 1971 draft of the *Lex* stated clearly that "a fundamental law is required, on which all other laws in the Church will depend.... Laws promulgated by the supreme authority of the Church are to be understood according to the prescriptions of the *Lex Ecclesiae Fundamentalis....* Laws promulgated by inferior ecclesiastical authority contrary to the *Lex Ecclesiae Fundamentalis* lack all power."[59]

Concerning the second point, Father Coriden wrote referring to the *Lex Fundamentalis* as key portions of it were imbedded in the 1983 Code of Canon Law: "The bill of rights is part of the bedrock upon which is based the rest of our canonical system.... The Coetus's communication to the episcopal synod of 1967 described the enumeration of rights of the faithful as fulfilling one of the chief purposes of the 'fundamental code.' "[60] Already in 1967 the Coetus told the Synod of Bishops in its ten guiding principles the following:

> The principal and essential object of canon law is to define and safeguard the rights and obligations of each person toward others and toward society.... A very important problem is proposed to be solved in the future Code, namely how the rights of persons can be defined and safeguarded.... The use of power in the Church must not be arbitrary, because that is prohibited by the natural law, by divine positive law, and by ecclesiastical law. The rights of each one of Christ's faithful must be acknowledged and protected.[61]

A further aspect of the *Lex Fundamentalis* is worth noting here. As mentioned, from the inception of the Coetus in 1965 until the press leak in 1971, its work was all done *sub secreto.* Why it should have been so is not clear, except that that was the way things had always been done. However, after the leak Msgr. Onclin held a press conference in which he "recalled that the draft text was only a working paper which will probably be modified in conformity with the wishes of the bishops. These, in turn, may consult priests and laymen, and the result will therefore be a truly Church-wide consultation."[62]

As Peter Hebblethwaite mentioned in his biography of Pope Paul VI, the Vatican instruction *Communio et progressio,* on the implementation of the Vatican II decree on the mass media, was issued less than two months before the *Lex* leak in *Il Regno.* It made a clear argument in favor of open government in the Catholic Church:

> The spiritual riches which are an essential attribute of the Church demand that the news she gives out of her intentions as well as her works be distinguished by integrity, truth and openness. When ecclesiastical authorities are unwilling to give information or are unable to do so, then rumor is unloosed and rumor is not a bearer of truth but carries dangerous half-truths. Secrecy should therefore be restricted to matters involving the good name of individuals or that touch on the rights of people whether singly or collectively.[63]

Then unfortunately, shortly after John Paul II became pope, "the whole *Lex* project was put to death, without explanation, in 1981 after it had been approved by a specially convened international commission earlier in the year."[64] Nevertheless, a number of the canons of the *Lex Ecclesiae Fundamentalis* were transferred to the new 1983 Code of Canon Law and became its canons 208–23, providing a contemporary beginning of a "Catholic Constitution."

National Reform Councils

It was not only on the international level that the movement toward "participatory democracy" gained momentum in the aftermath of Vatican Council II; it also happened in a number of instances on the national level, especially in the U.S. and the Germanic-speaking countries, namely, the Netherlands, West Germany, East Germany, Austria, Switzerland, and Luxemburg.[65]

The Dutch Pastoral Council ran in several phases from 1968 to 1979. The West German Synod went from 1971 to 1975; the East German Pastoral Synod was shorter during the same period. The Austrian Synod held three sessions, two in 1973 and one in 1974. The Swiss Synod was held in 1972 and provisions were made for subsequent national level Interdiocesan Pastoral Forums from 1978 onward. The Luxemburg Synod was the longest running, lasting from 1972 to 1981. In almost all these instances the surveys which were stimulated and the discussions which were held were extremely responsible and progressive.

The attempt to call a National Pastoral Council in the U.S. got as far as a committee being set up, but no further. However, the equivalent emerged under the leadership of Cardinal John Dearden of Detroit, who spearheaded the organization of the 1976 "Call to Action," as the National Conference of Catholic Bishops' contribution to the American Bicentennial Celebration. Besides employing clerical and lay representation and majority rule voting at the 1976 assembly, the "Call to Action" stimulated widespread grassroots consultation, including through travelling "hearings" by a committee of bishops. Finally a large number of very responsible and progressive resolutions were democratically passed at the Detroit assembly.

However, in the end, Rome was so resistant to serious democratizing developments, whether stemming from Europe or from America, that the initial general enthusiasm flowing from Vatican II progressively waned. As the French theologian Bernard Franck put it, it gave way to a "general moroseness characteristic of the Western countries and the discouragement of a great many laity, who, here as elsewhere, watch helplessly as the church is again taken over by clergy who, as always, are jealous of their prerogatives and find it difficult to share responsibilities."[66] This was written in 1991. Now, however, chastened progressive Catholics are beginning to strive once again for participatory democratization of the Catholic Church.

# Limited Term of Office

There is nothing in either Scripture or theology which necessitates an unlimited term of office for any position in the Catholic Church. Every position, including that of pope, is "resignable" — in fact, Pope St. Celestine V resigned as pope in 1294 C.E. On the positive side, it should be noted that there are many positions which have had time limitations set to them in a variety of ways. Various positions within a diocese, e.g., vicar general, dean, pastor, all depend for their longevity on the will of the presiding bishop. The temporal limitation of office in these cases is known only "after the fact," not "before the fact." Bishops and cardinals now have a specific "before the fact" temporal limitation, namely, they must retire from their posts at age seventy-five. Further, the position of a bishop as an "Ordinary" in a particular diocese is not infrequently temporally also limited by his leaving that diocese and going to another.

There has not been a tradition of diocesan bishops being selected for their positions for a specific period of time. However, there has been the tradition for many, many centuries in the Catholic Church of the superiors of religious orders — including abbots and abbesses who often held ecclesiastical geographical jurisdiction powers comparable to those of bishops — being elected for specific limited terms of office. And all this has been duly approved by Rome.

Suffice it to recall the immense benefits of a limited term of office in the modern civil experience. The prospect of soon or at least eventually being "among" those about whom one is now making decisions is a healthy tempering thought for the decision-maker. Unfettered power, with the best of will, tempts the realization of the famous saying of Lord Acton: "Power corrupts, and absolute power corrupts absolutely." Hence, it is no surprise to note that in the wake of the liberating winds of Vatican II the Catholic theological faculty of the University of Tübingen in Germany produced a special issue of their periodical, the *Tübinger Theologische Quartalschrift* 2 (1969), devoted to the questions of the election and limited term of office of bishops and that the whole faculty signed a careful argument in favor of the notion of a limited term of office of eight years for resident bishops. What is perhaps surprising, however, is not that Hans Küng was one of the signers of that document (which he was) but that Joseph Ratzinger (now cardinal and head of the Congregation for the Doctrine of the Faith) was also![67]

## Separation of Powers

When we think of the modern democratic principle of the "separation of powers," from the time of Montesquieu's *De l'Esprit des Lois* (1734), we normally think of the legislative, executive, and judicial powers being separated. In the ancient and medieval Catholic Church there was for long stretches of time a similar separation of powers, though the terms used were not precisely those of Montesquieu or of today. The holders of powers were: (1) bishops, (2) teachers, and in the Middle Ages, (3) canon lawyers. I will deal briefly only with the first two.

It will probably come as somewhat of a shock for many Catholics to learn that in the history of the Catholic Church the pope and bishops were not always the supreme teachers of what was true Catholic doctrine. For well over nine centuries of Catholic history it was the "teachers," the theologians who were the supreme arbiters in deciding what was correct Catholic teaching. This occurred in the first three centuries of the Christian era and again from the thirteenth through the eighteenth centuries. Concerning the first three centuries one need only remember such outstanding "teachers," who were not even priests, let alone bishops, as Clement of Alexandria (150–215) and his successor Origen (185–254). It is clear that there were lay teachers in the Roman Church as well in this early period, for we find the Roman priest Hippolytus (170–236) stating such in his *Apostolic Tradition:* "When the teacher...whether the one who teaches be cleric or lay, he will do so."[68]

The highly regarded Cardinal Jean Daniélou clearly described the situation at the first half of the third century in Alexandria when, in writing about Origen, he stated:

> There were two distinct types of authority in the early Church....The visible hierarchy of presbyters [clergy] and the visible hierarchy of doctors [free teachers]....There were two distinct types of authority in the early Church. Both could be traced back to the charismata of the early days, but they were each derived from different ones. The two hierarchies took up different attitudes on certain points. The presbyters turned more towards the worship of God, the *didaskaloi* [free teachers] rather to the ministry of the word and to Scripture. Clearly Origen represents the viewpoint of the *didaskaloi*.[69]

Concerning the Middle Ages from the thirteenth century on no less a person than St. Thomas Aquinas clearly distinguishes between the professorial chair, *cathedra magistralis,* and the episcopal throne, the *cathedra pontificalis vel pastoralis.* "The first conferred the authority to teach, *auctoritas docendi;* the second, the power to govern and, if necessary, to punish, *eminentia potestatis.*"[70] There was no subordination of the magisterium of the teacher to that of the bishop; they were on an equal plane: "Teachers of sacred Scripture adhere to the ministry of the word as do also prelates."[71]

In the fourteenth century we find the French theologian Godefroid de Fontaines posing the following question (and note how he poses it): "Whether the theologian *must* contradict the statement of the bishop if he believes it to be opposed to the truth?" He answers that if the matter is not concerned with faith or morals, then he should dissent only in private, but if it is a matter of faith or morals, "the teacher must take a stand, regardless of the episcopal decree...even though some will be scandalized by this action. It is better to preserve the truth, even at the cost of a scandal than to let it be suppressed through fear of a scandal." And, Godefroid pointed out, this would be true even if the bishop in question were the pope, "for in this situation the pope can be doubted."[72]

Thus from the medieval Scholastic perspective the theologians were supposed to determine truth and error and it was then up to the bishops to

punish the offenders. That is why from the thirteenth century onward episcopal decrees were often issued "with the counsel of teachers (*de consilio
doctorum*)." For example, the bishop of Paris, Etienne I, condemned several propositions as heretical "with the counsel of the teachers of theology"
(*de consilio magistrorum theologiae*).[73] The Western Schism (late fourteenth/
early fifteenth centuries, when there were two and even three popes simultaneously!) further reinforced the prestige and authority of the theologians,
so that at the two ecumenical councils which resolved the Western Schism,
Constance (1314–18 C.E.) and especially Basel (1431–49 C.E.), there were often hundreds of theologians present and only a handful of ignorant bishops
and abbots.

Hence, as Roger Gryson put it, "one can not find any question on which
the universal Church's ultimate criterion of truth did not come around to the
unanimous opinion of the Scholastics [theologians], through faith in their
authority (*eorum auctoritate mota*)." And by the middle of the sixteenth century the famous Spanish Dominican theologian Melchior Cano applied to
theologians the words of Jesus, "Whoever hears you hears me, who rejects
you rejects me": "When the Lord said: 'Who hears you hears me, and who
rejects you rejects me,' he did not refer with these words to the first theologians, i.e., the apostles, but to the future teachers in the Church so long as
the sheep need to be pastured in knowledge and doctrine."[74]

This "separation of powers," wherein the theologians exercised the teaching power and, as St. Thomas described it, the bishops *Regimen* or "manage-
ment," continued through the end of the "Old *Regimen*," the French *Ancien
Régime*, at the beginning of the last century.

## Dialogue — Means to Mutual Understanding and Creative Decisions

Question: Can there not be, indeed, ought there not be different opinions,
followed by possible dissent, then dialogue, and only thereafter decision in
the Church, even on matters of the greatest religious significance? Indeed,
should not this sequence of actions be adhered to especially in matters of the
greatest religious significance?

Response: "The Christian faithful... have the right and even at times *a
duty* to manifest to the sacred pastors their opinion on matters which pertain
to the good of the Church." "Those who are engaged in the sacred disciplines
enjoy a lawful freedom of inquiry and of prudently expressing their opinions
on matters in which they have expertise." These are not the wild words of
a radical group of non-Catholics, or even of a group of liberal Catholics.
They are the canons 212,3 and 218 of the new Code of Canon Law. This
might seem to some to seal the argument, but there is more. Recall what was
cited earlier:

Christ summons the Church, as she goes her pilgrim way, to that continual reformation of which she always has need. . . . Let everyone in the Church . . . preserve a proper freedom . . . even in the theological elaborations of revealed truth. . . . All are led . . . wherever necessary, to undertake with vigor the task of renewal and reform. . . . [All] Catholics' . . . primary *duty* is to make a careful and honest appraisal of whatever needs to be renewed and done in the Catholic household itself.

Who this time are the radical advocates of freedom and reformation "even in the theological elaborations of revealed truth"? All the Catholic bishops of the world gathered together in Ecumenical Council Vatican II (Decree on Ecumenism, no. 4).

Recall again that the same Council also declared that "the human person has a right to religious freedom. This freedom means that all human beings are to be immune from coercion on the part of individuals, social groups and every human power. . . . *Nobody is forced to act against his convictions in religious matters in private or in public*. . . . Truth can impose itself on the mind of humans only in virtue of its own truth" (Declaration on Religious Freedom, nos. 1, 2). The Council further stated that the "search for truth" should be carried out "by free enquiry . . . and dialogue. . . . Human beings are bound to follow their consciences faithfully in all their activity. . . . They must not be forced to act contrary to their conscience, *especially in religious matters*" (ibid., no. 3).

There is still more: in 1973 the Congregation for the Doctrine of the Faith stated that the "conceptions" by which Church teaching is expressed are changeable: "The truths which the Church intends to teach through her dogmatic formulas are distinct from the changeable conceptions of a given epoch and can be expressed without them" (the Congregation for the Doctrine of the Faith's 1973 declaration *Mysterium ecclesiae*). But how can these "conceptions" be changed unless someone points out that they might be improved, might even be defective, that is, unless there is deliberation, possibly dissent, and then dialogue leading to a new decision on how to express the matter?

And a real mind boggler: "Doctrinal discussion requires perceptiveness, both in honestly setting out one's own opinion and in recognizing the truth everywhere, even if the truth demolishes one so that one is forced to reconsider one's own position, in theory and in practice" — Words of the Vatican Curia(!) in 1968 (Vatican Secretariat for Unbelievers' document *Humanae personae dignitatem*).

Even Pope John Paul II encouraged responsible dissent and supported theologians in their invaluable service done in freedom. In 1969, then archbishop of Cracow, he said: "Conformity means death for any community. A loyal opposition is a necessity in any community." A decade later, as pope, he declared that "the Church needs her theologians, particularly in this time and age. . . . We desire to listen to you and we are eager to receive the valued assistance of your responsible scholarship.... We will never tire of insisting on the eminent role of the university... a place of scientific research, constantly updating its methods and working instruments... *in freedom of investigation*" ("Address to Catholic Theologians and Scholars at the Catholic University of America," October 7, 1979; emphasis added — standing ten feet away, I heard these words with my own ears). A little later he even went so far as to remark: "Truth is the power of peace.... What should one say of the practice of combatting or silencing those who do not share the same views?" (More than ironically, even as a countersign, that statement was issued on December 18, 1979, three days after the close of the "interrogation" of Schillebeeckx in Rome and on the very day of the quasi-silencing of Hans Küng.)

One of the main functions of the magisterium, and especially the Congregation for the Doctrine of the Faith, therefore, ought not be to put a stop to deliberation, dissent, dialogue, and then decision, but instead precisely to encourage, promote, and direct it in the most creative possible channels. As a 1979 petition in support of Father Schillebeeckx signed by hundreds of theologians urged,

> The function of the Congregation for the Doctrine of the Faith should be to *promote dialogue* among theologians of varying methodologies and approaches so that the most enlightening, helpful, and authentic expressions of theology could ultimately find acceptance. Hence, we call upon the Congregation for the Doctrine of the Faith to eliminate from its procedures "hearings," and the like, substituting for them dialogues that would be either issue-oriented, or if it is deemed important to focus on the work of a particular theologian, would bring together not only the theologian in question and the consultors of the Congregation for the Doctrine of the Faith, but also a worldwide selection of the best pertinent theological scholars of varying methodologies and approaches. These dialogues could well be conducted with the collaboration of the International Theological Commission, the Pontifical Biblical Commission, universities, theological faculties, and theological organizations. Thus, the best experts on the issues concerned would work until acceptable resolutions were arrived at. Such a procedure of course is by no means new; it is precisely the procedure utilized at the Second Vatican Council.[75]

Indeed, even the pope and the Curia wrote of the absolute necessity of dialogue and sketched out how it should be conducted. As recalled earlier, Pope Paul VI in his first encyclical, *Ecclesiam suam* (1964), wrote that dialogue

> is *demanded* nowadays.... It is *demanded* by the dynamic course of action which is changing the face of modern society. It is *demanded* by the... maturity humanity has reached in this day and age.... This desire to impress upon the internal relationships of the Church the character of a dialogue.... It is, therefore, our ardent desire that the dialogue within the Church should take on new fervor, new themes and new participants, so that the holiness and vitality of the Mystical Body of Christ on earth may be increased.

Then in 1968 the Vatican declared that

> the willingness to engage in dialogue is the measure and strength of that general renewal which must be carried out in the Church, which *implies a still greater appreciation of liberty.*... Doctrinal dialogue should be initiated with courage and sincerity, *with the greatest freedom*... recognizing the truth everywhere, even if the truth demolishes one so that one is forced to reconsider one's own position.... Therefore the *liberty of the participants* must be ensured by law and reverenced in practice (*Humanae personae dignitatem*, emphasis added).

## Summary

Thus, in summary, one can say that in the beginning the Church was the people, who naturally chose their leaders out of their midst; they also took an active role in deciding about a whole range of things, including doctrinal matters. It is only in the late Middle Ages and the modern period of history that the rights of the laity to choose their own Church leaders and actively to participate in Church decision-making were eroded to the tiny remnant which those of us born before Vatican II experienced growing up. We were told, however, that the way things were in our childhood was the way they had always been! This erosion of democratic rights of the laity reached its high point in the middle of this century just before Vatican II. That council, of course, started the process of restoring the ancient tradition of shared responsibility, and in fact was followed up in this regard by the 1971 Synod of Bishops when it stated:

> The members of the Church should have some share in the drawing up of decisions, in accordance with the rules given by the Second Vatican Ecumenical Council and the Holy See, for instance with regard to the setting up of councils at all levels.[76]

Unfortunately, for almost two decades thereafter we appeared more and more to be returning to a preconciliar mode.

Nevertheless, we must conclude that the Catholic Church not only could be a democracy; it in fact *was* a limited democracy — which has been dismantled. It needs to be reestablished.

# 16

# Suggestions for *Intermediate* Steps to Be Taken

Structures that could support many of the rights Catholics have, or should have, already exist, but, as mentioned, they are inadequately developed and, for millions of Catholics, they do not exist in actuality.[1] Hence, as steps to be taken now, the following are urged:

## Structures for Decision-Making and Due Process

1. That in every parish and diocese

   a. the establishment of pastoral councils be made mandatory,

   b. these councils be representatively elected, and

   c. they have real decision-making power so that responsibility for the welfare of the community and its mission will be truly shared among clergy, religious, and laity.

2. That every diocese have courts to redress grievances of all types according to due process (following the detailed recommendations of the Canon Law Society of America); this might be handled by

   a. extending the scope of existing marriage tribunals, contemplated by the 1983 Code, or by

   b. new administrative tribunals, also allowed and even recommended by the 1983 Code. In any case, a truly just and effective system must be made mandatory, widely promulgated, and implemented.

3. That there be set up on both the national and international levels representatively elected synods of clergy and laity with real decision-making responsibility along with the national bishops conferences, synod of bishops, and the papacy as ongoing constitutive parts of the collegial governance of the national and universal Church.

## The Status of Women

The most widespread and pervasive example of divisive dualism in the Catholic Church, and in society at large, is that between women and men, resulting in regular discrimination against women. This clearly contradicts Christian baptism, which initiates equally all, women and men, into the community of the followers of Jesus: "There is neither male nor female...but all are one in Christ Jesus" (Gal. 3:28).

Thus, although all people have the right to define themselves, women regularly cannot exercise this right in the Church; the 1971 Bishops' Synod saw this when it felt the need to state: "We also urge that women should have their own share of responsibility and participation in the community life of society and likewise of the Church." Unfortunately that recommendation has not yet been effectively implemented; until it is and until sufficient and adequate role models of women in leadership in the Church are provided, many women will not be able, or willing, to join actively in Church life. Therefore, the following are urged:

4. That every parish, diocese, national, international and other appropriate organizational unit move immediately within the present possibilities of canon law to place competent women in positions of leadership and decision-making in numbers proportional to their membership: "All Catholic women have an equal right with men to the resources and the exercise of all the powers of the Church" (ARCC *Charter of the Rights of Catholics in the Church*, Right 26).

5. That every parish, diocese, national, international and other appropriate organizational unit move immediately to appoint competent women in all liturgical offices within the present possibilities of canon law in numbers proportional to their membership. This includes readers, commentators, cantors, leaders of prayers, ministers of baptism and Communion, and Mass servers.[2]

6. That laity, priests, and bishops through every appropriate agency urge the Vatican to move to bring competent women as quickly as possible into the diaconate, presbyterate, and episcopacy: "All Catholics, regardless of...sex... have the right to exercise all ministries in the Church for which they are adequately prepared, according to the needs and with the approval of the community" (*Charter*, Right 16).

7. That every parish, diocese, national and international unit move immediately to eliminate all sexist and other non-inclusive language in its documents: "All Catholics have the right to expect that Church documents and materials will avoid sexist language and that symbols and imagery of God will not be exclusively masculine" (*Charter*, Right 32).

8. That every unit of the Church, and particularly the bishop, adopt a prophetic stance in the local, regional, national, and international communities on issues of social justice, especially concerning what is usually the most voiceless element of society— women.

# 17

# Suggestions for the Organization and Action of the Catholic Constitutional Convention — 2000/2001 C.E.

The beginning of not just a new century but of a new millennium provides a fantastic psychological moment to call for a dramatic breakthrough. Further, the goal of a Convention in the year 2000 or 2001 provides both adequate time to build momentum for such a momentous project while at the same time not so much time that ennui would set in. In brief, the time is ripe now to launch the calling of a "Catholic Constitutional Convention." The beginning of the third millennium should be viewed as a *kairos*, a special moment of "salvation" (i.e., of full "health," "[w]holiness," which, as noted above, the Latin root *salus* means).

## Considerations Concerning a Catholic Constitutional Convention

A Catholic Constitutional Convention Committee has been formed by the National Board of the Association for the Rights of Catholics in the Church (ARCC) to strategize on the steps to be taken in launching and guiding the project. It is working in conjunction with the European Catholic reform organizations. That committee is committed to at least the following:

1. The Catholic Constitutional Convention is not being called in opposition to the pope, bishops, or priests. Every effort has been made from the very beginning and will continue to be made to include every element of the Church in the shaping of the Catholic Constitution and the structure and spirit of the Church flowing from it. All Catholic organizations, papal, episcopal, presbyteral, religious and lay, local, national, and international, are invited and urged to participate in the project. As at Vatican II, observers from other Christian churches and other religions are also invited to assist; this dimension of Vatican II proved to be extremely helpful and creative.

2. The tone of the whole project is totally positive. For example, a formal invitation might read as follows: "As the civil world at large is dramatically moving toward democracy, framing anew the fundamental principles of humanity, which is 'created in the image of God,' in constitutions, so too is the Catholic Church.... Following the inspiration of Vatican II and Popes John XXIII, Paul VI, and John Paul II in their vigorous advocacy throughout the world of Human Rights, we committed Catholics are issuing a call to a 'Catholic Constitutional Convention'...."

3. Also as in Vatican II, full utilization of the theological and other experts is vital. Hence, specific invitations have gone out, and will go out again, to the organizations of the various theological disciplines (e.g., the Catholic Historical Society, Catholic Biblical Society, Catholic Theological Society of America, Canon Law Society of America, and the many parallels in other countries) to join in the project at least by focusing a portion of their programs on research into the various aspects of the question of democracy and the Catholic Church and related renewal/reform issues and by responding to a proposed draft of a Catholic Constitution. The Catholic organizations, national and international, of other disciplines and professions are likewise invited to contribute their charisms.

4. Following the example of the National Conference of Catholic Bishops (U.S.) in preparing for the 1976 "Call to Action" and the pastoral letter on economics, a series of "hearings" around the country (and in other countries) will be organized at a later phase.

5. A focused plan will be developed for the writing and publishing of not only scholarly articles and books on various aspects of the question of democracy and the Catholic Church and related renewal/reform issues, but also popular-level articles, books, textbooks, study-group materials, and audio and video materials.

6. The Catholic Constitutional Convention Committee has already been distributing as widely as possible a tentative proposed draft of a Catholic Constitution, inviting all Catholic groups and individuals to respond and make further suggestions, written and oral, on how the Constitution should be formed, with specifics on its form and contents. The purpose of the "Proposed Catholic Constitution" is to provide a possible structure into which to fit suggestions.

7. The "Proposed Catholic Constitution," of course, is subject not only to revision but even complete rejection by the participants. Ultimately an International Drafting Committee will be responsible to assimilate submitted responses and materials and begin to draft a "Revised Catholic Constitution" on their basis, to be submitted to the Convention for debate, revision, and eventual adoption.

## Suggestions to Promote a Catholic Constitution

I first laid the project of a "Catholic Constitutional Convention" before the Association for the Rights of Catholics in the Church (ARCC) in 1990 and under its auspices presented the proposal to a national meeting in Washington, D.C., on June 25, 1993, of Catholics Organizing Renewal (COR), where it won unanimous support and encouragement for ARCC to take the lead in launching the project. The German Organization of Catholic Academics (*Neudeutschland*) also gave strong support (*nachdrückliche Zustimmung*),[1] as did also the Fourth Annual Assembly of the European Conference on Human Rights in the Church in Brussels,[2] and once again at the January 1996 meeting of the same in London.[3]

Therefore, mindful of the stated purpose of ARCC ("to institutionalize a collegial understanding of Church in which decision-making is shared and accountability is realized among Catholics of every kind and condition"), I offer the following suggestions as an initial stimulus for all Catholics to think creatively about, discuss widely — and then send ideas back to ARCC for processing:

1. The Charter of the Rights of Catholics in the Church, along with the full *Lex Ecclesiae Fundamentalis* already approved but then mysteriously set aside in 1981, and the residue from the *Lex* imbedded in canons 208–23 of the 1983 Code of Canon Law are obvious sources for the Constitution of the Catholic Church.

2. Mindful of the 1971 Bishops' Synod's statement that "the members of the Church should have some share in the drawing up of decisions...for instance, with regard to the setting up of *councils at all levels,*" and its own Charter, ARCC claims that "all Catholics have the right to a voice in decisions that affect them" (*Charter,* Right 5), "the right to be dealt with fairly" (*Charter,* Right 9), and "the right to timely redress of grievances" (*Charter,* Right 10).

Structures that could support many of the above rights already exist, but are inadequately developed, and for millions of Catholics they do not exist in actuality because of the lack of adequate structures to make them real.[4] Hence, whatever structures for the governance of the Church are arrived at, they should include these principles:

a. Election of leaders, including pastors, bishops, and pope, through an appropriate structure giving serious voice to all respective "constituents."

b. A limited term of office for such leaders, as has been the case for centuries in religious orders.

c. A separation of powers, along with a system of checks and balances, including parish, diocesan, national and international councils, and a separate judicial system, to share the responsibility in appropriate ways with pastors, bishops, and pope.

    d. Establishment of the principle of dialogue to arrive at the most helpful formulations and applications of the teachings of the tradition from the local through to the highest universal level.

    e. Equitable representation of all elements of the faithful, including women and minorities, in all positions of leadership and decision-making.

3. Just as there were "state"-level constitutional conventions during the American colonial period which led up to and contributed significantly to the national constitutional conventions in Philadelphia (the first "Constitution," the "Articles of Federation," turned out to be a failure), so too would it be wise to hold various "Regional Catholic Constitutional Conventions." These would lead up to "National Catholic Conventions," climaxing on the world level in the *"Katholikos* Constitutional Convention" (and beyond that, an *"Oikumenikos* Constitutional Convention" including all the Christian churches?). Hence, I would urge:

    a. That all Catholics encourage their bishop not to wait for action either from above or below, but immediately to start in motion a process of bringing together all the elements of his diocese to draw up a Diocesan Constitution by which the diocese will be governed. According to the 1983 Code of Canon Law, this lies completely in the hands of the local bishop to undertake without any permissions needed. Moreover, there is the shining example of the Constitution of Bishop John England, arguably the most outstanding bishop in American Catholic history.

       While it is true that the succeeding bishop would not have to honor his predecessor's Constitution, a successful momentum would be in its favor. This is especially true if several American bishops were successfully to inaugurate diocesan constitutions.

       Clearly a successfully drafted and implemented Diocesan Constitution would have a very positive imitative effect on the parishes in the diocese and on other dioceses.

       To facilitate this process a sample "Proposed Diocesan Constitution" is included as an appendix at the end of this volume. It can be used to launch the process of creating a Constitution for a diocese.

    b. That all Catholics encourage their pastor not to wait for action from above or below, but immediately to start in motion a process bringing together all the elements of his parish to draw up a Parish Constitution by which the parish will be governed. According to the 1983 Code of Canon Law, this lies completely in the hands of the pastor to undertake without any permissions needed.

       While it is true that the succeeding pastor would not have to honor his predecessor's Constitution, a successful momentum would be in its favor. This is especially true if several pastors were successfully to inaugurate parish constitutions.

       Clearly a successfully drafted and implemented Parish Constitution would have a very positive imitative effect on other parishes and on the diocesan level.

To facilitate this process a sample "Proposed Parish Constitution" is included as an appendix at the end of this volume. It can be used to launch the process of creating a Constitution for a parish.

4. Perhaps the most important change that must be brought about in order to make a Catholic Constitution a reality is the change in consciousness or mentality in the Catholic people, laity and clergy. The Catholic tradition and community must be seen and experienced as a living source of how to make life meaningful and vital — whole, (w)holy as discussed above. It must be seen and experienced as something liberating and for which the mature Christian feels a reciprocal sense of responsibility. That obviously essentially includes an adult sharing in rights and responsibilities, in short, in democracy — a Constitution.

Therefore, I would urge:

a. That all Catholic individuals, organizations, and groups focus their attention on a deep and wide reflection, thorough discussion, and (not *too*) eventual action on the idea, principles, and specifics of Catholic responsibility-sharing, of a democratic Catholicism and a Constitution for it.

b. That all constructive suggestions on how to improve the Constitution be submitted in writing (addresses at the end of the Proposed Catholic Constitution). Remember, this is a Constitution, not a compendium of all theology or desirable laws; it is therefore brief and limited to essential principles, procedures, and structures.

c. That all Catholic individuals, organizations, and groups use every creative means to disseminate and publicize the idea, principles, and specifics of Catholic democracy and Constitution — e.g., newspaper and periodical articles, newsletters, letters to the editor, lectures, textbooks, homilies, lectures, classes, radio and TV broadcasts, Internet, World Wide Web.

# Conclusion

Let this suffice for an initial stimulus for launching us on the road to the "Catholic Constitutional Convention." Of course it will not happen without an immense effort by large numbers of Catholics on all levels, nor will the Establishment initially move to bring it about. But, thinking about it, discussing and debating it and its possible content will raise it and all it stands for — a mature, free and responsible, democratic Catholic Church — in the consciousness of Catholics throughout the world. Then, the "Catholic Constitutional Convention" (and what better target date than the beginning of the third millennium?), even if it is not participated in and recognized by the official structures of the Catholic Church, will nevertheless debate and develop creative, responsible ideas and projects for further democratizing and renewing the Church, which eventually are bound to have a significant effect on the Establishment.

Would this lead to a schism in the Catholic Church? No, no one is interested in starting a new Church or anything like it, but hundreds of millions of Catholics *are* interested in a *renewed* Church!

Impossible? Who in 1958 would have thought the Vatican II revolution of 1962–65 was remotely possible, or the Eastern Europe revolution of 1989? We need as a motto a paraphrase of one on the American penny, that is, "Trust in God," and then work with all the creativity and energy we can muster to realize in a contemporary democratic manner the other motto on the penny: "A unity flowing from the many," *E pluribus unum!*

I want to end with the draft of "A Proposed Constitution of the Catholic Church" of which the "Catholic Constitutional Convention Coordinating Committee" is asking for constructive criticisms and suggestions for improvement. But before I set it forth, let me provide one additional, very negative, reason of why we need to work to draw up a Constitution of the Catholic Church which embodies the basic principles of democracy outlined above. The reason is the horrible example of "what not to do" which has been provided us by the 1993 Diocesan Statutes of the Diocese of Camden, N.J., which include the following provisions — and be assured, these are not fantasy or invention:

199. Every parish corporation is to have a Board of Trustees composed of five persons, three of whom are members *ex officio*, namely the Bishop of Camden, the Vicar General, and the pastor of the Church, and two lay trustees elected each year by the three *ex officio* clerical members.

142

203. Should there be uncertainty or disagreement between the pastor and the lay members of the Board of Trustees, the diocesan bishop or Vicar General will settle the matter and all must yield to his decision.

207. For the conduct of business of the parish civil corporation...no proceeding, order or act shall be deemed valid or of any effect without the written approval of the diocesan bishop or the Vicar General.

Breathtaking! Where, we might ask, do we find here respected the principles of dialogue, subsidiarity, proportional representation, democratic election of officers, accountability of officers, separation of powers, and checks and balances?

# Appendix A

# A Proposed Constitution
# of the Catholic Church

*The following is a draft of "A Proposed Constitution of the Catholic Church." Although it has been carefully researched, thought through, submitted to many, many groups and individuals, and re-revised numerous times, it is obviously intended as Proposed Draft to launch the discussion which must range long, wide, and deep before the Constitution will begin to be an effective and acceptable instrument to guide the governance of the Catholic Church. It needs to include the experience and wisdom of the best of vital professions such as constitutional lawyers, experts in political science, canon lawyers, theologians, church historians, pastors, bishops, popes, business people, sociologists, psychologists, educators, etc., as well as parents, young persons, older persons, women, men — in short, all categories of the members of the Catholic Church. We will also want to learn from the experience of persons of other Churches which have developed various forms of democratic structures in their own governance — to learn by their positive and negative experiences.*

*The journey to a written and adopted "Constitution of the Catholic Church" will doubtless be long, arduous, and probably also serpentine. But it is a journey that a growing number of Catholics increasingly feel must be undertaken. Those of us so convinced now have not only the privilege but also the responsibility to push on in the journey, even though we personally may not arrive at the final destination.*

•

This Constitution provides the framework within which the Catholic Church governs itself. It sets forth the fundamental rights and corresponding responsibilities of members and basic structure for decision-making and action within the Catholic Church. All laws, regulations, and customs of the Catholic Church shall be carried out within its framework and in its spirit.

## I. Preamble

1. We the people of the Catholic Church hold that because all men and women are created in "God's image" and the same divine teaching on how they should live is written in every human heart, all persons are to be treated with dignity and equality, each person having the same fundamental rights and responsibilities.

2. We hold that by our faith in God through Jesus and our baptism with water and the Holy Spirit, all Christians become "members of the body of Christ," that is, the Church universal, and are committed to living out the Gospel taught and lived by Jesus. We further hold that all Christians who recognize the Petrine apostolic ministry of the Bishop of Rome, the Pope, are members of the Catholic Church (hereafter, simply, the Church).

3. We hold that the Church's mission, grounded in the Gospel, is to proclaim and show forth Jesus' Good News of how to live a fully human life as images of God in individual and communal justice and love. We hold that the Church realizes this mission within the context of the laws which it enacts to foster and preserve the spirit of the Gospel and to assist its members as they endeavor to live in the love of God and neighbor.

Fundamental to the Church's mission are certain rights and responsibilities (*listed below*) which pertain to all members.

## II. Rights and Responsibilities

1. All persons fit into one or more categories according to state of life, for example, adult or minor, male or female, single, married, widowed, divorced, office-holder. In addition to these, in the Church there are other states of life, for example, laity, clergy, vowed religious. All states of life carry with them specific rights and corresponding responsibilities.

2. The following are the Church members' fundamental rights, flowing either from their basic human rights or their basic baptismal rights. Each right entails a corresponding responsibility on the part of the rights holders, some of which are so obvious that they do not require specific articulation. In all instances these rights and responsibilities apply to all Catholics, regardless of race, age, nationality, sex, sexual orientation, state of life, social or economic position.

### A. Basic Human Rights and Responsibilities

1. All Catholics have the basic human rights — e.g., (a) freedom of action, (b) freedom of conscience, (c) freedom of opinion and expression, (d) right to receive and impart information, (e) freedom of association, (f) right to due process of law, (g) right of participation in self-governance, (h) to the accountability of chosen leaders, (i) right to the safeguarding of one's reputation and privacy, (j) right to marry, (k) right to education — and the corresponding duty to exercise them responsibly.

2. As a consequence of the basic human right of freedom of action, all Catholics have the right to engage in any activity which does not violate Christian ethics and does not infringe on the rights of others.

3. As a consequence of the basic human right of freedom of conscience,

all Catholics have the right, and responsibility, to follow their informed consciences in all matters.

4. As a consequence of the basic human right to receive and impart information, all Catholics have the right of access to all information possessed by Church authorities concerning their own spiritual and temporal welfare, provided such access does not infringe on the rights of others.

5. As a consequence of the basic human right of freedom of opinion and expression, all Catholics have the right to express publicly their agreement or disagreement in a responsible manner regarding decisions made by Church authorities.

    a. Laity have the right and responsibility to make their opinions known in a responsible manner, especially where they have first-hand experience of the issue at hand.

    b. Catholic teachers and scholars of theology have a right to, and responsibility for, academic freedom; the acceptability of their teaching is to be judged in dialogue with their peers — and, when appropriate, Church authorities. Such scholars and teachers will keep in mind that the search for the truth and its expression entails following wherever the evidence leads, and hence, the legitimacy of responsible dissent and pluralism of thought and its expression.

6. As a consequence of the basic human right of freedom of association, all Catholics have the right to form voluntary associations to pursue Catholic aims, including the right to worship together; such associations have the right to decide on their own rules of governance.

7. As a consequence of the basic human right to due process of law, all Catholics have the right to be dealt with according to commonly accepted norms of fair administrative and judicial procedures without undue delay, and to redress of grievances through regular procedures of law.

8. As a consequence of the basic human right of participation in self-governance, all Catholics have the right to a voice in decisions that affect them, including the choosing of their leaders, and a duty to exercise those rights responsibly.

9. As a consequence of the basic human right to the accountability of chosen leaders, all Catholics have the right to have their leaders render an account to them.

10. As a consequence of the basic human right to the safeguarding of one's reputation and privacy, all Catholics have the right not to have their good reputations impugned or their privacy violated.

11. As a consequence of the basic human right to marry, all Catholics have the right to choose their state in life; this includes the right for both laity and clergy to marry, remain single, or embrace celibacy.

12. As a consequence of the basic human right to marry, with each spouse retaining full and equal rights each during marriage, all Catholics have the right to withdraw from a marriage which has irretrievably broken down.

a. All such Catholics retain the radical right to remarry; and

b. All divorced and remarried Catholics who are in conscience reconciled to the Church retain the right to the same ministries, including all the sacraments, as do other Catholics.

13. As a consequence of the basic human rights to marry and to education, all married Catholics have the right and responsibility,

a. To determine in conscience the size of their families,

b. To choose appropriate methods of family planning, and

c. To see to the education of their children.

## B. Basic Baptismal Rights and Responsibilities

1. As a consequence of their baptism, all Catholics have the right to receive in the Church those ministries which are needed for the living of a fully Christian life, including:

a. Worship which reflects the joys and concerns of the gathered community and instructs and inspires it;

b. Instruction in the Christian tradition and the presentation of spirituality and moral teaching in a way that promotes the helpfulness and relevance of Christian values to contemporary life; and

c. Pastoral care that applies with concern and effectiveness the Christian heritage to persons in particular situations.

2. As a consequence of their baptism, all Catholics have the right,

a. To receive all the sacraments for which they are adequately prepared,

b. To exercise all ministries in the Church for which they are adequately prepared, according to the needs and with the approval of the community.

3. As a consequence of their baptism, all Catholics have the right to expect that the resources of the Church expended within the Church will be fairly distributed on their behalf. Among other concerns, this implies that,

a. All Catholic women have an equal right with men to the resources and the exercise of all the powers of the Church;

b. All Catholic parents have the right to expect fair material and other assistance from Church leaders in the religious education of their children; and

c. All single Catholics have the right to expect that the resources of the Church be fairly expended on their behalf.

## C. Basic Responsibility

All Catholics have the corresponding responsibility to support the Church appropriately.

# III. Governance Structures

## A. Fundamental Insights

1. Through the centuries the Church has wrestled with the concrete issues of the exercise of power and law, without which no society can survive, let alone develop humanly. In this long period the Church both benefitted and suffered from many human experiments with power and law in a great variety of cultures. In testing them for itself the Church gained wisdom in both negative and positive ways, i.e., it learned much about what works well and what does not.

2. Two key insights gained from all these experiences are fundamental for the governance of the Church in the third millennium. One is that shared responsibility and corresponding freedom are at the heart of being human, both individually and communally. The second is that the most effective means of arriving at an ever fuller understanding of reality is through dialogue — which should be carried on both within the Church and with those outside the Church. It is on this long experience and wisdom of the Church, especially these two key insights, that the Constitution draws and builds in its governance structures.

## B. Principles

1. It is of the essence of the Church to be a community. The most basic unit of that Church community is where members daily live their lives, beginning with the family and other intimate associations. Beyond this the fundamental unit of the Church is a local community, most often but not exclusively the geographical Parish.

2. It is, however, also of the essence of the Church that it is a community of communities, so that the local communities are also united in a regional community, most often but not exclusively called Diocese. Beyond that, Dioceses are united in provincial and then national communities, and at times continental communities, and these in turn in the international community of the Catholic Church.

3. In keeping with the spirit of the Gospel, developing human experience, and the dynamic Christian tradition, especially its two key insights of shared responsibility–corresponding freedom and dialogue, the following basic principles shall shape the governing structures and regulations of the Church:

a. The principle of subsidiarity shall rule throughout the Church, that is, all decision-making rights and responsibilities shall remain with the smaller community unless the good of the broader community specifically demands that it exercise those rights and responsibilities.

b. At all levels of the Church the formulations and applications of the teachings of the tradition shall be arrived at through a process of charitable and respectful dialogue.

c. Each local, regional, national, continental, and international community shall form its own body of governing regulations.

d. Local, regional, national, continental, and international leaders shall be elected to office through appropriate structures, giving serious voice to all respective constituents.

e. Leaders shall hold office for a specified, limited term.

f. A separation of legislative, executive, and judicial powers, along with a system of checks and balances, shall be observed. This entails (1) representatively elected local, regional, national, continental, and international councils, (2) elected local, regional, national, continental, and international leaders, and (3) a separate local, regional, national, continental, and international judicial system. All branches share responsibility in ways appropriate to the spirit of the Gospel and this Constitution.

g. All groupings of the faithful, including women and minorities, shall be equitably represented in all positions of leadership and decision-making.

## C. Councils

1. At every circle in a series of concentric circles — local, regional, national, continental, and international — representative councils shall be established which shall serve as the main decision-making bodies at each circle, the principle of subsidiarity being borne in mind. The spirit of the Gospel and the principle of dialogue are to characterize the deliberations and decisions of each council, preserving intact the principle of one person, one vote — with none having veto power.

### a. Local Circle

2. On the local circle every Parish (or equivalent) shall elect a Parish Council, which shall be the main decision-making body of the Parish. The Parish Council shall be elected in as representative a manner as possible, including when appropriate various organizations within the Parish. How that is carried out specifically shall be determined by the Parish's Constitution and statutes. Those two will determine how the Chair of the Parish Council is chosen. Members of the Council shall serve for a specified term of office.

3. If there is not already a Parish Constitution, the Parish Council shall formulate such, to be approved by the Parish, bearing in mind the appropriate regulations of the regional and broader communities. The Parish Constitution shall determine Parish procedures and how decision-making re-

sponsibilities are to be distributed, preserving the basic governance principles expressed in this Constitution.

4. The Parish Council with the Pastor, either directly or through committees, shall bear ultimate responsibility for Parish worship, education, social outreach, administration, finances, and other activities carried out in the name of the Parish. Any local decision must have the approval of the Parish Council.

### b. Regional Circle

5. At the regional circle every Diocese shall elect a Diocesan Council, which shall be the main decision-making body of the Diocese. The Bishop of the Diocese and a layperson elected by the Diocesan Council shall be Co-Chairs of the Diocesan Council.

6. If there is not already a Diocesan Constitution, the Diocesan Council shall formulate one, to be approved by the Parish Councils of the Diocese, bearing in mind the appropriate regulations of the national and international communities. The Diocesan Constitution shall determine diocesan procedures and how decision-making responsibilities are to be distributed, preserving the basic governance principles expressed in this Constitution.

7. The Diocesan Council shall be elected as representatively as possible, including various organizations within the Diocese when appropriate. It shall be composed of an equal number of clergy and laity. Specific procedures for elections and voting shall be determined by the Diocesan Constitution and diocesan statutes. Those regulations will determine how the lay Co-Chair of the Diocesan Council is chosen. Members of the Diocesan Council shall serve for a specified term of office.

8. The Diocesan Council with the Bishop, either directly or through committees or agencies, shall bear ultimate responsibility for diocesan worship, education, social outreach, administration, finances, and other activities carried out in the name of the Diocese.

### c. National Circle

9. At the national circle every national Church shall elect a National Council, which shall be the main decision-making body of the national Church. A Bishop and a layperson elected by the National Council shall be Co-Chairs of the National Council.

10. If there is not already a National Constitution, the National Council shall formulate one, to be approved by the Diocesan Councils of the nation, bearing in mind the appropriate regulations of the Universal Church. The National Constitution shall determine national procedures and how decision-making responsibilities are to be distributed, preserving the basic governance principles expressed in this Constitution.

11. The National Council shall be elected as representatively as possible, including, when appropriate, various organizations within the nation. Specific procedures for elections and voting shall be determined by the National Constitution and national statutes. Members of the National Council shall serve for a specified term of office.

12. The National Council, either directly or through committees or agencies, shall bear ultimate responsibility for national worship, education, social outreach, administration, finances, and other activities carried out in the name of the National Council.

### d. Continental Circle

13. If the National Councils of a continent or discrete geographical area decide it would be helpful to gather formally, they will formulate a Continental Constitution by which to regulate themselves, preserving the basic governance principles expressed in this Constitution.

### e. International Circle

14. On the international level the National Councils shall every ten years elect a General Council, which shall be responsible for the formulation of the laws governing the Universal Church. This General Council shall function as the main decision-making body of the Universal Church. The Bishop of Rome, the Pope, or papal delegate, and a layperson elected by the General Council shall be Co-Chairs of the General Council.

15. If there is not already a General Council Constitution, the first General Council shall formulate one to determine its procedures, preserving the basic governance principles expressed in this Constitution.

16. The General Council shall be elected as representatively as possible, including, when appropriate, various international organizations. How the elections and voting are carried out shall be determined by the International Constitution and international statutes.

17. The General Council, either directly or through committees or agencies, shall bear ultimate responsibility for passing the laws governing the Universal Church and setting policy concerning doctrine, morals, worship, education, social outreach, administration, finances, and other activities carried out in the name of the Universal Church, bearing especially in mind the principle of subsidiarity.

## C. Leaders

### a. General

1. Leaders at all circles shall be appropriately trained and experienced. They shall be chosen in a manner which shall give a representative voice

to all those who are to be led by them. This is especially true of the local Pastor, the Diocesan Bishop, and the Pope. At least concerning these three, both laity and clergy are to be representatively involved in their elections.

2. All leaders shall serve for specified terms of office. That of Pastor is for five years, renewable once. That of Diocesan Bishop, and Pope is for ten years, nonrenewable.

3. All leaders can be removed from office only for cause, following a procedure of due process spelled out elsewhere in this Constitution and appropriate statutes.

4. All leaders have responsibilities and corresponding rights; those of Pastor, Bishop and Pope are especially laid out here.

## b. Pastor

5. Pastors shall be chosen with the approval of both the Parish Council and the Bishop in accordance with the procedures set forth in the Diocesan Constitution.

6. The Pastor shall serve as the leader of the Parish pastoral team. Together with the Parish Council, the Pastor bears the main responsibility for the worship, spiritual and moral instruction, and pastoral care dimensions of the Parish. This responsibility entails:

   a. Worship that reflects the joys and concerns of the gathered community and instructs and inspires it;

   b. Instruction in the Christian tradition and the presentation of spirituality and moral teaching in a way that promotes the helpfulness and relevance of Christian values to contemporary life; and

   c. Pastoral care that applies with love and effectiveness the Christian heritage to persons in particular situations.

7. Pastors have both a right to and responsibility for proper training and continuation of their education throughout the term of their office.

8. Pastors have a right to fair financial support for the exercise of their office, as well as the requisite liberty needed for the proper exercise thereof.

## c. Bishop

9. The Bishop shall be chosen by the Diocesan Council in accordance with the Diocesan Constitution, bearing in mind the appropriate regulations of the national and international communities, including consultation with the appropriate committees of the National Council and General Council.

10. The Bishop together with the Diocesan Council bears the main responsibility for the worship, spiritual and moral instruction, and pastoral care dimensions of the Diocese, bearing in mind the principle of subsidiarity.

11. The Bishop together with the Diocesan Council is responsible for the appointment of Pastors and other clergy, with the appropriate approval of the Parish Council, in accordance with the procedures of the Diocesan Constitution.

### d. Pope

12. The Bishop of Rome, who is the Patriarch of the Western Church and the Pope of the Universal Church, shall be elected for a single ten-year term by Delegates selected by the National Councils.

   a. The number of Delegates from National Councils to the Papal Election Congress shall be proportional to the number of registered Catholics in a nation, to be determined by an appropriate international committee.

   b. The Delegates shall be chosen as representatively as possible, one-third being Bishops, one-third clergy, and one-third laity.

13. The Pope together with the General Council bears the main responsibility for carrying out the policies set by the General Council, especially in the areas of the worship, spiritual and moral instruction, and pastoral care functions of the Universal Church, bearing in mind the principle of subsidiarity.

## IV. Judicial System

### A. *Principles*

1. The Catholic Church is a pilgrim Church, always in need of reform and correction. Disputes, contentions, and crimes against the rights of members will regrettably occur. These are to be resolved by processes of conciliation and arbitration. Where this proves impossible, Catholics may take such cases to the Church's tribunals for adjudication. All Catholics are entitled to fair and due process under ecclesiastical law. All personnel involved in the Church's judicial system shall be appropriately trained and competent.

2. A system of diocesan, provincial, national, and international tribunals shall be established which shall serve as courts of first instance, each with designated courts of appeal. These tribunals shall be governed by this Constitution and subsequent laws in keeping with it.

### B. *Tribunals*

#### a. Local and Regional

1. Every Diocese shall establish a tribunal, or make other arrangements, for the judicial hearing of contentious and criminal cases which are brought before it by its people.

a. Diocesan Tribunals shall have competence over all matters which pertain to the internal order of the local and regional Church. These include all acts defined by the general ecclesiastical law as administrative acts, crimes, jurisdictional disputes, and matters of equity and restitution.

b. Diocesan Tribunals shall conduct their operations according to the procedural law established by the Universal Church.

c. Appeals against the judgment of the Diocesan Tribunal shall be heard by the tribunal of the respective ecclesiastical province.

2. All cases involving a diocesan Bishop shall be heard by the tribunal of the Bishop's ecclesiastical province.

3. Cases involving an Archbishop shall be heard by the National Tribunal.

## b. National

1. The National Council shall establish an appellate tribunal which shall serve as court of second instance for all cases, judicial or administrative, which are brought before it by its provincial tribunals.

2. Appeals from the decisions of this tribunal shall be heard by the Supreme Tribunal.

## c. International

1. The General Council shall establish a Supreme Tribunal which shall serve as the court of final appeal for all cases brought before it by lower courts.

2. The Supreme Tribunal shall hear cases charging illegal or unconstitutional actions by the Pope.

3. There shall be no judicial appeal from the judgments of the Supreme Tribunal.

## C. Continued Fitness for Office of Leaders

Church leaders shall serve out their elected term of office unless the question of competence and continued fitness for office is formally raised in accordance with constitutionally established norms. Determination of such competence and fitness for office may be made by the office-holder's ecclesiastical superior or by the appropriate Council, due process being observed. In the case of the Pope, such determination is to be made by a regular or special session of the General Council.

# V. Amendments

This Constitution can be amended by a three-quarter vote of the General Council and a subsequent ratification by three-fourths of the National Coun-

cils within a five-year period after the passage of the amendment by the
General Council.

*October 30, 1995 Version*

Send with your name and address: (1) agreement, (2) disagreement, (3) agreement with modifications specified to:

Professor Leonard Swidler
Religion Department, Temple University
Philadelphia, PA 19122
Tel.: 215-204-7251; Fax: 215-477-5928;
E-mail: DIALOGUE@VM.TEMPLE.EDU

# Appendix B

# A Proposed Constitution
# for the Parish (or similar local unit)

This Constitution provides the framework within which the local Catholic Church governs itself. It sets forth the fundamental rights and corresponding responsibilities of members and basic structure for decision-making and action within the local Church. All laws, regulations, and customs of the local Church shall be carried out within its framework and in its spirit.

## I. Preamble

1. We the people of the local Catholic Church hold that because all men and women are created in God's image and likeness and that the same divine teaching on how they should live is written in every human heart, all persons are to be treated with dignity and equality, each person having the same fundamental rights and responsibilities.

2. We hold that by our faith in God through Jesus and our baptism with water and the Holy Spirit, all Christians become "members of the body of Christ," that is, the Church universal, and are committed to living out the Gospel taught and lived by Jesus. We further hold that all Christians who recognize the Petrine apostolic ministry of the Bishop of Rome, the Pope, are members of the Catholic Church (hereafter, simply, the Church).

3. We hold that the Church's mission, grounded in the Gospel, is to proclaim and show forth Jesus' Good News of how to live a fully human life as images of God in individual and communal justice and love. We hold that the Church realizes this mission within the context of the laws which it enacts to foster and preserve the spirit of the Gospel and to assist its members as they endeavor to live in the love of God and neighbor.

Fundamental to the Church's mission are certain rights and responsibilities (*listed below*) which pertain to all members.

## II. Rights and Responsibilities

1. All persons belong to one or more categories according to state of life, for example, adult or minor, male or female, single, married, widowed, divorced. In addition to these, in the Church there are other states of life,

for example, laity, clergy, vowed religious. All states of life carry with them specific rights and corresponding responsibilities.

2. The following are the Church members' fundamental rights, flowing either from their basic human rights or their basic baptismal rights. Each right entails a corresponding responsibility on the part of the rights holders, some of which are so obvious that they do not require specific articulation. In all instances these rights and responsibilities apply to all Catholics, regardless of race, age, nationality, sex, sexual orientation, state of life, social or economic position.

## A. Basic Human Rights and Responsibilities

1. All Catholics have the basic human rights — e.g., (a) freedom of action, (b) freedom of conscience, (c) freedom of opinion and expression, (d) the right to receive and impart information, (e) freedom of association, (f) the right to due process of law, (g) the right of participation in self-governance, (h) the right to the accountability of chosen leaders, (i) the right to the safeguarding of one's reputation and privacy, (j) the right to marry, (k) the right to education — and the corresponding duty to exercise them responsibly.

2. As a consequence of the basic human right of freedom of action, all Catholics have the right to engage in any activity which does not violate Christian ethics and does not infringe on the rights of others.

3. As a consequence of the basic human right of freedom of conscience, all Catholics have the right and responsibility to follow their informed consciences in all matters.

4. As a consequence of the basic human right to receive and impart information, all Catholics have the right of access to all information possessed by Church authorities concerning their own spiritual and temporal welfare, provided such access does not infringe on the rights of others.

5. As a consequence of the basic human right of freedom of opinion and expression, all Catholics have the right to express publicly in a responsible manner their agreement or disagreement regarding decisions made by Church authorities.

    a. Laity have the right and responsibility to make their opinions known in a responsible manner, especially where they have first-hand experience of the issue at hand.

    b. Catholic teachers and scholars of theology have a right to, and responsibility for, academic freedom; the acceptability of their teaching is to be judged in dialogue with their peers — and, when appropriate, Church authorities. Such scholars and teachers will keep in mind that the search for truth and its expression entails following wherever the evidence leads, and hence, the legitimacy of responsible dissent and pluralism of thought and its expression.

6. As a consequence of the basic human right of freedom of association, all Catholics have the right to form voluntary associations to pursue Catholic aims, including the right to worship together; such associations have the right to decide on their own rules of governance.

7. As a consequence of the basic human right to due process of law, all Catholics have the right to be dealt with according to commonly accepted norms of fair administrative and judicial procedures without undue delay, and to redress of grievances through regular procedures of law.

8. As a consequence of the basic human right of participation in self-governance, all Catholics have the right to a voice in decisions that affect them, including the choosing of their leaders, and a duty to exercise those rights responsibly.

9. As a consequence of the basic human right to the accountability of chosen leaders, all Catholics have the right to have their leaders render an account to them.

10. As a consequence of the basic human right to the safeguarding of one's reputation and privacy, all Catholics have the right not to have their good reputations impugned or their privacy violated.

11. As a consequence of the basic human right to marry, all Catholics have the right to choose their state in life; this includes the right for both laity and clergy to marry, remain single, or embrace celibacy.

12. As a consequence of the basic human right to marry, with each spouse retaining full and equal rights during marriage, all Catholics have the right to withdraw from a marriage which has irretrievably broken down.

   a. All such Catholics retain the radical right to remarry; and

   b. All divorced and remarried Catholics who are in conscience reconciled to the Church retain the right to the same ministries, including all the sacraments, as do other Catholics.

13. As a consequence of the basic human rights to marry and to education, all married Catholics have the right and responsibility,

   a. To determine in conscience the size of their families,

   b. To choose appropriate methods of family planning, and

   c. To see to the education of their children.

## B. Basic Baptismal Rights and Responsibilities

1. As a consequence of their baptism, all Catholics have the right to receive in the Church those ministries which are needed for the living of a fully Christian life, including:

   a. Worship which reflects the joys and concerns of the gathered community and instructs and inspires it;

b. Instruction in the Christian tradition and the presentation of spirituality and moral teaching in a way that promotes the helpfulness and relevance of Christian values to contemporary life; and

c. Pastoral care that applies with concern and effectiveness the Christian heritage to persons in particular situations.

2. As a consequence of their baptism, all Catholics have the right,

a. To receive all the sacraments for which they are adequately prepared,

b. To exercise all ministries in the Church for which they are adequately prepared, according to the needs and with the approval of the community.

3. As a consequence of their baptism, all Catholics have the right to expect that the resources of the Church expended within the Church will be fairly distributed on their behalf. Among other concerns, this implies that,

a. All Catholic women have an equal right with men to the resources and the exercise of all the powers of the Church;

b. All Catholic parents have the right to expect fair material and other assistance from Church leaders in the religious education of their children; and

c. All single Catholics have the right to expect that the resources of the Church be fairly expended on their behalf.

## C. Basic Responsibility

All Catholics have the corresponding responsibility to support the Church appropriately.

# III. Governance Structures

## A. Fundamental Insights

1. Through the centuries the Church has wrestled with the concrete issues of the exercise of power and law, without which no society can survive, let alone develop humanly. In this long period the Church both benefitted and suffered from many experiments with power and law in a great variety of cultures. In testing them for itself the Church gained wisdom in both negative and positive ways, i.e., it learned much about what works well and what does not.

2. Two key insights gained from all these experiences are fundamental for the governance of the Church in the third millennium. One is that shared responsibility and corresponding freedom are at the heart of being human, both individually and communally. The second is that the most effective means of arriving at an ever fuller understanding of reality is through dialogue — which should be carried on both within the Church and with those outside the Church. It is on this long experience and wisdom of the Church,

especially these two key insights, that this Constitution draws and builds in its governance structures.

## B. Principles

1. It is of the essence of the Church to be a community. The most basic unit of that Church community is where members daily live their lives, beginning with the family and other intimate associations. Beyond this the fundamental unit of the Church is a local community, most often but not exclusively the geographical Parish.

2. It is, however, also of the essence of the Church that it is a communion of communities, so that the local communities are also united in a regional community, most often but not exclusively called Diocese. Beyond that, Dioceses are united in provincial and then national communities, and at times continental communities, and these in turn in the international community of the Catholic Church.

3. In keeping with the spirit of the Gospel, developing human experience, and the dynamic Christian tradition, especially its two key insights of shared responsibility–corresponding freedom and dialogue, the following basic principles shall shape the governing structures and regulations of the Church:

a. The principle of subsidiarity shall rule throughout the Church, that is, all decision-making rights and responsibilities shall remain with the smaller community unless the good of the broader community specifically demands that it exercise those rights and responsibilities.

b. At all levels of the Church, including the local, the formulations and applications of the teachings of the tradition shall be arrived at through a process of charitable and respectful dialogue.

c. Each community, including this local one, shall form its own body of governing regulations.

d. Local leaders shall be elected to office through appropriate structures, giving voice to all respective constituents.

e. Leaders shall hold office for a specified, limited term.

f. A separation of legislative, executive, and judicial powers, along with a system of checks and balances, shall be observed. This entails (1) a representatively elected local council, (2) elected local leaders, and (3) a separate local judicial system. All branches share responsibility in ways appropriate to the spirit of the Gospel and this Constitution.

g. All groupings of the faithful, including women and minorities, shall be equitably represented in all positions of leadership and decision-making.

## C. Local Council

1. Every Parish (or local equivalent) shall elect a Parish Council, which shall be the main decision-making body of the Parish. The Parish Council shall be elected in as representative a manner as possible, including, when appropriate, representatives of various organizations within the Parish. How all this is carried out specifically shall be determined by statutes of the Parish. Those statutes will determine how the Chair of the Parish Council is chosen. Members of the Council shall serve for a specified term of office.

2. The statutes shall be formulated by the Parish Council and approved by the vote of the entire Parish membership. The statutes shall determine Parish procedures and how decision-making responsibilities are to be distributed, preserving the basic governance principles expressed in this Constitution.

3. The Parish Council with the Pastor, either directly or through committees, shall bear ultimate responsibility for Parish worship, education, social outreach, administration, finances, and other activities carried out in the name of the Parish. All decisions will be in accord with the Parish Council.

## C. Leaders

### a. General

1. Leaders shall be appropriately trained and experienced. They shall be chosen in a manner which shall give a representative voice to all those who are to be led by them. This is especially true of the local Pastor.

2. All leaders shall serve for specified terms of office. That of Pastor is for five years, renewable once.

3. All leaders can be removed from office only for cause, following a procedure of due process spelled out elsewhere in this Constitution and appropriate statutes.

4. All leaders have responsibilities and corresponding rights; those of Pastor are especially laid out here.

### b. Pastor

5. Pastors shall be chosen with the approval of both the Parish Council and the Bishop in accordance with the procedures set forth in the Diocesan Constitution.

6. The Pastor shall serve as the leader of the Parish pastoral team. Together with the Parish Council, the Pastor bears the main responsibility for the worship, spiritual and moral instruction, and pastoral care dimensions of the Parish. This responsibility entails:

a. Worship that reflects the joys and concerns of the gathered community and instructs and inspires it;

b. Instruction in the Christian tradition and the presentation of spirituality and moral teaching in a way that promotes the helpfulness and relevance of Christian values to contemporary life; and

c. Pastoral care that applies with love and effectiveness the Christian heritage to persons in particular situations.

7. Pastors have both a right to and responsibility for proper training and continuation of their education throughout the term of their office.

8. Pastors have a right to fair financial support for the exercise of their office, as well as the requisite liberty needed for the proper exercise thereof.

# IV. Judicial System

## A. Principles

1. The Catholic Church is a pilgrim Church, always in need of reform and correction. Disputes, contentions, and crimes against the rights of members will regrettably occur. These are to be resolved by processes of conciliation and arbitration. Where this proves impossible, Catholics may take such cases to the Church's tribunals for adjudication. All Catholics are entitled to fair and due process under ecclesiastical law. All personnel involved in the Church's judicial system shall be appropriately trained and competent.

2. A system of diocesan, provincial, national, and international tribunals shall be established, which shall serve as courts of first instance, each with designated courts of appeal. These tribunals shall be governed by their appropriate Constitutions and subsequent laws in keeping with them.

## B. Tribunals

Every Parish shall establish a Judicial Committee to hear Parish-level cases brought before it, and judge whether the Parish Constitution and statutes have been violated, and provide the appropriate redress.

## C. Continued Fitness for Office of Leaders

Church leaders shall serve out their elected term of office unless the question of competence and continued fitness for office is formally raised in accordance with constitutionally established norms. Determination of such competence and fitness for office may be made by the office-holder's ecclesiastical superior or by the Parish Council, due process being observed.

## V. Amendments

This Constitution can be amended by a three-quarter vote of the Parish Council and a subsequent ratification by three-fourths of the Parish membership within a six-week period after the passage of the amendment by the Parish Council.

# Appendix C

# A Proposed Constitution for the Diocese

This Constitution provides the framework within which the regional Catholic Church governs itself. It sets forth the fundamental rights and corresponding responsibilities of members and basic structure for decision-making and action within the Diocese. All laws, regulations, and customs of the regional Church shall be carried out within its framework and in its spirit.

## I. Preamble

1. We the people of the regional Catholic Church hold that because all men and women are created in God's image and likeness and that the same divine teaching on how they should live is written in every human heart, all persons are to be treated with dignity and equality, each person having the same fundamental rights and responsibilities.

2. We hold that by our faith in God through Jesus and our baptism with water and the Holy Spirit, all Christians become "members of the body of Christ," that is, the Church universal, and are committed to living out the Gospel taught and lived by Jesus. We further hold that all Christians who recognize the Petrine apostolic ministry of the Bishop of Rome, the Pope, are members of the Catholic Church (hereafter, simply, the Church).

3. We hold that the Church's mission, grounded in the Gospel, is to proclaim and show forth Jesus' Good News of how to live a fully human life as images of God in individual and communal justice and love. We hold that the Church realizes this mission within the context of the laws which it enacts to foster and preserve the spirit of the Gospel and to assist its members as they endeavor to live in the love of God and neighbor.

Fundamental to the Church's mission are certain rights and responsibilities (*listed below*) which pertain to all members.

## II. Rights and Responsibilities

1. All persons belong to one or more categories according to state of life, for example, adult or minor, male or female, single, married, widowed, divorced. In addition to these, in the Church there are other states of life,

for example, laity, clergy, vowed religious. All states of life carry with them specific rights and corresponding responsibilities.

2. The following are the Church members' fundamental rights, flowing either from their basic human rights or their basic baptismal rights. Each right entails a corresponding responsibility on the part of the rights holders, some of which are so obvious that they do not require specific articulation. In all instances these rights and responsibilities apply to all Catholics, regardless of race, age, nationality, sex, sexual orientation, state of life, social or economic position.

## A. Basic Human Rights and Responsibilities

1. All Catholics have the basic human rights — e.g., (a) freedom of action, (b) freedom of conscience, (c) freedom of opinion and expression, (d) the right to receive and impart information, (e) freedom of association, (f) the right to due process of law, (g) the right of participation in self-governance, (h) the right to the accountability of chosen leaders, (i) the right to the safeguarding of one's reputation and privacy, (j) the right to marry, (k) the right to education — and the corresponding duty to exercise them responsibly.

2. As a consequence of the basic human right of freedom of action, all Catholics have the right to engage in any activity which does not violate Christian ethics and does not infringe on the rights of others.

3. As a consequence of the basic human right of freedom of conscience, all Catholics have the right and responsibility to follow their informed consciences in all matters.

4. As a consequence of the basic human right to receive and impart information, all Catholics have the right of access to all information possessed by Church authorities concerning their own spiritual and temporal welfare, provided such access does not infringe on the rights of others.

5. As a consequence of the basic human right of freedom of opinion and expression, all Catholics have the right to express publicly in a responsible manner their agreement or disagreement regarding decisions made by Church authorities.

   a. Laity have the right and responsibility to make their opinions known in a responsible manner, especially where they have first-hand experience of the issue at hand.

   b. Catholic teachers and scholars of theology have a right to, and responsibility for, academic freedom; the acceptability of their teaching is to be judged in dialogue with their peers — and, when appropriate, Church authorities. Such scholars and teachers will keep in mind that the search for truth and its expression entails following wherever the evidence leads, and hence, the legitimacy of responsible dissent and pluralism of thought and its expression.

6. As a consequence of the basic human right of freedom of association, all Catholics have the right to form voluntary associations to pursue Catholic aims, including the right to worship together; such associations have the right to decide on their own rules of governance.

7. As a consequence of the basic human right to due process of law, all Catholics have the right to be dealt with according to commonly accepted norms of fair administrative and judicial procedures without undue delay, and to redress of grievances through regular procedures of law.

8. As a consequence of the basic human right of participation in self-governance, all Catholics have the right to a voice in decisions that affect them, including the choosing of their leaders, and a duty to exercise those rights responsibly.

9. As a consequence of the basic human right to the accountability of chosen leaders, all Catholics have the right to have their leaders render an account to them.

10. As a consequence of the basic human right to the safeguarding of one's reputation and privacy, all Catholics have the right not to have their good reputations impugned or their privacy violated.

11. As a consequence of the basic human right to marry, all Catholics have the right to choose their state in life; this includes the right for both laity and clergy to marry, remain single, or embrace celibacy.

12. As a consequence of the basic human right to marry, with each spouse retaining full and equal rights during marriage, all Catholics have the right to withdraw from a marriage which has irretrievably broken down.

a. All such Catholics retain the radical right to remarry; and

b. All divorced and remarried Catholics who are in conscience reconciled to the Church retain the right to the same ministries, including all the sacraments, as do other Catholics.

13. As a consequence of the basic human rights to marry and to education, all married Catholics have the right and responsibility,

a. To determine in conscience the size of their families,

b. To choose appropriate methods of family planning, and

c. To see to the education of their children.

## B. Basic Baptismal Rights and Responsibilities

1. As a consequence of their baptism, all Catholics have the right to receive in the Church those ministries which are needed for the living of a fully Christian life, including:

a. Worship which reflects the joys and concerns of the gathered community and instructs and inspires it;

b. Instruction in the Christian tradition and the presentation of spirituality and moral teaching in a way that promotes the helpfulness and relevance of Christian values to contemporary life; and

c. Pastoral care that applies with concern and effectiveness the Christian heritage to persons in particular situations.

2. As a consequence of their baptism, all Catholics have the right,

a. To receive all the sacraments for which they are adequately prepared,

b. To exercise all ministries in the Church for which they are adequately prepared, according to the needs and with the approval of the community.

3. As a consequence of their baptism, all Catholics have the right to expect that the resources of the Church expended within the Church will be fairly distributed on their behalf. Among other concerns, this implies that,

a. All Catholic women have an equal right with men to the resources and the exercise of all the powers of the Church;

b. All Catholic parents have the right to expect fair material and other assistance from Church leaders in the religious education of their children; and

c. All single Catholics have the right to expect that the resources of the Church be fairly expended on their behalf.

## C. Basic Responsibility

All Catholics have the corresponding responsibility to support the Church appropriately.

# III. Governance Structures

## A. Fundamental Insights

1. Through the centuries the Church has wrestled with the concrete issues of the exercise of power and law, without which no society can survive, let alone develop humanly. In this long period the Church both benefitted and suffered from many experiments with power and law in a great variety of cultures. In testing them for itself the Church gained wisdom in both negative and positive ways, i.e., it learned much about what works well and what does not.

2. Two key insights gained from all these experiences are fundamental for the governance of the Church in the third millennium. One is that shared responsibility and corresponding freedom are at the heart of being human, both individually and communally. The second is that the most effective means of arriving at an ever fuller understanding of reality is through dialogue — which should be carried on both within the Church and with those outside the Church. It is on this long experience and wisdom of the Church,

especially these two key insights, that this Constitution draws and builds in its governance structures.

## B. Principles

1. It is of the essence of the Church to be a community. The most basic unit of that Church community is where members daily live their lives, beginning with the family and other intimate associations. Beyond this the fundamental unit of the Church is a local community, most often but not exclusively the geographical Parish.

2. It is, however, also of the essence of the Church that it is a communion of communities, so that the local communities are also united in a regional community, most often but not exclusively called Diocese. Beyond that, Dioceses are united in provincial and then national communities, and at times continental communities, and these in turn in the international community of the Catholic Church.

3. In keeping with the spirit of the Gospel, developing human experience, and the dynamic Christian tradition, especially its two key insights of shared responsibility—corresponding freedom and dialogue, the following basic principles shall shape the governing structures and regulations of the Church:

a. The principle of subsidiarity shall rule throughout the Church, that is, all decision-making rights and responsibilities shall remain with the smaller community unless the good of the broader community specifically demands that it exercise those rights and responsibilities.

b. At all levels of the Church, including the diocesan, the formulations and applications of the teachings of the tradition shall be arrived at through a process of charitable and respectful dialogue.

c. Each community, including the diocesan, shall form its own body of governing regulations.

d. Diocesan leaders shall be elected to office through appropriate structures, giving voice to all respective constituents.

e. Leaders shall hold office for a specified, limited term.

f. A separation of legislative, executive, and judicial powers, along with a system of checks and balances, shall be observed. This entails (1) a representatively elected Diocesan Council, (2) elected diocesan leaders, and (3) a separate diocesan judicial system. All branches share responsibility in ways appropriate to the spirit of the Gospel and this Constitution.

g, All groupings of the faithful, including women and minorities, shall be equitably represented in all positions of leadership and decision-making.

## C. Diocesan Council

4. Every Diocese shall elect a Diocesan Council, which shall be the main decision-making body of the Diocese. The Bishop of the Diocese and a layperson elected by the Diocesan Council shall be Co-Chairs of the Diocesan Council.

5. If there is not already a Diocesan Constitution, the Diocesan Council shall formulate one, to be approved by the Parish Councils of the Diocese, bearing in mind the appropriate regulations of the national and international communities. The Diocesan Constitution shall determine diocesan procedures and how decision-making responsibilities are to be distributed, preserving the basic governance principles expressed in this Constitution.

6. The Diocesan Council shall be elected as representatively as possible, including, when appropriate, representatives of various organizations within the Diocese. It shall be composed of an equal number of clergy and laity. Specific procedures for elections and voting shall be determined by the Diocesan Constitution and diocesan statutes. Those regulations will determine how the lay Co-Chair of the Diocesan Council is chosen. Members of the Diocesan Council shall serve for a specified term of office.

7. The Diocesan Council with the Bishop, either directly or through committees or agencies, shall bear ultimate responsibility for diocesan worship, education, social outreach, administration, finances, and other activities carried out in the name of the Diocese.

## C. Leaders

### a. General

1. Leaders shall be appropriately trained and experienced. They shall be chosen in a manner which shall give a representative voice to all those who are to be led by them. This is especially true of the local Pastor and Bishop.

2. All leaders shall serve for specified terms of office. That of Diocesan Bishop is for ten years, nonrenewable.

3. All leaders can be removed from office only for cause, following a procedure of due process spelled out elsewhere in this Constitution and appropriate statutes.

4. All leaders have responsibilities and corresponding rights; those of Bishop are especially laid out here.

### b. Bishop

5. The Bishop shall be chosen by the Diocesan Council in accordance with the Diocesan Constitution, bearing in mind the appropriate regulations of the national and international communities, including consultation with the appropriate committees of the National Council and General Council.

6. The Bishop together with the Diocesan Council bears the main responsibility for the worship, spiritual and moral instruction, and pastoral care dimensions of the Diocese, bearing in mind the principle of subsidiarity.

7. The Bishop together with the Diocesan Council is responsible for the appointment of Pastors and other clergy, with the approval of the Parish Council, in accordance with the procedures of the Diocesan Constitution.

# IV. Judicial System

## A. Principles

1. The Catholic Church is a pilgrim Church, always in need of reform and correction. Disputes, contentions, and crimes against the rights of members will regrettably occur. These are to be resolved by processes of conciliation and arbitration. Where this proves impossible, Catholics may take such cases to the Church's tribunals for adjudication. All Catholics are entitled to fair and due process under ecclesiastical law. All personnel involved in the Church's judicial system shall be appropriately trained and competent.

2. A system of diocesan, provincial, national, and international tribunals shall be established, which shall serve as courts of first instance, each with designated courts of appeal. These tribunals shall be governed by the appropriate Constitutions and subsequent laws in keeping with them.

## B. Tribunals

1. Every Diocese shall establish a Tribunal for the judicial hearing of contentious and criminal cases which are brought before it by its people.

   a. Diocesan Tribunals shall have competence over all matters which pertain to the internal order of the local and regional Church. These include all acts defined by the general ecclesiastical law as administrative acts, crimes, jurisdictional disputes, and matters of equity and restitution.

   b. Diocesan Tribunals shall conduct their operations according to the procedural law established by the universal Church.

   c. Appeals against the judgment of the Diocesan Tribunal shall be heard by the tribunal of the respective ecclesiastical province.

2. All cases involving a diocesan Bishop shall be heard by the tribunal of the Bishop's ecclesiastical province.

3. Cases involving an Archbishop shall be heard by the National Tribunal.

## C. Continued Fitness for Office of Leaders

Church leaders shall serve out their elected term of office unless the question of competence and continued fitness for office is formally raised in accordance with constitutionally established norms. Determination of such competence and fitness for office may be made by the office-holder's ecclesiastical superior or by the Diocesan Council, due process being observed.

## V. Amendments

This Constitution can be amended by a three-quarter vote of the Diocesan Council and a subsequent ratification by three-fourths of the Parish Councils within a one-year period after the passage of the amendment by the Diocesan Council.

# Notes

## Chapter 1: The Copernican Turn of Vatican II

1. For a discussion of "salvation" and other key terms about the ultimate goal of life see Leonard Swidler, *The Meaning of Life at the Edge of the Third Millennium* (Mahwah, N.J., 1992).

2. *Humanae personae dignitatem*, "On Dialogue with Unbelievers," in Austin Flannery, ed., *Vatican Council II* (Collegeville, Minn., 1975), 1002–14, 1010.

3. See, e.g., Hans Küng and Leonard Swidler, eds., *The Church in Anguish: Has the Vatican Betrayed Vatican II?* (San Francisco, 1987); Bernard Häring, *My Witness for the Church*, trans. and introduction Leonard Swidler (Mahwah, N.J., 1992); Heinrich Fries, *Suffering from the Church*, trans. and introduction Arlene and Leonard Swidler (Collegeville, Minn., 1995).

4. See, e.g., Leonard Swidler, *Freedom in the Church* (Dayton, Oh., 1969); Leonard Swidler, *Aufklärung Catholicism 1780–1850* (Missoula, Mont., 1978); Leonard and Arlene Swidler, *Bishops and People* (Philadelphia, Press, 1970).

## Chapter 2: Vatican II and the Turn Toward This World

1. Laszlo Lukacs, "Changing Forms of Religiosity in a Changing Society," an unpublished paper prepared for a Christian-Marxist dialogue between Americans and Hungarians in Budapest, June 1988.

2. Ibid.

## Chapter 3: Vatican II and the Turn Toward Dialogue

1. Thomas Aquinas, *Summa Theologiae*, II–II, q. 1, a. 2.

2. Oswald Spengler, *Der Untergang des Abendlandes*, 2 vols. (Munich, 1922–23); *The Decline of the West* (New York, 1928–28); abridged edition, *Der Untergang des Abendlandes, Gekürzte Ausgabe* by Helmut Werner (Munich, 1959); abridged English edition by Arthur Helps from the translation by Charles Francis Atkinson (New York, 1962).

3. Pitirim A. Sorokin, *The Crisis of Our Age* (New York, 1941).

4. See, among others, Hans Küng, *Theologie im Aufbruch* (Munich, 1987), esp. 153ff. A "paradigm" here means the bundle of intellectual assumptions which form the intellectual "lens" through which we view and interpret data. For example, the assumption that the earth is the center of the universe was the "paradigm" of geocentrism through which all astronomical data was interpreted, whereas the "paradigm-shift" to the heliocentric paradigm, reversing the celestial order of bod-

ies, made the sun the center of the solar system. It occurred as a result of the studies of Copernicus — hence the term "Copernican turn."

5. See especially Ewert Cousins, "Judaism-Christianity-Islam: Facing Modernity Together," *Journal of Ecumenical Studies* 30, nos. 3–4 (Summer–Fall 1993): 417–25. It was Karl Jaspers, the German philosopher, who some forty-five years ago pointed out the significance of this phenomenon in his book *The Origin and Goal of History* (Karl Jaspers, *Vom Ursprung und Ziel der Geschichte* [Zurich, 1949], 19–43). He called the period from 800 to 200 B.C.E. the Axial Period because "it gave birth to everything which, since then, man has been able to be." It is here in this period "that we meet with the most deepcut dividing line in history. Man, as we know him today, came into being. For short, we may style this the 'Axial Period'" (ibid., 19; trans. Michael Bullock, *The Origin and Goal of History* [New Haven, 1953], 1). For the ongoing academic discussion of Jaspers's position on the Axial Period, see S. N. Eisenstadt, ed., *Wisdom, Revelation, and Doubt: Perspectives on the First Millennium B.C.*, *Daedalus* (Spring 1975); and *The Origins and Diversity of Axial Age Civilizations* (New York, 1989).

6. See my forthcoming *Toward a Universal Declaration of a Global Ethic: An Interreligious Dialogue.*

7. Leonard Swidler, John Cobb, Monika Hellwig, and Paul Knitter, *Death or Dialogue* (Philadelphia, 1990).

## Chapter 4: Vatican II and the Turn Toward History: A New Freedom

1. Gallicanism is a doctrine that grew up in France (previously known as Gaul; hence the name Gallican) starting in the thirteenth century as taught at the Sorbonne (founded 1257). It developed further during the fourteenth- and fifteenth-century "Western Schism" when there were two or three popes simultaneously, and still more in the wake of the sixteenth-century Protestant Reformation. The basic teaching was that the decrees of Rome could take effect in France only with the appropriate French approvals. One version was "Royal Gallicanism," wherein the king had the right of (dis)approval; a second was "Episcopal Gallicanism," wherein the assembly of French bishops had the right of (dis)approval; and the third was "Parliamentarian Gallicanism," wherein the French Parliament had the right of (dis)approval. Gallicanism was dominant in France until after the Napoleonic period (ended 1815).

2. George Lindbeck, "Reform and Infallibility," *Cross Currents* 11 (1961): 353.

## Chapter 6: Vatican II Attitude Toward History and Freedom

1. Herbert Butterfield, *Christianity and History* (London, 1949), passim; Herbert Butterfield, "Moral Judgments in History," in Hans Meyerhoff, ed., *The Philosophy of History in Our Time* (New York, 1959), 228–49.

2. Isaiah Berlin, "Historical Inevitability," Meyerhoff, *Philosophy*, 249–69.

3. Oskar Simmel, S.J., and Rudolf Stählin, eds., "Inquisition," *Christliche Religion* (Frankfurt, 1957).

4. Josef Lortz, *The Reformation in Germany*, 2 vols. (New York, 1969). Unfortunately the translation of these two volumes into English and other languages

after World War II (the German was published in 1939/40) was prohibited by Pope Pius XII and did not see the light of day until after Vatican II.

5. Bishop John J. Wright (later made cardinal), in a lecture at the University of Wisconsin, Fall 1956.

6. Heinrich Hermelink, *Die katholische Kirche unter den Pius-Päpsten des 20. Jahrhunderts* (Zurich, 1949), 105.

7. "Bibelverbot," *Die Religion in Geschichte and Gegenwart* (1957); Leonard Swidler, "The Catholic Bible Movement in Germany," *Interpretation* 15 (April 1961): 164.

8. Lortz, *The Reformation in Germany;* Ludwig Andreas Veit and Ludwig Lenhart, *Kirche and Volksfrömmigkeit im Zeitalter der Barock* (Freiburg, 1956).

9. Aelred Watkin and Herbert Butterfield, "Gasquet and the Acton Simpson Correspondence," *Cambridge Historical Journal* 10 (1950): 75–105; Josef Altholz, *The Liberal Catholic Movement in England* (London, 1962), 63.

10. See Hans Müller, "Zur Behandlung des Kirchenkampfes in der Nachkriegs-literatur," *Politische Studien* 12 (July 1961): 474–81; Gordon Zahn, *German Catholics and Hitler's Wars* (New York, 1962), 52.

11. Altholz, *The Liberal Catholic Movement in England*, 39.

12. Ibid., 18.

13. Gallicanism was already described above. Febronianism in many ways was a mid-eighteenth-century German counterpart of Gallicanism. The three Archbishop Electors of the Emperor of the Holy Roman Empire commissioned Bishop Nicholas von Hontheim of Trier to do an analysis of the German Church's grievances against Rome. The result was his essay published under the pen name Justinus Febronius. He advocated that as far as possible German Church affairs should be kept in German episcopal and civil hands.

Josephinism receives it name from Emperor Joseph II of Austria (sole emperor 1780–90) who not only basically followed the principles of Gallicanism and Febroni-anism but also was very active in reforming and restructuring the Church within his empire. He did so not only without waiting for permission from Rome but often in direct opposition to Rome. His aggressiveness in many ways put the Enlightenment and reform in a subsequent disadvantageous light.

14. Ibid., 86.

15. Mathew Arnold in his essay "The Function of Criticism at the Present Time" mentioned Acton's *Rambler* under its subsequent name, *The Home and Foreign Review*. "We saw this the other day in the extinction, so much to be regretted, of the *Home and Foreign Review*. Perhaps in no organ of criticism in this country was there so much knowledge, so much play of mind; but these could not save it. The *Dublin Review* [the journal of Cardinal Wiseman, one of the *Rambler*'s strongest opponents] subordinates play of mind to the practical businesses of English and Irish Catholicism, and lives."

16. Ernst-Wolfgang Böckenförde, "German Catholicism in 1933," *Cross Currents* 11 (1961): 283.

17. Hans Küng, *Konzil und Wiedervereinigung* (Freiburg, 1960); English translation, *The Council, Reform and Reunion* (New York, 1961).

18. See Rodger Van Allen, *The Commonweal and American Catholicism* (Philadelphia, 1974).

## Chapter 7: Religious Freedom and Religious Dialogue

1. See Leonard Swidler, *After the Absolute. The Dialogue Future of All Religious Reflection* (Minneapolis, Press, 1990).

2. Joannes Dominicus Mansi, *Sacrorum Conciliorum Nova et Amplissima Collectio* (Arnhem, 1926), 51: col. 75.

3. John Dalberg-Acton, *The History of Freedom and Other Essays* (London, 1909), 541.

4. As related to me between sessions by Father George Tavard, who was a member of the Secretariat for Christian Unity, and hence deeply involved in the regular committee meetings.

5. John Courtney Murray, "Introduction and Commentary on 'Declaration on Religious Freedom,'" in Walter M. Abbott, ed., *The Documents of Vatican II* (New York, 1966), 674 and 695.

6. See the 1917 *Codex Juris Canonici*, Canon 93, which was in force until 1983.

7. Abbott, *The Documents of Vatican II*, 675f.

## Chapter 8: Religious Freedom and Catholic Church-State Relations

1. Quoted in Albert Dondeyne, *Faith and the World* (Pittsburgh, 1963), 257.

2. *Summa Theol.*, IIa IIae, q. 11, art. 3. "Circa haereticos... meruerunt non solum ab Ecclesia per excommunicationem separari, sed etiam per mortem a mundo excludi. Multo enim gravius est corrumpere fidem, per quam est animae vita, quam falsare pecuniam, per quam temporali vitae subvenitur... relinquit eum iudicio saeculari a mundo exterminandum per mortem. Dicit enim Hieronymus: Resecandae sint putridae carnes" (Comm. sup. *Ep. ad Gal.*, Commentary on the Epistle to the Galatians).

3. See Alec R. Vidler, *Prophecy and Papacy* (New York, 1954), 213 ff.

4. Quoted in Roger Aubert, "Religious Liberty from 'Mirari vos' to the 'Syllabus'" in *Historical Problems of Church Renewal*, Concilium 7 (Glen Rock, N.J., 1965), 91f.

5. A. Simon, "Vues nouvelles sur Gregoire XVI," *Revue Générale Belge* (January 1951): 399ff.

6. Roger Aubert, *Le Pontificat de Pie IX* (Paris, 1963), 14–29, 505f.

7. Quoted in Christopher Hollis, "The Syllabus of Errors," in *Twentieth Century Catholicism*, no. 1, supplement to *The Twentieth Century Encyclopedia of Catholicism*, ed. Lancelot Sheppard (New York, 1965), 38–39.

8. See Leonard Swidler, "The Catholic Historian," in Samuel Hazo, ed., *The Christian Intellectual* (Pittsburgh, 1963), 134f.

9. Sheppard, *Encyclopedia*, 165.

10. Ibid., 143f.

11. Ibid., 145f.

12. Ibid., 151f.

13. Ibid., 164.

14. Ibid., 163f.

15. Ultramontanism means literally "beyond the mountains," referring to the Alps from a northern European perspective. This was a movement favoring the authority of the pope, who lived "beyond the mountains."

16. Quoted in Aubert, *Pontificat*, 103.

17. Quoted in Hollis, "Syllabus," 49.

18. See ibid., 39f.

19. Ibid., 41.

20. James Hastings Nichols, *History of Christianity 1650–1950* (New York, 1956), 214.

21. See Gregory Baum, "Doctrinal Renewal," *Journal of Ecumenical Studies* 2 (Fall 1965): 365–81.

22. See the speech Kenrick gave at the Council on June 8, 1870, and had printed privately in Naples (entitled "Concio," also reproduced without appendices in Mansi) and distributed at the Council. In it he vigorously argued in historical, scholarly fashion against papal infallibility, among other things, citing many bishops from Ireland, England, and the United States who rejected it in modern times — including his brother Francis, archbishop first of Philadelphia and then Baltimore until his death in 1863.

23. See E. A. Goerner, *Peter and Caesar* (New York, 1965), 153–72, for a thorough investigation of the writings of the three major "canonists," Fathers Joseph C. Fenton, Francis J. Connell, and George W. Shea.

24. See his 1302 *Tractatus de Potestate Regia et Papali.* Murray contended that John had found a genuine middle way that is "indeed 'the great Catholic tradition' and...if developed *in eodem sensu,* it may show the way to the solution of the contemporary problem" (John Courtney Murray, S.J., "Contemporary Orientations of Catholic Thought on Church and State in the Light of History," *Cross Currents* 5 [Fall 1951]: 24).

25. Alfredo Ottaviani, "Church and State: Some Present Problems in the Light of the Teaching of Pope Pius XII," *American Ecclesiastical Review* 128 (May 1953): 321–34.

26. Goerner, *Peter and Caesar,* 175f.

27. Dondeyne, *Faith and the World,* 258.

## Chapter 9: Doctrinal Authority and Freedom in the Church

1. Albert Outler, "The Sense of Tradition in the Ante-Nicene Church," *Journal of Ecumenical Studies* 1 (Fall 1964): 460–84.

2. In a letter to St. Boniface, dated November 22, 726, Pope Gregory II replied to a number of questions Boniface had put to him. Gregory used as solemn and definitive language in speaking of this matter of morals as it would seem possible to muster:

> ...You included a number of questions concerning the faith and teaching of the Holy Roman and Apostolic Church. This is a commendable practice, for here St. Peter held his see and the episcopate had its beginning. And since you seek our advice on matters dealing with ecclesiastical discipline, we will state with all the authority of apostolic tradition what you must hold, though we

speak not from our own insufficiency but relying on the grace of Him who opens the mouths of the dumb and makes eloquent the tongues of babes....

As to what a man shall do if his wife is unable through illness to allow him his marital rights, it would be better if he remained apart and practiced continence. But since this is practicable only in the case of men of high ideals, the best course if he is unable to be continent would be for him to marry. [This legislation is recorded by Gratian, *Decreta*, pt. ii, ch. 32, q. 7, can. 18, but attributed to Gregory III.] Nevertheless, he should continue to support the woman who is sick, unless she has contracted the disease through her own fault. (C. H. Talbot, *The Anglo-Saxon Missionaries in Germany* [New York, 1954], 81).

3. Colman J. Barry, ed., *Readings in Church History* (Westminster, Md., 1960), 1:504.

4. In his article on the "Konstanzer Dekrete" in the latest edition (1961, i.e., before Vatican II) of the Catholic *Lexikon für Theologie und Kirche (LTK)*, Dr. Remigius Bäumer, also the chief editor of the *LTK*, understates that "a dogmatically and historically completely satisfactory answer [concerning the reconciliation of Constance and Vatican I] does not yet exist."

5. *Nec mihi vos... superbae appellationis verbum universalem, me papam dicentes.* Migne, *Patrologia Latina*, vol. 77, col. 933.

6. Ibid. *Sed absit hoc. Recedant verba quae vanitatem inflant, et charitatem vulnerant.*

## Chapter 10: The Turn Toward Inner-Church Reform

1. For the above, see James H. Provost, "The Hierarchical Constitution of the Church," in James A. Coriden et al., *The Code of Canon Law: A Text and Commentary* (New York, 1985), esp. 260, 268.

2. Quoted in Albert Dondeyne, *Faith and the World* (Pittsburgh, 1963), 257; and Colman J. Barry, ed., *Readings in Church History* (Westminster, Md., 1960), 1:466f.

3. Barry, *Readings in Church History*, 1:504f.

4. Concerning Gallicanism, Febronianism, and Josephinism see chapter 4, note 1, p. 174, and chapter 6, note 13, p. 175. For Aufklärung Catholicism see Leonard Swidler, *Aufklärung Catholicism 1780–1850* (Missoula, Mont., 1978).

5. See F. Logan, "The 1875 Statement of the German Bishops on Episcopal Power," *The Jurist* 21 (1961): 285–95.

6. I am indebted in this whole section, and especially on this particular point, to James H. Provost, "The Hierarchical Constitution of the Church," Coriden, *The Code of Canon Law*, 258–310.

7. This position was held by a small minority at Vatican II. See A. Acerbi, *Due Ecclesiologie: Ecclesiologia giuridica ed ecclesiologia di communione nella "Lumen Gentium"* (Bologna, 1975), 243–54, 444–47.

## Chapter 11: Church Reform: Vatican II and Aftermath

1. See Jean-Pierre Jossua, "Jacques Pohier: A Theologian Destroyed," in Hans Küng and Leonard Swidler, eds., *The Church in Anguish: Has the Vatican Betrayed Vatican II?* (San Francisco, 1987), 205–11.

2. See Ad Willems, "The Endless Case of Edward Schillebeeckx," ibid., 212–22.

3. See Leonardo and Clodovis Boff, "Summons to Rome," ibid., 223–34.

## Chapter 12: The Maturation of American Catholicism

1. See Gerhard Lenski, "The Religious Factor, 1961, Referred to in NCR Gallup Poll," *National Catholic Reporter*, September 11, 1987, 10.

2. See Leonard Swidler, "Roma Locuta, Causa Finita?" in Leonard Swidler and Arlene Swidler, eds., *Women Priests: A Catholic Commentary on the Vatican Declaration* (New York, 1977), 3.

3. "NCR Gallup Poll," 10.

4. Ibid.

5. Joseph H. Fichter, "Restructuring Catholicism: Symposium on Thomas O'Dea," *Sociological Analysis* 38 (1977): 163f.

6. See the Ph.D. dissertation by Pamela Monaco, "A History and Sociological Analysis of Catholic Reform Movements in Contemporary North America," Religion Department, Temple University, 1995.

## Chapter 13: European Church Renewal Movements

1. November 28, 1990, typed notes from a European trip by Terry Dosh.

2. *Eighth of May Newsletter*, Acht Mei Beweging, Brigittenstraat 15; NL-3512 KJ Utrecht, Netherlands.

3. "Aufbruch-Bewegung" publishes (in German) an impressive newspaper six times a year with a circulation of 34,000. It is entitled *Aufbruch. Forum für eine offene Kirche*, Postfach 169, 1700 Fribourg 7, Switzerland.

4. At least one of the regional organizations publishes a newsletter, whose address is: KIRCHE SIND WIR ALLE, Postfach 107, 6800 Feldkirch, Austria. A progressive Catholic monthly periodical in Austria, which regularly reports on the activities of these and other renewal movements, is *Kirche Intern. Forum für eine offene Kirche*, Floriangasse 1, A-2440 Reisenberg, Austria.

5. The Ikvu also puts out a quarterly periodical: *Rundbriefe Initiative Kirche von unten*, Heerstr. 205, 5300 Bonn 1, Germany.

6. "Dialog statt Dialogverweigerung. Wie in der Kirche miteinander umgehen?" The committee was made up of thirty-three members, including men and women, laity, clergy, religious, and a bishop. Copies can be obtained from the Generalsekretariat des ZdK, Hochkreuzallee 246, 5300 Bonn 2, Germany.

7. *Macht teilen, Gleichheit anerkennen. Ein Demokratieförderplan für die katholische Kirche in Deutschland* (Düsseldorf: BDKJ-Bundesstelle, 1994), 3.

8. Ibid., 6.

9. Ibid., 12–15.

10. The countries and organizations involved in Kirche im Aufbruch are:

- The Netherlands: Acht Mei Beweging — Commissie Mensenrechte (Eighth of May Movement–Human Rights Committee)

- Belgium: Priesters en Religieuzen voor Gerechtiggheid en Vrede (Priests and Religious for Justice and Freedom)

- France: Femmes et Hommes en l'Eglise — Section française (Women and Men in the Church — French Section)

- Luxemburg: Luxemburg Gruppe (Luxemburg Group)

- Germany: Maria von Magdala — Initiative Gleichberechtigung (Mary Magdalene — Movement for Equal Rights)

- Switzerland: Aufbruch-Bewegung (The Breaking Forth Movement)

- Austria: Aufbruch (Breaking Forth)

- Italy: Secretaria Tecnica delle Communità Christiane de Base (Technical Secretariat of the Christian Base Communities)

- United Kingdom: Catholics for a Changing Church

- Ireland: Vatican II Laity Alliance

- Spain: Comunidades Cristianas Populares Españolas (Spanish Christian Popular Communities)

- Poland: Nasza Droga (Our Way)

- Hungary: Hungarian Catholic Base Communities — BOKOR

- Czech Republic: Emmaus

Up-to-date information on the addresses of the various organizations can be obtained from Josée Reichling, Sekretariat des Europäischen Netzwerkes, 12, rue des champs, L-5953 Itzig, Luxembourg; Tel./Fax: 011-352-369-743; or Gerd Wild, Christenrechte in der Kirche, Commission for International Contacts; Mithrasstr. 45, 6000 Frankfurt 50, Germany; Tel. 011-49-69-586-516; Fax: 011-49-6173-652-20.

11. *The Tablet* (London), January 15, 1994, 56. See also *Euronews. Informationsblatt für das "Europäische Netzwerk Kirche im Aufbruch,"* no. 3 (June 1994), ed., Josée Reichling, 12, rue des champs, L-5953 Itzig, Luxembourg, Tel./Fax: 011-352-369-743.

12. See Ingrid Shafer, "500,000 Petition for Church Tolerance," *National Catholic Reporter*, July 14, 1995.

## Chapter 14: Call for a Catholic Constitutional Convention

1. Paul VI used the phrase *novus habitus mentis* (Paul VI, allocution of November 20, 1965, *Communicationes* 1 [1969]: 38–42).

2. James Provost, "Prospects for a More 'Democratized' Church," in James Provost and Knut Walf, eds., *The Tabu of Democracy within the Church*, Concilium 1992/5 (London, 1992), 132. See John Paul II's Apostolic Constitution *Sacrae disciplinae leges*, January 25, 1983; *Acta Apostolicae Sedis* 75, no. 2 (1983): xii.

3. Provost, "Prospects."

4. Provost and Walf, *The Tabu of Democracy within the Church.*

5. *Centesimus annus,* no. 46; in James Provost, "Prospects for a More 'Democratized' Church," in Provost and Walf, *The Tabu of Democracy within the Church,* 141.

6. "Message to Humanity," issued at the beginning of the Second Vatican Council by its Fathers, with the endorsement of the Supreme Pontiff, cited in Walter Abbott, ed., *The Documents of Vatican II* (New York, 1966), 6.

7. *Acta Apostolicae Sedis* 57 (1965): 988.

8. *Acta Apostolicae Sedis* 75 (1983): 556; *Origins* 12 (1983): 631.

9. See Peter Clarke, *A Free Church in a Free Society* (Greenwood, S.C.: Attic Press, 1982).

10. "A Declaration of Human Rights: A Statement Just Drafted by a Committee Appointed by the National Catholic Welfare Conference," *The Catholic Action,* 29 (February 1947), 4f. and 17; and "A Declaration of Rights: Drafted by a Committee Appointed by the National Catholic Welfare Conference," *Catholic Mind* 45, no. 1012 (April 1947): 193–96. A German translation appeared in "Eine Charta der Menschenrechte: Eine Denkschrift der Katholiken Amerikas," *Die Furche,* 8 (February 1947): 4f.

Both the original American and a German translation as well as an interesting analysis can be found in Gertraud Putz, *Christentum und Menschenrechte* (Innsbruck, 1991), 322–30, 388–97.

11. See "Basic Schedule of Rights," *Commonweal* 45 (February 14, 1947): 435; "NCWC on Human Rights," *The N.C.W.C. News Service* 860 (February 15, 1947): 538; Dies Villeneuve, "Recent Events," *Catholic World* 164 (March 1947): 562f.

12. Dr. Gertraud Putz noted how accidental and labyrinthine her discovery of the document was: "The difficult search for the English text shall not remain hidden from the reader. Through a personal contact with Professor Johannes Schwartländer of the University of Tübingen, doubtless the most knowledgeable scholar of the history of human rights, I was directed to an American human rights expert, Professor Leonard Swidler in Philadelphia. The accident that he — who at first also knew nothing of the existence of this declaration — is married to a historian with whom he discussed the matter made it possible that she then took up the search. In a letter dated April 18, 1990, she responded to my letter and explained the difficulty in finding the declaration, for it had no listed author under which it could be indexed. However, the fact that Professor Arlene Swidler precisely at that time was giving a course on "American Catholic History" at Villanova University led her to search further, and she ended by writing: "However, I am quite sure I have found the important material by paging through the significant periodicals" (Putz, *Christentum und Menschenrechte,* 325).

## Chapter 15: Democracy in the Catholic Church

1. Eusebius, *History of the Church,* 3, 2.

2. Ibid., 3, 36.

3. See T. Patrick Burke, "The Monarchical Episcopate at the End of the First Century," *Journal of Ecumenical Studies* 11 (1970): 499–518.

4. Eusebius's account of the Easter controversy describes Anicetus in a monoepiscopal role in Rome shortly before the death of Polycarp in 155 (*History of the Church,* 4.22.1–3). See James F. McCue, "The Roman Primacy in the Patristic Era: The Beginnings through Nicea," in Paul Empie and T. Austin Murphy, eds., *Papal Primacy and the Universal Church: Lutherans and Catholics in Dialogue V* (Minneapolis, 1974), 44–72.

5. *Didache,* 15:1–2.

6. *1 Clement,* 44, 5.

7. Hippolytus, *Traditio Apostolica,* 2, 7, 8.

8. Migne, *Patrologia Latina* (*PL*), 4, 317–18. "Cyprianus presbyterio et diaconibus et plebi universae salutem. In ordinationibus clericis, fratres charissimi, solemus vos ante consulere, et mores ac merita singulorum communi consilia ponderare."

9. Ibid., 3, 796–97

10. Cyprian, Epistle, 67, 3, *Corpus scriptorum ecclesiasticorum Latinorum* (*CSEL*), 3.2.737. "Plebs . . . ipsa maxime habeat potestatem uel eligendi dignos sacerdotes uel indignos recusandi."

11. Optatus, *CSEL,* 34.2.407. "Tunc suffragio totius populi Caecilianus elegitur et manum imponente Felice Autumnitano episcopus ordinatur."

12. Canon 18. See C. J. von Hefele, *Conciliengeschichte,* I (Freiburg, 1873), 237.

13. Celestine, Epistle, iv, 5; *PL,* 50, 431. "Nullus invitis detur episcopus. Cleri, plebis, et ordinis, consensus ac desiderium requiratur."

14. Leo, *Epistle,* x, 4; *PL,* 54, 634. "Qui praefuturus est omnibus ab omnibus eligatur."

15. See Jean Harduin, *Acta Conciliorum et Epistolae Decretales ac Constitutiones Summorum Pontificum,* 4:1289 ff.

16. See Leonard Swidler, "People, Priests, and Bishops in U.S. Catholic History," in Leonard Swidler and Arlene Swidler, eds., *Bishops and People* (Philadelphia: Westminster, 1970), 113–35.

17. Carroll to Charles Plowden, December 22, 1791, Thomas O'Brien Hanley, ed., *The John Carroll Papers,* 3 vols. (Notre Dame, Ind., 1976), 1:548.

18. This was expressed in a letter from a trustee, Benedict Fenwick, in Charleston, South Carolina, to the then bishop of the area, Archbishop Ambrose Maréchal of Baltimore, on August 11, 1819 (Archdiocesan Archives of Baltimore, 1-0-15).

19. Quoted in Patrick W. Carey, *People, Priests, and Prelates: Ecclesiastical Democracy and the Tensions of Trusteeism* (Notre Dame, Ind., 1987), 171.

20. Mathew Carey, *Address to the Right Reverend the Bishop of Pennsylvania, the Catholic Clergy of Philadelphia, and the Congregation of St. Mary's in the City* (Philadelphia: H. C. Carey & I. Lea, 1822), 30.

21. Patrick Carey, *People,* 5.

22. Ibid., 224.

23. Ibid., 2f.

24. Ibid., 3.

25. John Carroll to Dominick Lynch and Thomas Stoughton, January 24, 1786, Hanley, *John Carroll Papers,* 1:203; and John Carroll to Andrew Nugent, July 18, 1786, ibid., 214. Concerning Father Andrew Nugent, matters became so turbulent that the trustees went to civil court in order to remove Nugent — with Carroll's obvious ap-

proval. "Thus, Nugent was removed as pastor by use of the secular arm when recourse to the voluntary measures of ecclesiastical discipline had failed" (Carey, *Priests,* 15).

26. Quoted in Peter Guilday, *The Life and Times of John Carroll* (New York, 1922), 293; italics added.

27. Letter of John Carroll to Cardinal Antonelli, February 17, 1785, quoted in Annabelle M. Melville, *John Carroll of Baltimore* (New York, 1955), 230.

28. Eusebius, *History of the Church, Patrologia Graeca,* 20, 468.

29. Cyprian, Epistle, xxvi.

30. Cyprian, *PL,* 4, 256–57. "Cyprianus fratribus in plebe consistentibus salutem ... examinabuntur singula praesentibus et judicantibus vobis."

31. Cyprian, Epistle, liv, quoted in Johann Baptist Hirscher, *Sympathies of the Continent,* trans. of *Die kirchlichen Zustände der Gegenwart,* 1849, by Arthur C. Coxe (Oxford, 1852), 123. "Singulorum tractanda ratio, non tantum cum collegis meis, sed cum plebe ipsa universa."

32. Cyprian, *PL,* 4, 234. "Quando a primordio episcopatus mei statuerim, nihil sine consilio vestro, et sine consensu plebis, mea privatim, sententia gerere."

33. Cyprian, *PL,* 4, 312. "Sic collatione consiliorum cum episcopis, presbyteris, diaconis, confessoribus pariter ac stantibus laicis facta, lapsorum tractare rationem.... quoniam nec firmum decretum potest esse quod non plurimorum videbitur habuisse consensum."

34. Canon 7, in J. B. Chabot, *Synodicon Orientale* (Paris, 1902), 358f.

35. Joseph L. O'Brien, *John England, Bishop of Charleston: Apostle to Democracy* (New York, 1934).

36. Quoted in Andrew M. Greeley, *The Catholic Experience* (New York: Image Books, 1969), 81

37. Carey, *People,* 222.

38. Hanley, *Carroll Papers,* 1:59–76.

39. Carey, *People,* 166.

40. Ibid., 168.

41. Quoted in Greeley, *Catholic Experience,* 82

42. Sebastian Messmer, *The Works of the Right Reverend John England,* 7 vols. (Cleveland, 1908), 6:238.

43. *The Records of the American Church History Society of Philadelphia (ACHSP)* vol. 8 (1897), 458f.

44. *Concilia Provincialia Baltimore habita* (Baltimore, 1851), 74.

45. *Records of the American Catholic Historical Society of Philadelphia,* vol. 7 (1896), 290, 293.

46. Greeley, *Catholic Experience,* 85.

47. The bulk of the Constitution is published in Patrick W. Carey, ed., *American Catholic Religious Thought* (New York, 1987), 73–93.

48. Peter Guilday, *Life and Times of John England, 1786–1842* (New York, 1927), 1:131.

49. See ibid., 2:214.

50. Theodore Maynard, *The Story of American Catholicism* (New York, 1954), 241.

51. *Brownson's Quarterly Review,* vol. 50, 158. See Peter Clarke, *A Free Church in a Free Society* (Greenwood, S.C.: Attic Press, 1982), 131.

52. Quoted in Greeley, *Catholic Experience,* 91f.

53. Ibid., 92.

54. *Records ACHSP,* vol. 8, 460.

55. Messmer, *Works,* vol. 7, 32.

56. John Ireland, "The Church and the Age" (October 18, 1893); *The Church and Modern Society* (New York, 1903), 114f., quoted in Carey, *American Catholic Religious Thought,* 183f.

57. See Pope John Paul II, *Apostolic Constitution Sacrae disciplinae leges,* in *Code of Canon Law. Latin-English Edition* (Washington, D.C., 1983), ix.

58. James A. Coriden, "A Challenge: Making the Rights Real," in Leonard Swidler and Herbert O'Brien (a pseudonym for protective purposes), *A Catholic Bill of Rights* (Kansas City, 1988), 11; also in *The Jurist* 45, no. 1 (1985).

59. *Textus Emendatus,* Vatican Press, 119–20, 123, cited in Peter Hebblethwaite, *Pope Paul VI* (New York: Paulist Press, 1993), 573.

60. Coriden, "A Challenge," 11.

61. *Communicationes* 1 (1969), 77–100. *Patribus synodi episcoporum habenda* (Vatican, 1969), 80, 79.

62. Report by Peter Nichols in the *Times* (London), July 6, 1971.

63. *Communio et progressio,* published in Austin Flannery, ed., *Vatican Council II* (Collegeville, Minn., 1975), 332.

64. Coriden, "A Challenge," 11.

65. For information on the "national" synods in the Germanic-speaking countries see the detailed essay by the priest/theologian Bernard Franck, "Experiences of National Synods in Europe after the Council," in James Provost and Knut Walf, eds., *The Tabu of Democracy within the Church,* Concilium, 1992/5 (London, 1992), 82–97. For further analysis of the West German Synod and its aftermath as well as the U.S. equivalent, the 1976 "Call to Action," see Heinrich Fries, *Suffering from the Church,* introduction and translation by Leonard and Arlene Swidler (Collegeville, Minn., 1994).

66. Franck, "National Synods," 92.

67. See the English translation in Leonard and Arlene Swidler, *Bishops and People.*

68. *Apostolic Tradition* (Hippolytus), XIX.

69. Jean Daniélou, *Origen* (New York, 1955), 50.

70. Roger Gryson, "The Authority of the Teacher in the Ancient and Medieval Church," in Leonard Swidler and Piet Fransen, eds., *Authority in the Church and the Schillebeeckx Case* (New York, 1982), 184.

71. Thomas Aquinas, *Quodlibitales,* III, a. 9. "Doctores sacrae scripturae adhibentur ministerio verbi Dei, sicut et praelati."

72. References and fuller discussion in Gryson, "The Authority of the Teacher," 176–87.

73. Ibid., 186.

74. Citation found in ibid., 186f. The original reads: "Cum Dominus dixit: Qui vos audit me audit, et qui vos spernit me spernit, non modo ad primos theologos, i.e. apostolos verba illa referebat, sed ad doctores etiam in Ecclesia futuros, quamdiu pascendae essent oves in scientia et doctrina."

75. Reprinted in Leonard Swidler, *Küng in Conflict* (New York: Doubleday, 1981), 516f.

76. Reprinted in part in the Charter of the Rights of Catholics in the Church of the Association for the Rights of Catholics in the Church (ARCC, P.O.Box 912, Delran, NJ 08075), 2nd ed., January 1985, 17.

## Chapter 16: Suggestions for Intermediate Steps to Be Taken

1. See the excellent introductory essay on the realization of rights already existing in the new 1983 Code of Canon Law by James Coriden in Leonard Swidler and Patrick O'Brien, eds., *A Catholic Bill of Rights* (Kansas City, Mo., 1988).

2. On the latter see John M. Huels, "The Most Holy Eucharist," in James A. Coriden et al., eds., *The Code of Canon Law: A Text and Commentary*, commissioned by the Canon Law Society of America (New York, 1985), 648: "The revised Code, unlike the 1917 Code, does not prohibit females from serving Mass.... There is no solid legal basis for excluding female altar servers." This matter was finally satisfactorily resolved by the Vatican in 1994.

## Chapter 17: Suggestions for the Organization and Action of the Catholic Constitutional Convention

1. This was a result of the presentation of the idea of a Catholic Constitutional Convention in Leonard Swidler, "Aufruf zur einer Katholischen Verfassungsgebenden Versammlung," *Diakonia* 24, no. 2 (March 1993): 133–39.

2. *Tablet* (London), January 15, 1994, 56.

3. See report in *ARCC Light*, newsletter of the Association for the Rights of Catholics in the Church, 18, no. 2, March 1996.

4. See above chapter 16, n. 1.

# Index

*Of Related Interest...*

# The Future Church of 140 B.C.E.:
# A Hidden Revolution
*by Bernard J. Lee*

A century and a half before the time of Jesus, a movement of educated Jewish laity initiated a profound transformation of Judaism. Bernard Lee uses this as a metaphor for a hidden revolution in the U.S. Catholic Church today: *the development of a lay interpretation of Catholic Christian identity.* He proposes an ecclesiology that believes that the Spirit is God's gift to the entire people of God without privilege or prejudice. Accordingly, some form of dialogic community is ecclesiologically appropriate to give the lay experience of faith a legitimated voice in the telling of the Catholic story, i.e., a place in the interpretive structure of Catholic community.

BERNARD J. LEE, S.M., is Professor of Theology at Loyola's Institute for Ministry in New Orleans. An early Catholic pioneer in process theology, he has also been involved nationally and internationally with the basic Christian community movement. His books include *The Becoming of the Church, Dangerous Memories,* and *Jesus and the Metaphors of God.*

*"Bernard Lee charts, with clarity and force, a revolution taking place in the American Catholic Church."*
— James D. and Evelyn Eaton Whitehead

ISBN 0-8245-1529-3 (paper)
$17.95

At your bookstore or, to order direct, send check or money order, including $3.00 for shipping and handling, to Crossroad, 370 Lexington Avenue, New York, NY 10017.

If you would like a free catalog of Crossroad books, please write to us at 370 Lexington Avenue, New York, NY 10017.